Primary Language Arts

NSC Edition

Grade 4

Jennifer Peek
Heather Raymond
Mitzie-Ann Jackson

The Publishers would like to thank the following for permission to reproduce copyright material.

Text credits

p.32: © Familycookbookproject, LLC, © Tim Palmer, "America by rivers", Island Press. May 1996, © Emily Bone, "The Solar System", Usborne Publishing Ltd. 2010; p.130: © Seafood's Off by Valerie Bloom; p.180: © Rain by Valerie Bloom; p.232: © Jamaicans warned be guard water borne diseases, The Gleaner; p.233: © Getting it clean water treatment process, The Gleaner.

Photo credits

t = top, b = below, l = left, r = right, c = centre, b/g = background

p.8: © Viktar Malyshchyts/stock.adobe.com; p.13: (t) © Lunja/stock.adobe.com, (b) © Josu Ozkaritz/stock.adobe.com; p.18: © Debbie Ann Powell/stock.adobe.com; p.28: (l) © myviewpoint/stock.adobe.com, (c) © Brent Hofacker/stock.adobe.com, (r) © uckyo/stock.adobe.com; p.39: © Prachaya Roekdeethaweesab/Shutterstock, © Prachaya/stock.adobe.com, © Everett Collection/Shutterstock, © Georgios Kollidas/stock.adobe.com, © Janusz Pienkowski/Shutterstock; p.44: © Georgios Kollidas/stock.adobe.com; p.53: © Petr Toman/Shutterstock; p.58: © arrowsmith2/stock.adobe.com; p.62: © Wangkun Jia/stock.adobe.com; p.78: © Sergey Novikov/stock.adobe.com; p.92: (t) © aomvector/stock.adobe.com, (c) © Tarik GOK/stock.adobe.com, (b) © teresinagoia/stock.adobe.com; p.95: © Peter Hermes Furian/stock.adobe.com; p.96: © rocketclips/stock.adobe.com; p.122: © Michael Gray/stock.adobe.com; p.147: © alvincadiz/stock.adobe.com; p.150: © david_franklin/stock.adobe.com; p.152: © Heronim/stock.adobe.com; p.155: (l) © Ruth P. Peterkin/stock.adobe.com, (c) © Konstantin Kulikov/stock.adobe.com, (r) © Greg Meland/stock.adobe.com; p.157: © PhotoSpirit/stock.adobe.com; p.169: © pavalena/stock.adobe.com; p.189: (l) © Bruno/stock.adobe.com; (c) © David Biagi/stock.adobe.com, (r) © PhotoSpirit/stock.adobe.com; p.199: (l) © Konstantin Kulikov/stock.adobe.com, (c) © Konstantin Kulikov/stock.adobe.com, (r) © Cavan/stock.adobe.com; p.206: © erllre/stock.adobe.com; p.221: (l) © vystekimages/stock.adobe.com, (cl) © Wayhome Studio/stock.adobe.com, (cr) © amorn/stock.adobe.com, (r) © wavebreak3/stock.adobe.com; p.238: © Cyril Lutsenko/stock.adobe.com; p.245: © Peter Hermes Furian/stock.adobe.com; p.269: (l) © Q/stock.adobe.com, (r) © Mike Dot/stock.adobe.com; p.277: © vectorgoods/stock.adobe.com; p.278: (l) © amadeustx/stock.adobe.com, (c) © Mario Hoppmann/stock.adobe.com, (r) © nikkytok/stock.adobe.com; p.278: © vectorgoods/stock.adobe.com; p.292: © mikesilent/stock.adobe.com, © YummyBuum/stock.adobe.com, © Liliya/stock.adobe.com, © Kateina/stock.adobe.com; p.296: (l) © N_studio/stock.adobe.com, (c) © Photozi/stock.adobe.com, (r) © Stanislav Pepeliaev/stock.adobe.com; p.310: © nezezon/stock.adobe.com; p.314: © Aide/stock.adobe.com; p.321: © Pixel-Shot/stock.adobe.com; p.326: © BlueRingMedia/Shutterstock; p.334: © Mike Mareen/stock.adobe.com.

Although every effort has been made to ensure that website addresses are correct at time of going to press, Hodder Education cannot be held responsible for the content of any website mentioned in this book. It is sometimes possible to find a relocated web page by typing in the address of the home page for a website in the URL window of your browser.

Hachette UK's policy is to use papers that are natural, renewable and recyclable products and made from wood grown in well-managed forests and other controlled sources. The logging and manufacturing processes are expected to conform to the environmental regulations of the country of origin.

To order, please visit www.hoddereducation.com or contact Customer Service at education@hachette.co.uk / +44 (0)1235 827827.

ISBN: 9781398356283

© Jennifer Peek, Heather Raymond, Mitzie-Ann Jackson and Hodder & Stoughton Limited 2024

This edition published in 2024 by

Hodder Education,

An Hachette UK Company

Carmelite House

50 Victoria Embankment

London EC4Y 0DZ

www.hoddereducation.com

Impression number 10 9 8 7 6 5 4 3 2 1

Year 2027 2026 2025 2024

All rights reserved. Apart from any use permitted under UK copyright law, no part of this publication may be reproduced or transmitted in any form or by any means, electronic or mechanical, including photocopying and recording, or held within any information storage and retrieval system, without permission in writing from the publisher or under licence from the Copyright Licensing Agency Limited. Further details of such licences (for reprographic reproduction) may be obtained from the Copyright Licensing Agency Limited, www.cla.co.uk

Cover illustration by Heather Clarke c/o D'Avila Illustration Agency

Illustrations by Jane Commin, Claudia Eckard, Samantha van Riet, Heather Clarke c/o D'Avila Illustration Agency and Hyphen S.A.

Typeset by Hyphen S.A.

Printed in Spain

A catalogue record for this title is available from the British Library.

Contents

Contents.. 3

Term 1 **Unit 1**

Cultural traditions which shape our national and regional identity

Project 1: Our music and dance 8

Speaking and listening: Jamaican Creole and Standard Jamaican English; ask and answer questions 8

Word builder: Song and dance vocabulary; *-tion* words 10

Research and study skills: Skim and scan 12

Grammar builder: Proper nouns and common nouns 14

Let's write: Music and dance; compare and contrast; transitional words and phrases 15

Project 2: Folktales, news stories and documentary texts 18

Speaking and listening: Compare versions of folktales; respond to documentary texts; verb and subject agreement 18

Word builder: Folktales and stories vocabulary; match syllables 20

Let's read: Anansi and Goat; characterisation and inference; story outcomes 22

Grammar builder: Positive, comparative and superlative adjectives 24

Let's write: Characterisation, setting, message; comparative adjectives; plan, write and revise 26

Project 3: Food and cooking 28

Speaking and listening: Answer *true* or *false*; read bar graphs, present findings 28

Word builder: Vocabulary about food; spell, sort and segment words 30

Let's read: Fiction and non-fiction; read a recipe; make lists 32

Grammar builder: Fiction, non-fiction and tenses (present and past) 35

Research and study skills: Compare and contrast fiction and non-fiction 36

Let's write: Write a recipe; proofread and check 37

Project 4: Jamaican heroes 39

Speaking and listening: Identify key information; in groups, plan and prepare a presentation to the class 39

Word builder: Vocabulary about history and heroes; pronunciation, meaning, spelling; prefix, root, suffix 41

Research and study skills: Understand text features and how information is organised; research the life of Samuel Sharpe 43

Grammar builder: Conjunctions and compound sentences 46

Let's write: Write a speech in the voice of a Jamaican national hero 48

Project 5: Jamaican sports and sporting achievements 50

Speaking and listening: Answer *true* or *false*; read, discuss and report back 50

Word builder: Sports vocabulary; segment, blend, spell; crossword 51

Let's read: Biography; skim and scan; answer questions 53

Grammar builder: Punctuate sentences 55

Let's write: Plan and write an email using sports vocabulary, adjectives, conjunctions, transitional phrases and correct punctuation 56

Project 6: Tourism in Jamaica 58

Speaking and listening: Listen and respond to a poem; make a class performance 58

Word builder: Tourism vocabulary; pronunciation; compound words 60

Let's read: Comprehension, answer questions; identify and list positives and negatives 62

Research and study skills: Read informational texts and understand text features; use a graphic organiser 64

Grammar builder: End-of-unit check: adjectives, transitional words, conjunctions, nouns 65

Let's write: Plan and write a factual report 67

Term 1 Unit 1 Review and assessment 69

Term 1 — Unit 2
Our five senses

Project 7: Introduction to the five senses 73

- **Speaking and listening:** Question and answer; conduct a conversation 73
- **Word builder:** Use sense words; conduct a conversation; alphabetical orders 75
- **Let's read / Research and study skills:** Skim and scan; headings and sub-headings; read and discuss an information text 77
- **Grammar builder:** Apostrophes 79
- **Let's write:** Use the RAFT strategy (role, audience, format, topic); plan, write, reflect, review 81

Project 8: About the nose and sense of smell 83

- **Speaking and listening:** Read aloud; role playing; use Jamaican Creole 83
- **Word builder:** Nose and sense of smell; spelling; double letters; code-breaking 84
- **Let's read:** Skim and scan a story about the sense of smell; apostrophes of possession; reflect on own experience 86
- **Grammar builder:** More on apostrophes; pronoun contractions 88
- **Let's write:** Plan, write and review a story about the senses 90

Project 9: About the tongue and sense of taste 92

- **Speaking and listening:** Form words; different languages spoken in the Caribbean; how we communicate 92
- **Word builder:** Tongue and sense of taste; compound words, antonyms and synonyms; label a diagram 94
- **Let's read:** Information texts; diagrams; tongue-twisters 96
- **Grammar builder:** Adverbs of manner 98
- **Let's write:** Use adverbs of manner; write and compare paragraphs 100

Project 10: About the skin and the sense of touch 102

- **Speaking and listening:** Write and perform a role play set in a doctor's office 102
- **Word builder:** Vocabulary about the skin; segmenting; consonant blends and clusters 104
- **Let's read:** Read and evaluate an advertisement 107
- **Grammar builder:** Noun substitutes – pronouns 110
- **Let's write:** Plan, write and evaluate an advertisement, using the RAFT strategy 112

Project 11: Symptoms and treatments 115

- **Speaking and listening:** Homophones; play language games 115
- **Word builder:** Vocabulary about symptoms and treatments; syllables; sequence; prefixes and suffixes 117
- **Let's read:** Use dictionaries; definitions; comprehension; diaries and journals 119
- **Grammar builder:** More about pronouns 123
- **Let's write:** Plan, write and evaluate a letter of complaint 124

Project 12: Poetry to stimulate the senses 126

- **Speaking and listening:** Read poetry aloud, varying tone of voice 126
- **Word builder:** Poetic vocabulary; consonant clusters; spelling challenge 128
- **Let's read:** Read poetry aloud with actions; common nouns, proper nouns; rhyming words 130
- **Grammar builder:** Apostrophes for possession and contraction; noun substitutes; adverbs of manner; self-check 133
- **Let's write:** Plan, write and read aloud a poem; acrostic poems 135

Term 1 Unit 2 Review and assessment 138

Term 2 — Unit 1
The Jamaican landscape and natural environment

Project 13: Natural places of Jamaica 142

- **Speaking and listening:** Interpret a comic strip; plan and perform a role play of the story; evaluate performances 142
- **Word builder:** Vocabulary about the natural landscape; segmenting; syllables; plurals; spelling; categories 145

Let's read / Research and study skills: Read graphs and charts; use data; mind map; using RAFT to assess text; summarise 148

Grammar builder: Collective nouns; use a dictionary 152

Let's write: Plan, write and review a journal entry 154

Project 14: Our mountains 157

Speaking and listening: Listen attentively; listen for information; share and discuss ideas 157

Word builder: Vocabulary about mountains; spelling challenge; sort words; synonyms, antonyms, homophones 159

Let's read: Read an information text; assess/categorise text types; comprehension skills 161

Research and study skills: Use charts and graphs for information; write information texts 162

Grammar builder: Commas 164

Let's write: Plan and write a non-fiction text; write a leaflet about mountains in Jamaica ... 167

Project 15: Famous rivers 169

Speaking and listening: Plan and hold a debate 169

Word builder: Vocabulary about rivers; spelling; proper nouns; homographs 172

Let's read: Read a story; predict what will happen; alliteration; personification; comprehension; sequencings 174

Grammar builder: Adverbs of time 176

Let's write: Write fiction; plan and write a story including alliteration and personification 178

Project 16: The natural world in stories and poems 180

Speaking and listening: Read aloud and compare two poems 180

Word builder: Vocabulary about landscape and weather; consonant clusters; alphabetical order; common noun; verb; adjective; synonym 182

Let's read: Read poetry; personification; comprehension 184

Grammar builder: Prepositions of time 187

Let's write: Plan and write a poem about the Jamaican landscape; write a journal entry to reflect on the process of writing the poem 189

Project 17: The environment and pollution 191

Speaking and listening: Work in groups, using an online search engine to research, plan and write a presentation to be given to the rest of the class 191

Word builder: Vocabulary about our environment; segmenting/blending; suffixes; definitions 194

Let's read: Read a non-fiction text; comprehension; *true* or *false* 197

Grammar builder: Collective nouns 199

Let's write: Plan, draft and write a formal letter, respond to feedback from a partner 201

Project 18: Other Caribbean countries 203

Speaking and listening: Research and discuss Caribbean countries; play a quick-fire game naming countries 203

Word builder: Vocabulary about Caribbean places; proper nouns; suffixes; homographs ... 204

Let's read: Read a non-fiction text about Cuba; comprehension 206

Grammar builder: Commas; collective nouns; prepositions of time; adverbs of time 207

Let's write: Design a poster featuring a fact file about one Caribbean country; write a richly descriptive, information text describing a Caribbean country; facts, figures and dates; headings and subheadings, conjunctions, vivid, descriptive language; reflect and review 209

Term 2 Unit 1 Review and assessment 212

Term 2 Unit 2

Water and the Jamaican environment

Project 19: We all need water 216

Speaking and listening: Discussion and role play about water and how we use it 216

Word builder: Vocabulary about water; word definitions; prefix, suffix, root; synonyms; homographs 218

Let's read: Match titles to plays; summarise; characterisation in plays 221

Grammar builder: Object pronouns; subject, object, verb agreement 223

Let's write: Plan and write interview questions; conduct an interview and writing notes; write a report after the interview 225

Project 20: Clean water is safe water 227

Speaking and listening: Read a report aloud; ask and answer questions; summarise; plan and role play a meeting about water quality 227

Word builder: Vocabulary about making water clean and safe; syllables; spelling; prefix, suffix, root; sentence construction 229

Let's read: Read extracts; comprehension; identify words or phrases with similar meanings 231

Research and study skills: Complete a summary table; understand cause and effect; summarise and create a table of information to be presented to the class 234

Grammar builder: Signal words; sentence construction; compare using signal words and phrases; link using signal words and phrases; sequence using signal words and phrases 235

Let's write: Sequence an information text; relay the key pieces of information in comic strip form 237

Project 21: Water in our community 240

Speaking and listening: Work in teams to plan, construct and conduct a debate 240

Word builder: Vocabulary about water in the community; homophones; suffix; synonyms .. 243

Let's read / Research and study skills: Read maps and tables; comprehension; questions and answers 245

Grammar builder: Present simple and present continuous tenses; past tense 248

Let's write: Plan, make notes, describe events; write a paragraph; summarise a text message 251

Project 22: A school water project 253

Speaking and listening: Read aloud; discuss; plan, practise and perform a role play; use Standard Jamaican English and Jamaican Creole 253

Word builder: Vocabulary about water; suffix; spelling; alphabetical order 256

Let's read: Read a newspaper article; comprehension; respond to text; expressing a view 258

Grammar builder: Sentence signposts; statements, interrogatives, exclamations 259

Let's write: Plan a whole-school project and write a draft of your plan 260

Project 23: Time of drought 262

Speaking and listening: Class discussion: discuss and practise reading a script of a television news broadcast 262

Word builder: Vocabulary about drought; definitions; pronunciation; select the right word to complete a sentence 264

Let's read: Introduce the QAR strategy; different levels of comprehension skills 266

Grammar builder: Parts of speech: nouns, verbs, adjectives, adverbs, pronouns, conjunctions, prepositions 268

Let's write: Describe a landscape from photographs; plan and write a news report using writing strategies 269

Project 24: The properties of water 272

Speaking and listening: Discuss and share ideas; research, plan and present your research to the class 272

Word builder: Vocabulary about the properties of water; suffix; synonyms 274

Let's read: Read about the scientific properties of water; identify facts; summarise information; fill in the gap 276

Grammar builder: Object pronouns; parts of speech; tenses; sentence types 280

Let's write: Make a science poster showing how to carry out an experiment; step-by-step instructions; add research 282

Term 2 Unit 2 Review and assessment ... 284

Term 3 Unit 1
Talking and writing about the weather

Project 25: Weather 288

Speaking and listening: Share weather lore through rhymes and discussion 288

Word builder: Vocabulary about the weather; stressed syllables in nouns and verbs; pronunciation; mnemonics 290

Let's read: Ancient myths and legends about the weather 292

Grammar builder: Contractions with "will" and "shall"; modal verbs 294

Let's write / Research and study skills: Record weather conditions; complete a weather chart; draw a graph recording findings; make a poster; write a review of your findings 296

Contents

Project 26: Weather reports and forecasts 299

- **Speaking and listening:** Read weather forecasts; vary speed and pitch of voice; give feedback 299
- **Word builder:** Vocabulary about weather report; use a dictionary; proper nouns; suffixes; compound words 301
- **Let's read:** Weather forecasts; read text and weather maps (synoptic charts); design weather symbols; summarise; read a chart 303
- **Grammar builder:** Reflexive pronouns 305
- **Let's write:** Write synoptic and prognostic weather forecasts using present and future tenses; draw a map with symbols; plan, write and review a script 307

Project 27: Our Caribbean weather 310

- **Speaking and listening:** Read a short text aloud, discuss ask and answer questions; discuss thoughts and feelings 310
- **Word builder:** Vocabulary about describing the weather; definitions; pronunciation; consonant clusters; infinitive verb form; play charades; alphabetical order 312
- **Let's read:** Read an informal letter; use similes 314
- **Grammar builder:** Present simple, present continuous, past simple, future simple tenses; perfect tenses, past, present and future 316
- **Let's write:** Write personal account including likes and dislikes; write with humour; write to present to class; use planning lists; draft, write, proofread, review 318

Project 28: Artists inspired by weather 321

- **Speaking and listening:** Discuss thoughts and feelings; song lyrics and singing songs 321
- **Word builder:** Descriptive vocabulary; use dictionaries; spelling; words ending -le; consonant blends; rhyming words 323
- **Let's read:** Read poems about the weather; reading aloud for different effects (stress, volume, intonation, rhythm); identify verbs, adverbs, adjectives; spell rhyming words; express and explain preferences 326
- **Grammar builder:** Modal auxiliary verbs 328

- **Let's write:** Rhyming poems; poems in stanzas; use adjectives and similes; use direct and indirect questions; use mind map/thought bubble/lists to plan writing; draft and review, respond to feedback 330

Project 29: Hurricanes 333

- **Speaking and listening:** Discuss your own and others' experiences sensitively; listen to song lyrics and discuss; ask questions and share stories 333
- **Word builder:** Vocabulary about wild weather; use a dictionary; words ending in -tion; use a thesaurus; unscramble words 335
- **Let's read:** Read a story extract; answer questions; exclamations; predict 337
- **Grammar builder:** More about modal auxiliaries; write sentences giving advice; design a poster listing tips and advice, make a class display 338
- **Let's write:** Draw on own experience to write a story; use a planning chart with three sections (background/details of problem or events/ outcome); use adjectives, adverbs, similes; redraft and correct; choose a title 340

Project 30: Flooding in the news 343

- **Speaking and listening:** Read a newspaper article aloud; be sensitive to others' experiences; answer questions based on the article 343
- **Word builder:** Vocabulary about flooding; hyphenated words; homographs; play word games 345
- **Let's read:** Read and answer questions on a news report; understand use of double letters; summarise in note form 347
- **Grammar builder:** Reflexive pronouns; modal auxiliary verbs; contractions; perfect tenses ... 348
- **Let's write:** Research and write a news report; use writing strategies like RAFT to help plan; write factual information; write in paragraphs 350

Term 3 Unit 1 Review and assessment 353

TERM 1

Unit 1

In this unit, you will share ideas about cultural traditions and heritage. This will include learning about traditional music, drama and folktales, food and other topics that shape our national and regional identity.

Project 1

Speaking and listening

1. Student A recites or sings the folk song to Student B. Student B takes notes about what is happening in each verse.

Mango Time

Mi nuh drink coffee tea – mango time
Care how nice it may be – mango time
In the heat of the mango crop
When di fruit dem a ripe an' drop
Wash yu pot, tun dem dung - mango time.

De terpentine large an fine, mango time
Robin mango so sweet, mango time
Number eleven an hairy skin
Pack di bankra an ram dem in
For di bankra mus' full, mango time

Mek wi go a mango walk, mango time
For is only di talk mango time
Mek wi jump pon di big jackass
Ride im dung an no tap a pass
Mek di best a di crop, mango time.

Folk song of Jamaica

1. In pairs, look at your notes and discuss what you think each verse means. How do you think the person singing the song is feeling?

2. With your partner, take turns to translate the poem out loud from Jamaican Creole (JC) into Standard Jamaican English (SJE).

L👀k and learn

Wh- questions are used to ask about: people (**who**), time (**when**), something (**what**), place (**where**), a specific choice (**which**).

2   Make questions using a question word from the vocabulary box. The first one is done for you. Then ask and answer the questions in pairs.

Vocabulary box

who   where   when   why   ~~which~~   what

1   <u>Which</u> kind of songs do you prefer, songs in SJE or songs in JC?
2   _____ was the last time you listened to the song *Mango Time*?
3   _____ do you usually listen to music?
4   _____ is your favourite singer?
5   _____ is music important to people and culture?

3   In pairs, take turns to ask your partner a question from Activity 2, but this time continue with a follow-up question.

Look and learn
Good listeners actively engage with the other person using **body language** and **follow-up questions**.

Example:

Which kind of songs do you prefer, songs in SJE or songs in JC?

I prefer songs in JC.

Oh, really, can you tell me why?

Because I can learn about our culture.

4   Did you focus on your partner while they were talking? Ask a question and a follow-up question from Activity 2 and check whether you are listening intentionally. Use body language to show your partner you are interested.

Word builder

This vocabulary is about song and dance:

Vocabulary box

celebration	clap	sound	dance
tradition	instrument	performance	verse
rhythm	musical	emotion	melody
tune	joyful	costume	

1 Read the words with a partner and organise them in the table. Are there any words you do not know yet?

I know the meaning and how to say them.	I can read them, but I do not know what they mean.

2 In each sentence, there is a missing word. Find the correct word in the vocabulary box above and complete the sentences. Check your answers with a partner.

1 Rebecca loves music because she thinks it is very _____.

2 The piano is Ian's favourite _____.

3 The dancer at the carnival had a beautiful _____.

4 The singer asked the crowd to _____ along with him.

3 Write two sentences of your own, like the ones in Activity 2. Then challenge your partner to find the missing word from the Word box.

Project 1 – Our music and dance

> For words ending in **-tion** as in *nation*, by learning the word ending you can spell other words more easily.
> For example: *addition, station, position.*

4 1 Find the words that end in *-tion* in the vocabulary box and write them below.

_____

2 Add two more words of your own that end in *-tion*.

_____

3 Compare your words with a partner and use a dictionary or online tool to check their spelling.

5 Look at the words in Activity 1 that you placed under the column titled *I can read them, but I do not know what they mean*. Use a dictionary or online tool to look up the meaning of these words and write a sentence for each in your notebook. Ask your teacher to check your sentences.

Let's read

Research and study skills

Skim

When you answer comprehension questions, you often need to **skim** the text first. This means **reading quickly** to see how the text is organised and to get the gist (general idea) of the content.

Scan

When you **scan**, you **read quickly**, but **more carefully** to find specific information. To scan, you move your eyes quickly across the text. You do not have to read every word. When you scan, you do many things at the same time.

- Think about the **specific information** you are looking for, for example, a date, a name or a key word.
- **Ignore information** you do not need and is therefore **not important** for your purpose.
- **Move your eyes quickly** across the text until you find the information and then stop reading.

1. In small groups, think of a time that someone would skim information. For example, people skim through recipes to get an idea of what to cook for dinner.

2. In pairs, discuss a time you needed to scan for information. For example, you see a sale sign for sports trainers in a shop window, but you are on a moving bus. You need to scan the information quickly for the price.

3. Report back to the class with examples of skimming and scanning.

---

1. Skim the text quickly and decide what the best topic is for the text below.

    1. music makes you dance
    2. a traditional dance

The Dinki Mini

The Dinki Mini is a dance for male and female dancers. It came to Jamaica from Africa and its name comes from the African word *ndingi*.

Traditionally, it was performed after a person had died to help to make their relatives and friends feel better. The music has a lively beat and it is a joyful dance to celebrate the life of the person. Sometimes, it is performed for up to nine nights after a person has died.

To dance the Dinki Mini, dancers must move in time to the music in a certain way. They need flexible knees and hips that jerk back and forth to the rhythm of the beat. The instruments used to play this dance are often home-made instruments such as shakers, tins beaten together for percussion, or graters played with forks or spoons. They can also be instruments like the tamboo, which is a drum in the shape of a cylinder that is beaten with a baton.

Tamboo

Grater and spoon

2 Scan the text and decide whether these statements are true (T) or false (F).

   1 The Dinki Mini is a dance only for girls. _____

   2 The Dinki Mini is dance for just two people. _____

   3 The Dinki Mini is a fast dance. _____

   4 The Dinki Mini is a dance to celebrate Easter. _____

   5 The Dinki Mini is a dance from Africa. _____

3 Why is the Dinki Mini dance traditionally performed?

4 Check out videos of young dancers performing the Dinki Mini dance on the Jamaica Cultural Development Commission's YouTube channel.

ICT opportunity

Remember that we have to keep ourselves safe when we are online.

Challenge:

- In pairs, use a search engine such as Google or Windows Explorer to search for information on safety rules for children using the internet. Write down three of these rules.
- Compare your answers with the YouTube website by searching for videos titled *5 Internet Safety Tips for Kids*.

Grammar builder

Proper nouns and common nouns

> **Look and learn**
>
> **Proper nouns** are names of people and places. They start with a capital letter, for example: *Helen, Mark, Kingston.*
>
> Nouns that are not proper nouns and do not start with a capital letter are called **common nouns**. Common nouns include the names of everyday items, for example: *table, car, school, house.*

1. With your partner, take turns to say nouns. Your partner must say whether each noun is a proper noun or a common noun. How do they know? Are they right?

   Student A: Kingston.

   Student B: Kingston is a proper noun. It is the name of a place and starts with a capital letter.

   Student A: Yes, you're right!

2. Sort the nouns in the vocabulary box into two categories: common nouns and proper nouns. Write them in two lists in your notebook.

   Vocabulary box

instrument	tune	plate	sound	Cuba
dance	Mr Smith	Portland	Joanna	performance

3. Look back at the text about the Dinki Mini dance. Find ten common nouns in the text and list them in your notebook.

4. Another student read the same text and he says that there are no proper nouns in it. Is he correct? Give a reason for your answer.

5. List ten common nouns you can see around you.

6. Think of the people you know and the places you have been. Then list ten proper nouns.

7. With your partner, compare your lists of nouns. Did you think of the same words or are they different? Count how many different common nouns and proper nouns you have together.

8. Choose two common nouns and two proper nouns from your list. Write four sentences, one for each noun you have chosen.

Project 1 – Our music and dance

Let's write

Our music and dance

In this project, you have learned about traditional music and dance of Jamaica. However, there are other types of music that come from the Caribbean. Popular types of Caribbean music include salsa, calypso and reggae.

Cuba

Salsa is a lively style of dance music with origins from Africa and Spain.

Trinidad and Tobago

Calypso was originally the national dance of Trinidad and Tobago. It is associated with carnival.

Jamaica

Mento is a kind of Jamaican folk music similar to calypso. It was most popular in the 1950s.

Reggae is a much slower type of music than **ska** which became popular in the 1960s.

Look and learn

- **Signal words to compare and contrast**

Compare	Contrast
Jamaican reggae is **similar to** some types of Trinidadian music, but it sounds more like ska.	Salsa music is **different from** reggae music.
alike resemble same as similar to	although different from however in contrast on the other hand

- **Transitional words and phrases to help your writing flow**

  The first way…, Another way…, Next…, Then…, In addition…, To conclude…, Finally…

- **A Venn diagram to compare data and identify common features**

A **Venn diagram** is used to show how things are the same or different. Things that are the same go in the middle section.

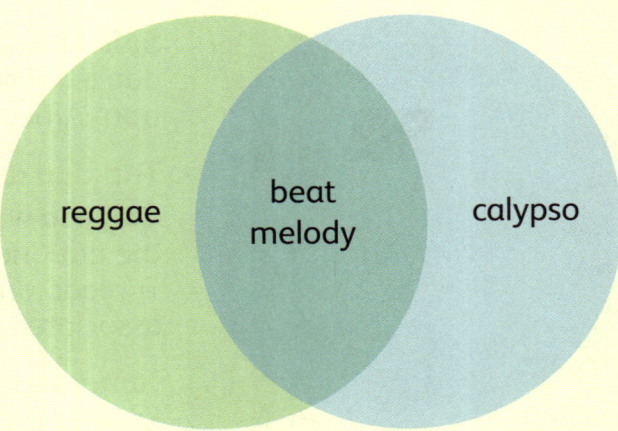

1. Write a paragraph to compare and contrast two types of music or dance from the Caribbean. Use signal words to **compare and contrast** and **transitional phrases** in your writing.

   1. Choose two different types of music or dance. Draw a Venn diagram in you notebook. Write the different features of what you will compare in the two Venn diagram circles. Then write the similar features in the middle section of the Venn diagram.

   2. Complete the gaps in the paragraph below, then use it to guide you in writing a draft for your own paragraph.

      - The topic sentence must state both topics you are writing about.

      When I researched _____ and _____

      music, I found there are some ways the two types of music are **alike** and

      different.

- The body of the paragraph should include the points you want to compare and contrast.

  The first way _____ and _____

  are alike is that they both have/sound/use _____

  in the music. Another way that they are similar is that

  _____.

  However, there are some ways _____

  and _____ are different. For example,

  _____.

- The conclusion summarises the information in your paragraph.

  In conclusion, after researching _____ and

  _____ music/dance, you can see that there are

  some ways they are the same and other ways that they are very

  different.

2. Revise and edit your draft. Make sure you have developed the correct structure of a paragraph (a topic sentence, the body and a concluding sentence). Check that you have used a variety of signal words to compare and contrast, as well as transitional phrases.

3. Write out your paragraph on a separate sheet of paper. You could illustrate your writing with a few drawings. Ask you teacher to display your work for others to read.

Term 1 Unit 1

Project 2

Speaking and listening

News stories

1 Annie Palmer was known as the *White Witch of Rose Hall*. Listen carefully as your teacher reads aloud two versions of the tale of Annie Palmer. Cover the texts while you listen and make notes on the main ideas.

Rose Hall

Text 1
Annie Palmer is said to haunt the grounds of Rose Hall Plantation near Montego Bay. She was born in Haiti where her English mother and Irish father lived. When her parents died of yellow fever, she was adopted by a nanny who taught her witchcraft and voodoo. She moved to Jamaica and married the owner of Rose Hall Plantation, John Palmer. Annie murdered Palmer as well as two subsequent husbands and many male plantation slaves. She was later murdered by a slave named "Takoo".
https://en.wikipedia.org/wiki/White_Witch_of_Rose_Hall

Text 2
Annie Palmer was born in Haiti. Her parents died of yellow fever and she was raised by a woman who taught her witchcraft and voodoo. However, recent research has cast doubt on the Annie Palmer legend. The real Annie Palmer married John Rose Palmer in 1820. He died in debt a few years later. Annie had no legal right to the plantation, so she had to leave. She died in 1846.
https://www.thepalmsjamaica.com/annie-palmer-white-witch-rose-hall/

2 With your partner, look at your notes and discuss these questions:

- What were the differences between the two versions you listened to? Read the texts to confirm the differences you identified.

- Why do you think that different versions of this tale exist?

3 Listen to your teacher read two extracts from documentaries about Jamaica. In small groups, answer the following questions and discuss your personal reactions.

Tourist harassment
Crime and tourist harassment [1]are increasing and being reported in both the local and foreign news. The result is that the tourism industry in Jamaica [2]has suffered, not only from bad publicity but also from people thinking that Jamaica is a dangerous place.

Project 2 – Folktales, news stories and documentary texts

Jamaica's dominance in track and field.
Jamaicans ³start running track at a young age. Track ⁴is a popular sport both in elementary schools and in clubs. The training is quite intense for children, but as it involves outdoor activities and sporting success, children are happy to work hard. Many think this to be the main reason for Jamaica being the best in the world in track and field.

1. How do you feel after listening to the information presented in the documentary on tourist harassment? Are the comments positive or negative? Do you agree that some tourists are harassed? Do you feel sorry, angry or fine about the reputation of Jamaica?

2. How do you feel after listening to the documentary on Jamaica's dominance in track and field? Do the comments make you feel proud and increase your self-respect and self-esteem?

I don't recognise some of these words. I think I'll use a dictionary or online tool to look them up.

3. Look at the underlined subjects in the documentary texts. Decide whether the subjects are singular or plural and look at how they agree with the verbs labelled 1 to 4.

Example:

*The subject **Crime and tourist harassment** is plural. The pronoun is **They** and agrees with the verb **are**.*

4. In groups, discuss the difference between the story of Annie Palmer and the news stories.

Word builder

This vocabulary is about folktales and stories. Work in pairs to learn to spell the words below.

Vocabulary box

setting	folktale	funny	ending
version	moral	character	favourite
myth	exciting	surprise	enjoyable
legend	frightening	plot	

1 1 Work with a partner. Each student creates a table with three columns in their notebook, as in the example below. Make sure your table is big enough for every word in the Vocabulary box.

1	2	3
setting version		

2 Copy the words from the vocabulary box into column 1.

3 Practise writing each word in column 2.

4 Then cover the first two columns and listen as your partner reads the words aloud, while you write the words in the last column. Then swap.

2 Keisha has been searching online for information about folktales. Here are some of the results that came up. Unfortunately, there is a word missing from each search result.

Find a word from the vocabulary box to complete each result.

Project 2 – Folktales, news stories and documentary texts

mysearch.jm   good Jamaican folktales

1   A _ _ _ _ _ _ _ _ _ _ _ story. Read on if you dare.
    www.readscarystories.jm
2   Somebody will get a big _ _ _ _ _ _ _ _ in this much-loved tale.
    www.folktalesforyou.jm
3   The _ _ _ _ of this story is full of twists and turns but eventually there is a happy _ _ _ _ _ _.
    www.storyoftheweek.jm
4   A real _ _ _ _ _ _ amongst Jamaicans, the oldest known folktale.
    www.historytales.jm

3   The syllables of the vocabulary box words are written below on separate pieces of paper. Without looking at the vocabulary box, match the different pieces together.

| set | ver | leg | folk | mor | fun | end | sur |

| sion | ting | tale | al | end | prise | ny | ing |

Example: *ver + sion = version*

| ex | char | fright | fav | en |

| en | our | ci | joy | ac |

| ter | ing | able | ting | ite |

Example: *fav + our + ite = favourite*

4   The words *myth* and *plot* are missing in Activity 3. In pairs, say why you think these words have been left out.

Let's read

1 Read this Anansi story and complete the following tasks.

> ### Anansi and Goat, Part 1
> *adapted from Go-Local Jamaica*
>
>
>
> Anansi and Goat had a little quarrel. Anansi said to Goat, "Brother Goat, I'm going to catch you." Goat answered, "You will never live, my friend, to catch me."
>
> Now Goat is afraid of rain. So, one wet night, Goat was coming from his field and had to pass Anansi's house. Drizzle, drizzle, the rain fell. The rain fell harder. The thunder rolled. The lightning flashed. Brother Goat had to run to Anansi's house.
>
> "Come in, my friend!", Anansi called. Goat went in. Anansi stepped into the room, took out his fiddle and began to sing: "Me thank Brother Rain fe run with meat from bush come a me house."
>
> Goat didn't like the song and kept close to the doorway. Anansi pretended not to notice him and just kept on playing the same song. The rain stopped.

1 Draw a picture of the scene you imagine on the night that Goat went to Anansi's house. What will the weather be like in your picture? What expression might there be on Goat's face?

2 Read the text again. Find and list five common nouns.

3 How do you think Goat is feeling when Anansi is singing? Find and write some quotes from the text as evidence to describe Goat's emotions.

A **quote** repeats the exact words in a text or that someone says. It can be used as an example or as part of an explanation: "Goat is afraid of the rain."

Inference chart		
Act like a detective. Use clues in the text (headings, sub-headings, pictures) and your own knowledge to guess information and make an inference.		
Inference What do you think will happen?	**Hint** A quote that leads you to the inferences.	**Outcome** A quote that proves whether or not your inference was correct.

Project 2 – Folktales, news stories and documentary texts

2 Read on to find out what happened next. Complete the following tasks.

> **Anansi and Goat, Part 2**
>
> Goat, without a word to Anansi, jumped out the door. Anansi, quick like lightning, chased after him. Goat ran and ran, but Anansi was right behind him. But Goat didn't give up. He kept on running, and before he realised it he was right in front of the river.
>
> But Goat could not cross the river. He was too afraid of water. So, he ran to the riverside and turned into a little white stone.
>
> Now Dog, who stood on the other side of the river, saw when Goat turned into a little stone. By this time, Anansi had reached the river. He shouted to Dog, "Brother Dog, you see Goat pass?"
>
> "Yes, Brother Anansi. You see the little stone by the riverside? Pick it up and throw it over here. I will show you where he is."
>
> Anansi took up the stone and threw it over the river. As the stone dropped, it turned back into Brother Goat. Brother Goat landed safe and sound, out of Anansi's way.
>
> Anansi shook his head and sighed, "Luck was in my hand but it got away."

1. Which new character do we meet in Part 2 of this tale?

2. How would the story ending be different without this new character?

3. Share some ideas about a new story ending without the new character.

> I think that…

> If Brother Dog was Anasi's friend, he would have…

> If Brother Dog had been sleeping, …

> If Goat had turned into a huge rock, then…

4. How do you know Brother Dog was looking after Goat? Find a quote from the story to use as evidence for your idea.

5. What do you think is the lesson of this tale? What are the things in the story that make you think that?

Grammar builder

Making comparisons with adjectives

Lk and learn

Adjectives can be used to **make comparisons**. Most adjectives have three different forms: **positive**, **comparative** and **superlative**.

Positive adjective	Comparative adjective	Superlative adjective
tall	taller	tallest

Comparative adjectives often end in **-er** or **-ier**.
Superlative adjectives often end in **-est** or **-iest**.

1. Read the sentences. Find and write the adjective in each sentence. For example: *Jamaica is warmer than Iceland.* The adjective is *warmer*.

    1. Goat was faster than Anansi.
    2. Dog was smarter than Anansi.
    3. Goat was the luckiest character.
    4. Dog was the kindest and friendliest character.
    5. Anansi was the unluckiest character.
    6. Some Jamaican folktales are funnier than others.

2 Look at these three sets of pictures. What are the missing adjectives?

1 fat _____ _____   2 dirty _____ _____

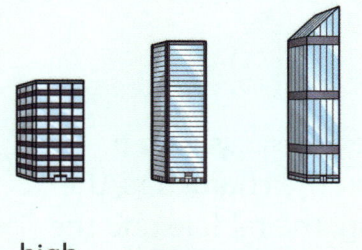

3 high _____ _____

> ### L👀k and learn
> Usually, **positive adjectives** are used to describe only one thing. **Comparative adjectives** are used to compare two things and **superlative adjectives** are used to compare three or more things.

3 What are the missing words?

Positive	Comparative	Superlative
1	prettier	prettiest
loud	2	loudest
busy	busier	3
cool	4	coolest
5	quieter	quietest
bright	brighter	6

Extra challenge
Create a table like the one in Activity 3 using four adjectives of your own choice from the Anansi story. Leave four boxes blank and challenge a partner to complete it.

Let's write

My favourite folktale

Using **adjectives** to make comparisons in stories is a great way to add detail. **Adjectives** help the reader imagine the scene.

1. Do you know many Anansi folktales or Duppy stories? Discuss with a partner which is your favourite and why. Think about the characters, the setting and the message. Think about the beginning, the middle and the end. This is a story chart for Anansi and Goat. Copy the chart and answer the questions for Anansi and Goat.

Characters	Setting	Message of the tale
Who is the main character? How do the characters behave? What do they look like?	Where is the story taking place? What time of day is it? What is the overall mood/feeling of the story? Will the mood/feeling change?	What lesson does the main character learn? Do the readers see the lesson?
What happens at the start?	**What happens in the middle?**	**What happens at the end?**
Write about the characters: *One day, there were two boys playing…* the setting: *It was getting dark and very cold…* the problem in the story: *Then they were in trouble, they were trapped…*	What do the characters do? What happens to make the plot exciting? How do the characters think they can deal with the problem?	How did the characters overcome the problem?

2. Write your own version of a folktale or story that you know. Then copy the story chart and fill it in for your own story. The questions are there to help you think of the important things to include.

Plan and write

- Use the information from your story chart to write a first draft.
- Swap your first draft with a partner and read each other's stories.

Revise

- Use the feedback from your partner to make any changes to your first draft.

Write up your final version

- You are going to write your own version of a folktale or story that you know.

When you write a story, it must have a beginning, a middle and an end!

Editor's checklist

Check your story carefully when you finish.

- Does the story have a title?
- Does the story have strong characters and a clear setting?
- Does the story have a clear beginning, middle and end?
- Do all sentences have a full stop?
- Are adjectives used to make comparisons?

ICT opportunity

On a computer, design an interesting title page or front cover for your story. Consider whether to type up your story. Think about how you can design the layout, so it looks like a book when it is printed out.

Term 1 Unit 1

Project 3

Speaking and listening

1. Listen to your teacher read aloud the text on food and decide whether the following sentences are true (T) or false (F).

Jamaican food and diets

Your diet is all the food and drink that you have each day. In Jamaica, we grow and make lots of delicious foods. We enjoy fresh fruits and vegetables such as bananas, mangoes and yams. We cook very tasty dishes, like rice and peas and we jerk meat or fish, which means it is marinated in spicy sauces or seasonings.

rice and peas jerk chicken ackee and saltfish

1. Everything you eat and drink is your diet. _____
2. Yams are grown in Jamaica. _____
3. Rice and peas are marinated in spicy sauces. _____

2. With your partner, discuss your favourite food and why you like it. Describe the way it looks, how it smells and how it tastes.

3. In pairs, look at the bar graph which shows information about Jamaican children's favourite dish. Answer the following questions.

28

Project 3 – Food and cooking

1   How **many children like** rice and peas? _____

2   Do **more children like** jerk chicken **than** ackee and saltfish?

    _____

3   Do **fewer children like** ackee and saltfish **than** jerk chicken?

    _____

4   Which dish is the **most popular**? _____

5   Which dish is the **least popular**? _____

6   How many **more children like** ackee and fish **than** jerk chicken?

    _____

4   Present your findings and report back to the class. Make sure you and your partner both speak. Use the language from Activities 1 to 4.

Example:
The bar graph shows the favourite dishes of Jamaican children in 2023. It is clear that the **most popular** dish is…

Word builder

This vocabulary is about food and cooking:

Vocabulary box

marinade	chicken	curry	thoroughly
slice	sauce	measure	plantain
ingredients	delicious	prepare	serve
chop	taste	stock	

1. With your partner, take turns to read the words. Discuss the word meanings as you go. Circle any words you do not recognise and look up the meaning at the end of the activity.

Example:
"Marinade" is to cover food with spices or a sauce before cooking. My mom always marinades chicken before she cooks it.

2. With your partner, have a spelling challenge. One of you calls out a word and your partner has to spell it out loud letter-by-letter. You must cover the list of words and try to get the spelling correct using your knowledge of phonics (word sounds). Swap roles so that you both have a chance to be the caller and the speller.

3. With your partner, explore different ways to sort the words. For example, you can sort them by word length, by meaning, by word class (noun, verb, adjective). Add some more words about food and cooking to each group. Share your ideas with a group or the class.

Remember

Nouns that do not start with a capital letter are called **common nouns**. Common nouns include the names of everyday items, for example: *table, car, school* and *house*.

4. Which words in the Vocabulary box are common nouns?

Extra challenge

Write a sentence that contains two common nouns from the list.

Project 3 – Food and cooking

L👀k and learn

- Words are made up of **sounds**. Identifying these sounds can help you to spell words.

  For example, the word *cat* has three sounds: /c/, /a/, /t/.

- The number of letters does not correspond to the number of sounds. For example *toe* has three letters, but only two sounds: /t/, /oe/.

5 1 In pairs, take turns to practise segmenting the following words. Student A ticks (✓) the box after Student B segments the word into sounds, then swap roles.

Word	Sounds	Student A ✓	Student B ✓
fat	/f/, /a/, /t/		
food	/f/, /oo/, /d/		
goat	/g/, /oa/, /t/		
milk	/m/, /i/, /l/, /k/		
butter	/b/, /u/, /tt/, /e/, /r/		
meat	/m/, /ea/, /t/		
rice	/r/, /i/, /ce/		

2 Here are some segmented words from the vocabulary box. Practise saying the sounds that make up these words to your partner. In pairs, complete the table with the number of letters and sounds in the words.

Word / letters	Sounds
marinade (8 letters)	/m/, /a/, /r/, /i/, /n/, /a/, /de/ (7 sounds)
chicken (7 letters)	/ch/, /i/, /ck/, /e/, /n/ (5 sounds)
slice (5 letters)	/sl/, /i/, /ce/ (_____ sounds)
chop (_____ letters)	(_____ sounds)
stock (_____ letters)	(_____ sounds)
plantain (_____ letters)	(_____ sounds)

31

Let's read

Fact or fiction?

Stories and poems are not the only types of text that we can read. We also read newspapers and magazines, instruction manuals, school text books and recipe books. In this project, you will be looking at non-fiction texts, starting with recipe books.

Look and learn

Text that describes something which has never actually happened in real life, such as *Peter Pan* by JM Barrie is called **fiction**. Fiction books are imaginary, which means they are not based on facts. They may have a few illustrations to set the scene.

Text that describes something that is true in real life such as a school history text book or a recipe book is called **non-fiction**. Non-fiction books provide facts and information. They often have many pictures or diagrams to explain the text. Sometimes, non-fiction books are called reference books.

- Which of these books are fiction?
- Which are non-fiction?

 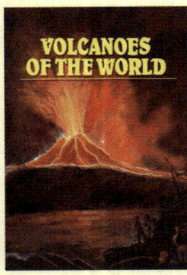 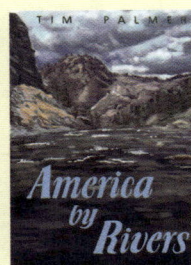 

- Which is your favourite fiction book?
- Which is your favourite type of non-fiction?
- Look around your classroom or a library and find more examples of fiction and non-fiction books that you think you will enjoy. Share your ideas with the class.

What's your view?
Think about fiction and non-fiction books.
Is one kind more important than the other?
Explain your ideas to your partner.

1 A recipe is a non-fiction text. It gives instructions about how to make something. Read this recipe and answer the questions that follow.

Jerk chicken recipe

Ingredients

1 large chicken
8 cloves of garlic
3 medium brown onions
6 sliced scotch bonnet or jalapeno peppers
2 tbsp. sugar
2 tbsp. salt
2 tsp. ground black pepper
1 or 2 tsp. ground cinnamon
1 or 2 tsp. ground nutmeg
1 or 2 tsp. ground ginger
2 tbsp. thyme
2 tbsp. ground allspice
½ cup olive oil
½ cup soy sauce
1 cup orange juice
1 cup white vinegar
juice of 1 lime

Remember ☆☆☆

Measure carefully. Look at numbers (3 onions), size (medium), cups and spoon measures. *Tbsp.* is short for tablespoon. *Tsp.* is short for teaspoon.

Kitchen caution! Handle knives safely. Always have dry hands and ask an adult to help.

Preparation

1. Cut up the onions, garlic and peppers.
2. Blend all the ingredients, except for the chicken, in a blender to make the jerk sauce.
3. Chop the chicken into quarters and rub the sauce into the meat. Save some sauce to use later.
4. Leave the chicken in a refrigerator overnight to marinate.

Cooking

Method 1: Bake the chicken in the oven for half an hour then turn the meat over and bake for another half hour.

Method 2: Grill the meat slowly, turning regularly until it is cooked thoroughly. During cooking, baste with some of the sauce that you saved.

Serving

1. Chop each chicken portion into smaller pieces using a meat cleaver.
2. Serve with salad, rice and peas, or hard dough bread and the jerk sauce left over for dipping.

Kitchen caution! Hold the chicken still with a fork instead of your hand, or you may end up chopping your fingers instead of chicken!

1. Imagine you are going to cook jerk chicken. Write a shopping list of what you would need to buy. Write your list under different headings.

Meat	Vegetables	Spices	Fruits	Liquids	Seasonings

2. Write a list of the kitchen equipment you would need to cook the dish. Write your list under different headings.

Measuring	Cutting	Liquids	Cooking	Other

3. Safety in the kitchen is important. Create a poster to share your ideas about how to keep safe in the kitchen when cooking. Give an example of how you could stay safe when following this recipe.

4. Look at the speech bubble and circle the correct word, *skim* or *scan*.

I can't remember if I need two or three onions. I'll need to **skim / scan** the jerk chicken recipe.

Grammar builder

Fiction, non-fiction and tenses

> **Remember** ☆ ☆ ☆
>
> **Fictional** texts often tell a story and usually use the past tense.
> **Non-fiction** texts are factual and true about life. Non-fiction texts about things that have already happened are usually in the past tense. Texts about things that are still happening are usually in the present tense.
> Find an example of the past tense in the "Folktales" project.
> Find an example of the present tense in this "Food" project.

1. Sort these sentences into present tense and past tense. Write them under the correct tense in your notebook.

    1. Finally, you need to stir the sauce into the rice and mix thoroughly.
    2. One day Brother Goat strolled along the river bank.
    3. First, cut up the onions, garlic and pepper.
    4. Leave the chicken in a refrigerator to marinade.
    5. Once upon a time, there was a strange creature that lived in the mountains.

2. Which of the sentences in Activity 1 are non-fiction? Which are fiction? How do you know?

3. Spot the mistake in each of these recipe book sentences and rewrite each sentence correctly.

    1. Chopped up the chicken into small pieces.
    2. After an hour, turned down the oven.
    3. When the meat is golden brown, added the other ingredients.
    4. Cooked until tender.
    5. Carefully poured the stock over the fish.

Research and study skills

Remember ☆☆☆

A **Venn diagram** is used to show what is the same and what is different. Things that are the same go in the middle section.

Fiction
front vs. back cover
chapter titles
illustrations
read from
beginning to end

Non-fiction
table of contents
titles/subtitles
photos/captions/
diagrams/maps
index

1. In a group and on a large sheet of paper, draw a Venn diagram like the one above to compare and contrast fiction and non-fiction texts.

   1. Add these features under the correct section of the diagram:
      - imaginary or fantasy
      - real life and true
      - add more points if your group agrees.

   2. As a group, agree on the common features between the two sections and write the details in the middle section of the Venn diagram. Report your groups findings to the class by explaining your points in the middle section of the Venn diagram.

Project 3 – Food and cooking

Let's write

Cook Caribbean

A website called *Cook Caribbean* is looking for recipes from Jamaica to feature on the site.

> A recipe starts with a list of ingredients (including measurements). Then it has a step-by-step method to follow for preparing, cooking and serving the dish.

Task

Write a recipe for the website. Choose your favourite dish or use a recipe that belongs to your family. Ask an adult if you are not sure about the measurements of the ingredients or method you need for the recipe.

Plan

Follow this sequence in your writing:

- Choose the dish and make the name of the dish clear. Be creative.
  ↓
- List the ingredients and say how much of each you need in teaspoons, tablespoons or cups.
  ↓
- List how to prepare the ingredients. Do any need to be washed, chopped, sliced or blended?
  ↓
- Explain how to mix the ingredients. Use numbers to make the order clear.
  ↓
- Explain how to cook the ingredients. For how long do you need to cook them?
  ↓
- Describe how to serve the cooked dish.
  - Is it served hot or cold?
  - What should it be served with?
  - Does it need any other sauce?

Extra challenge

The website is very aware of safety. Find two stages in your recipe where you can include some safety advice.

Editor's checklist

You must check your work carefully when you finish. This is called **proofreading**.

- Does the recipe have a title?
- Is the recipe written in the present tense?
- Does the recipe say what is needed and what to do in the correct order?
- Does the recipe use signal words, such as *first, next, then, after this*?
- Do all sentences begin with a capital letter and end with a full stop?
- Are adjectives used to make comparisons?

Project 4 – Jamaican heroes

Project 4

Speaking and listening

1. Your teacher will read aloud a text about Jamaican heroes.

   1. Make some notes about the text by writing key words to help you remember the details later.

      These seven people are national heroes. They were all awarded the greatest honour in the country: The Order of National Hero. In different ways and at different times, they helped to shape and develop the nation. Without them, the country of Jamaica would not be what it is today.

      For example, Sir Alexander Bustamante, who was born in Blenheim, in Hanover parish, on the 24th of February 1884 supported the poor and workers' rights. He formed the Jamaican Labour Party and became Jamaica's first chief minister.

   2. In groups, refer to your notes and discuss the following:
      - What is the main point of the text?
      - What do the people in the text have in common?
      - Who is mentioned as an example? What is special about this person?

2. In groups, choose one of the national heroes to study.

   1. Find information about these facts:
      - the years of birth and death
      - where in Jamaica they were born or lived
      - one thing that they are famous for and how they helped Jamaican people.

   2. Talk together about how this person has contributed to Jamaican culture.

3 Prepare to speak:
- Divide the information about your chosen national hero between each group member. For example, Student A will talk about the years of birth and death and family members. Student B may talk about the places the hero lived or where they went to school.
- Each student should prepare to speak about the hero using one or two sentences, including a fact from Activity 1.
- To ensure the information in your sentences is presented confidently and fluently, you should know your material (this means understand the information) and practise saying your sentences out loud several times. In addition, think about your body language by standing straight and using eye contact.

3 As a group, share the information about your hero with the class. Your class members will evaluate your performance using the table below. Copy the table into your notebooks and use it to evaluate the other groups when you are listening to their information.

Group evaluation	A good effort	Well done
Makes eye contact.		
Speaks clearly and loudly.		
The information is interesting and includes facts.		

Speak slowly and clearly.
Make eye contact.
Listen carefully.
Look interested.
Respect the other person's time to speak, meaning don't interrupt if it's not appropriate.

Word builder

This vocabulary is about history and heroes:

Vocabulary box

history	believe	develop	thought
challenge	bravery	fight	remember
hero	important	without	slavery
respect	figure	famous	

1. Read the vocabulary words slowly and clearly to a partner. Listen to your partner read the words to you. Help each other with the pronunciation of the words.

2. In pairs, circle any words you do not understand and use a dictionary or online tool to look up the meanings.

> Be careful! Some words can have more than one meaning. Remember that you are thinking about history and heroes, so, for example, the word *figure* doesn't refer to a number like the figure 8, it refers to historical figures — the national heroes.

3. In your notebook, rewrite the vocabulary words in alphabetical order. Swap your notebook with a partner and check each other's spelling.

Extra challenge

In pairs, take turns to read out a word to each other. Your partner should write down the word without looking at the vocabulary box. Award each other a point if you both agree the spelling is correct.

4. Read this paragraph about national heroes. How many of the words from the vocabulary box can you find in the paragraph?

The national heroes are famous historical figures in Jamaica. People remember them for their bravery. They are important because they played a role in our history and helped to develop our nation.

Term 1 Unit 1

Look and learn

- A **prefix** is a part of a word that comes at the **beginning** of a word and changes its meaning. For example: *like* → **dis**like   *happy* → **un**happy
- A **root word** is the **original meaning** of any word. It is what is left when the prefix and suffix is removed.
- A **suffix** is a part of a word that comes at the **end** and changes the meaning of the word.
- For example: *happy* → *happi***ness**   *option* → *option***al**

Extra challenge

1. How many words from the vocabulary box can you change the meaning of by adding *di-* or *un-* in front of them? How do they change the meaning?
2. Complete the spelling patterns.

    1 history   → historical
    2 _____ → national
    3 exception   → _____
    4 _____ → traditional

Notice how the root word *history* and the suffix *-al* changes the noun to an adjective. For example: *history* → **historical** *figures*.

42

Project 4 – Jamaican heroes

Let's read

Research and study skills

1 Here are the titles of three non-fiction books:

   Famous Jamaicans

   Port Royal: A Rich History

   The Incredible Life of Nat Turner

   What is the purpose of a book's title?

   _____

   _____

> **Look and learn**
> Text features are organised with a specific purpose in mind. The author wants the reader to find the information quickly so you continue to read with interest.

2 Look at the article below. Write the name of the **heading** in green that you would look at to learn about:

   what Samuel Sharpe believed in _____

   Samuel Sharpe's childhood _____

   how he helped others to make their voices heard _____

The life of Samuel Sharpe

Early years

Samuel Sharpe was born in Montego Bay in 1801. Samuel was born a slave, but learned to read and write. Later, his faith in the Bible helped him to become a Baptist deacon.

His message

He believed that slaves should be free because the Bible said "no man should serve two masters" and he travelled around to spread his message to others.

Protest

Samuel Sharpe used his church meetings to help other enslaved people understand what they could do to make their voices heard.

Peace

He did not believe in violence and did not want to fight, so he tried to arrange a **peaceful protest against slavery**.

Violence

Some of the other slaves, however, did not want to be peaceful and they started burning the estates and crops instead. Violence broke out all around the island. Samuel Sharpe was blamed because he had been the one who **preached about freedom** to the slaves, even though his plan was a peaceful one.

3 A **subheading** is smaller than a heading and organises information into smaller sections. What are the two subheadings under the heading *Protest*?

   _____

4 Another text feature is bold text. This is for important information the author thinks you need to know. What does the author think is the most important information in this text?

   _____

Read the information about the life and times of Samuel Sharpe and why he became a national hero of Jamaica.

The life of Samuel Sharpe

Samuel Sharpe was born in Montego Bay in 1801. For many years Samuel was a slave, but he was also a Baptist with great faith in the Bible. He believed that slaves should be free because the Bible said "no man should serve two masters" and he travelled around to spread his message to others. He did not believe in violence and did not want to fight, so he tried to arrange a peaceful protest against slavery. If the slaves refused to harvest the sugar cane when it was ready at Christmas time in 1831, then, he hoped, the landowners would give in and agree to pay them to work. Some of the other slaves, however, did not want to be peaceful and they started burning the estates and crops instead. Violence broke out all around the island. Samuel Sharpe was blamed because he had been the one who preached about freedom to the slaves, even though his plan was a peaceful one. Samuel gave himself up after ten days of violence had passed. He was charged with rebellion, found guilty and he was executed in 1832. Just two years later, slavery was abolished and Samuel's dream for freedom for all slaves was achieved. He inspired people to believe that they could work together in a peaceful way to bring about change. This is why he is a national hero.

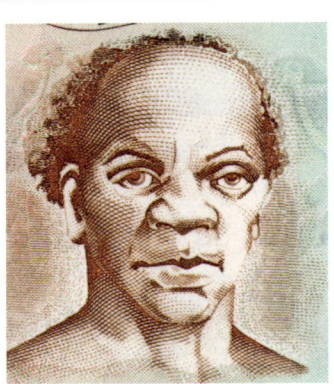

Samuel Sharpe (1801 – 1832) as seen on the $500 note

5 Use the text about Samuel Sharpe to fill the gaps in the sentences.

   1 Samuel Sharpe came from _____ in Jamaica.

   2 He believed in _____.

3   He disagreed with _____ and did not want to fight.

4   He tried to organise a _____ protest against slavery.

5   He was blamed for the _____. He was executed in 1832 because they found him guilty of _____.

6   Imagine you were a slave in 1831. What would you have thought about Samuel's peaceful plan? Give two points of view.

Example:

"I support Samuel Sharpe's peaceful plan because…"

"I do not agree that we should only refuse to harvest the sugar cane because…"

7   In pairs, make notes on the main ideas of the text above. Visit a library or use the internet to find out more about Samuel Sharpe. Summarise the main points of the information you have and give a short presentation to the class.

L👀k and learn

Libraries have different areas for fiction and non-fiction books. You will need to look in the history area of the non-fiction section for information about Samuel Sharpe.

Books in a library are often packed on the shelves in a particular order to make it easier to find them. Alphabetical order is commonly used.

Ask a librarian about the different sections and the ordering system that they use in the library you visit or research this online if you are unable to visit a library.

"A library is a great place to find information. Some libraries provide services like computers connected to the internet that you can use as well."

Grammar builder

Conjunctions

> **Look and learn**
>
> **Conjunctions** are connecting words. Common conjunctions include: *and, so, or, but, while, when, where.*
>
> Conjunctions can be used to join two parts of a sentence, two nouns or two verbs.
>
> Sentences: Peter went to the market **while** Rita stayed at home.
> Nouns: I would like a mango **and** a banana.
> Verbs: The boys were singing **and** dancing in the street.
>
> **Compound sentences and coordinating conjunctions**
>
> When a conjunction is used to join together two complete sentences, the sentence is called a **compound sentence**. Notice the **comma**. There is always a comma before a coordinating conjunction.
>
> | Sentence A | Conjunction | Sentence B |
> | --- | --- | --- |
> | The bus stopped | and | the children got off the bus. |
> | The bus stopped**,** and the children got off the bus. | | |

1 Conjunctions have different meanings. Match the conjunctions 1-5 against the functions (a-e). If there are any conjunctions or words you are not sure about, use a dictionary or an online tool to look up the meanings.

1 first, next, finally   a to add information

2 and, in addition   b express the result of something

3 but, however   c an alternative

4 or   d to contrast information

5 so   e to sequence points

2 Complete the sentences with *and*, *but*, *so*.

1 It was very hot, _____ she turned on the fan.

2 I wanted more jerk chicken, _____ it was all finished.

3 I wanted an ice cream, _____ I wanted a soda.

3 Write sentences about what you did yesterday using the conjunctions listed below.

1 (and) Yesterday I went shopping, and I bought some shoes.

2 (but) _____

3 (so) _____

4 (and) _____

Now I can use conjunctions to make longer sentences when I am writing.

4 Work in groups or as a whole class.

- Make a large drawing of a graphic organiser in the shape of a tree for the classroom wall.
- Add the following list of conjunctions to the tree:

  and, but, or, nor, for, yet, so, although, because, since, unless

- Look up the meaning and how to use any conjunctions you do not know.
- Every time you learn a new conjunction, if your group or whole class agree, add it to the tree.

Let's write

Speeches

Look again at the portraits of the seven national heroes. You know a lot about them now.

You have given a short presentation about them and listened to presentations by your classmates. You have read about and researched Samuel Sharpe. You have learned a lot of new vocabulary.

Task

Do a creative writing task about national heroes. Use all that you have studied in this project to help you.

- Choose one of the seven national heroes. You are going to imagine you are that person.
- Plan and write a speech that you will give to the people of that time about what you stand for.
- Use language that is powerful and descriptive. Remember, you want the people to follow you and believe in you. Use your words to convince them that you are a hero.

Plan

Here are some questions to help you get started with writing your speech:

- How will you introduce yourself? *"Hello everyone. My name is … and I am here today to tell you about… ."*
- What are your ideas and dreams for the people? *"I have a dream… . We can and we will… ."*
- How do you plan to achieve them? *"First, I plan to… . Then, I will… . In addition, I will… ."*
- What type of a future do you see for yourself and the people? *"In the future we will… . Together we can… ."*
- What can you do for the people that other leaders can't? *"Follow my lead and I will… . You will see that I am the best person for… because… . I will never let you down!"*

You may write a short paragraph for each answer to these questions or one or two longer paragraphs that include all your ideas.

Editor's checklist

Proofread your speech when you finish.

- Does the speech include powerful vocabulary to inspire listeners?
- Does the speech include adjectives to give details?
- Are conjunctions used to form compound sentences?
- Are short sentences used deliberately?
- Do all proper nouns have capital letters?
- Do all sentences end with a full stop or a question mark?
- Do powerful statements end with an exclamation mark?

It's great fun to imagine being a historical hero!

Project 5

Speaking and listening

1 Listen to your teacher read the text and decide whether the following statements are true (T) or false (F).

The Secret of Jamaica's Runners

The fastest times ever recorded in 100 metre races were mostly by Jamaicans. In the past ten years, male and female runners from the Caribbean island have **dominated** track and field events. Usain Bolt, Asafa Powell and Verona Campbell-Brown are all Jamaican and Olympic gold medallists. In the 2008 Olympics in Beijing, Jamaica was **ranked** first in sprints, with Usain Bolt winning three gold medals.

So how do Jamaicans do it? One reason is that the sport of running has changed in Jamaica. In the past, some sprinters got scholarships at overseas colleges. However, some felt **homesick**. Today, Jamaica employs top coaches, so Jamaican sprinters can stay in Jamaica.

The result is that sprinters can perform better because they are not stressed.

Another reason is that in Jamaica, children start running at a very early age. When they are at school, they have opportunities to train **alongside** their everyday studies. This way teachers and coaches can spot whether talented students should be sent to track and field clubs. At school, teenagers get together to compete with each other.

Jamaica is perhaps the only country in the world where a track and field meet is a top sporting event. Winning school championships is something really big. The competitive track and field competitions may be one of the reasons Jamaicans are so good.

1 Usain, Asafa and Verona won gold medals. ____

2 Running has changed in Jamaica. ____

3 Coaches employ Jamaican sprinters. ____

4 Jamaica is the only country that has a track and field meet. ____

2 1 With your partner, discuss the sporting achievements of Jamaica. Take turns to read a paragraph from the text and discuss the main points after each paragraph. Why do you think Jamaicans are the best in the world at track and field?

2 In pairs, report back to the class on the sporting achievements of Jamaica. Make sure you and your partner both speak.

Word builder

This vocabulary is about sport:

Vocabulary box

sport	training	hurdles	agility	podium
Olympics	determination	excel	team	result
athletics	example	speed	practice	achieve

1 In pairs, take turns to read the words to each other.

2 **1** Here are some segmented words from the vocabulary box. In pairs, practise saying the sounds that make up these words and complete the table. The first one is done for you.

Word / Letters	Sounds
team (4 letters)	/t/ /ea/ /m/ (__3__ sounds)
sport (_____ letters)	/s/ /p/ /or/ /t/ (_____ sounds)
speed (_____ letters)	/sp/ /ee/ /d/ (_____ sounds)
result (_____ letters)	/r/ /e/ /s/ /u/ /l/ /t/ (_____ sounds)
practice (_____ letters)	/pr/ /a/ /ct/ /i/ /ce/ (_____ sounds)

2 Now say the letter sounds together quickly. This is called blending.

Example:
Segment: Blend:
/t/ /ea/ /m/ → team

3 Here are some newspaper headlines. There is a spelling mistake in each one. Write out the headlines again and correct the mistakes.

> Spoort gets big investment

> Super sprinter hits top spead

> Cricket teem on the road to success

> High school student gets world class risult

Term 1 Unit 1

4 Stories about sporting achievements most often appear in newspapers. Newspapers also contain pages that have puzzles such as crosswords. This is a crossword about sport.

1 Work with a partner or group. Read the clues and write your answers.

2 Time yourselves to see who is the class champion. Who can complete the crossword fastest?

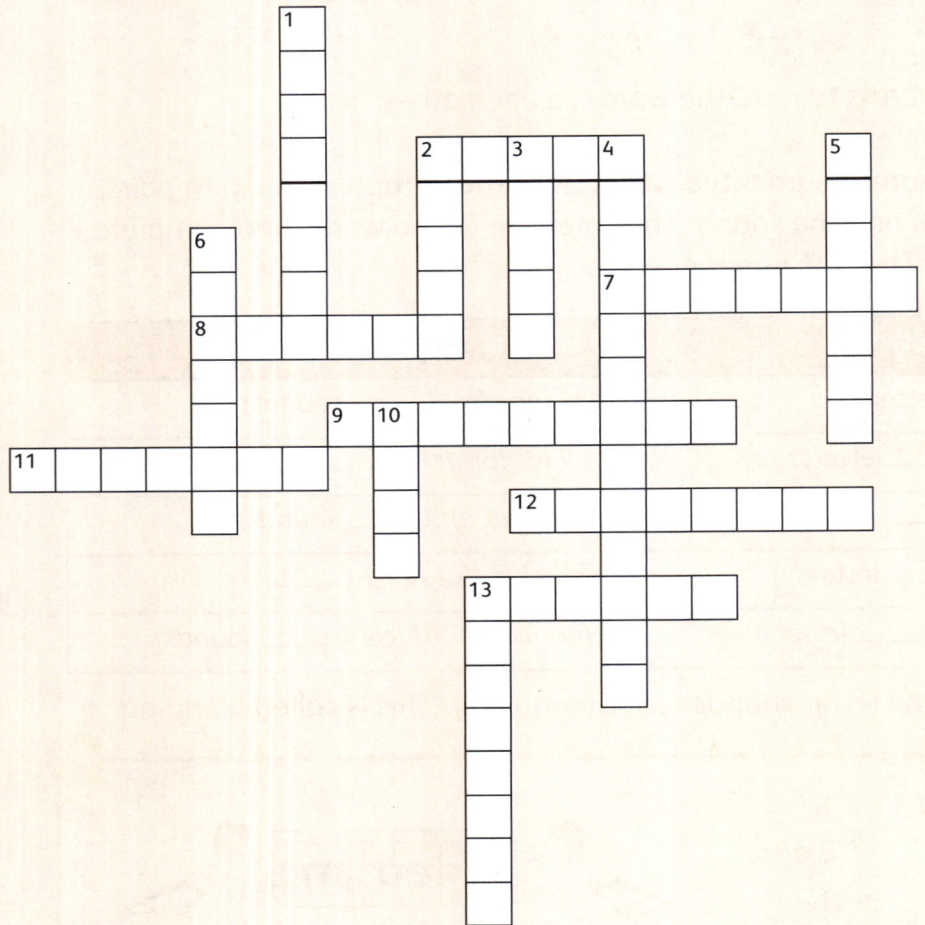

Across
2 how fast something is
7 used for comparison or explanation
8 an outcome
9 track and field
11 to obtain
12 preparation for an event or task
13 a stand for medal winners

Down
1 a global sporting event
2 an activity done for exercise or pleasure
3 to do very well
4 motivation to complete a task
5 ability to flex and move
6 an Olympic event
10 a group of people doing sport together
13 trying something many times to get better at it

52

Project 5 – Jamaican sports and sporting achievements

Let's read

Usain Bolt: the fastest man on Earth

This is a biography of Usain Bolt that appeared in a sports magazine. Read the biography and then complete the tasks that follow.

> A **biography** is a summary of a person's life and achievements.

1 Skim the text and answer the following question: How do you think Usain Bolt became such a good athlete?

Usain Bolt: the fastest man on Earth

Usain Bolt is a sprinter and he is the most well-known and world famous of all Jamaican athletes. He was born in Trelawny on 21st August 1986. He towers over most people he meets. Incredibly, he has been this tall since the age of 15!

He has the nickname "Lightning Bolt" because of the amazing speeds he reached on the athletics track. His fastest ever recorded speed is 23.7 mph. In 2012 at the London Olympics, he ran 100 metres in a time of 9.63 seconds! Wow!

Usain always loved sport as a child. He first began to compete when he was at high school. He won his first medal, a silver, at the Inter-Secondary Schools Boys and Girls Championship in 2001. After that, he was recognised as a promising athlete and went on to become a professional sprinter in 2004. His first Olympic Games participation was in Athens, in 2004. After this, he went to the games again in Beijing in 2008, London in 2012 and Rio de Janeiro in 2016. He has won eight gold medals in his career.

2 1 Read the text again. Write three sentences summarising the information about Usain Bolt.

2 Share your summary with your partner and listen to theirs. Which similar information did you include? What was different? Discuss how you chose what to include.

3 Create a Usain Bolt timeline to show his main achievements. Refer to the text as well as your own knowledge and experiences to help you.

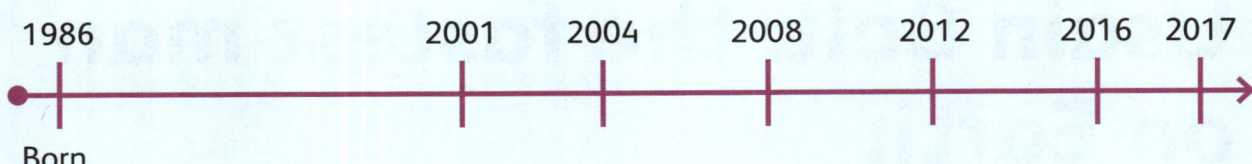

Born

Extra challenge

Usain Bolt is not the only famous Jamaican athlete. Name another Jamaican sports star and state their sport. Give two facts about your chosen sports star.

ICT opportunity

Find out more about Usain Bolt by reading the biography on his official website.
If possible, make a presentation with your information.
Step 1: Launch the PowerPoint™ program.
Step 2: Choose a design.
Step 3: Create a title page.
Step 4: Add another slide and display the timeline and information in Activity 2.
Step 5: Add pictures and text features to make the presentation clear.
Step 6: Present your work to a group or the class using your PowerPoint presentation.
Note: You could transfer your PowerPoint to a USB flash drive and then connect the USB flash drive to the classroom computer. You will then be able to project your presentation on the board. Ask your teacher to help you.

Grammar builder

Defining a sentence with punctuation

Whenever we read a text of any kind, the words we read are organised in a certain way by the punctuation used. **Punctuation** is important because it helps us to make sense of words that we read either on a page or on a screen. Without punctuation, words would be a long jumble and they wouldn't make sense.

Look and learn

Some of the most important parts of punctuation are the marks that we use to show when sentences start and end.

Start of sentences	End of sentences
New sentences always start with a **capital letter**.	All sentences must end with a punctuation mark. A **full stop** (.) is used at the end of a statement or fact. A **question mark** (?) is used at the end of a question. An **exclamation mark** (!) is used at the end of a powerful, funny, or angry sentence.

1 The following paragraph contains five sentences. However, the punctuation marks at the beginning and end of the sentences have been left out.

   1 Rewrite the paragraph and add the correct punctuation.

   2 Swap with a partner to check whether you have punctuated the paragraph in the same way.

> the country of Jamaica has a long history of success at the Olympic Games since we began competing in 1948 we have won medals at every games with both men and women of the nation winning several medals it's just amazing we are very proud of the sporting heroes that have represented us in the past and today wouldn't you agree that Jamaica is a great sporting nation

> **Punctuation marks** are an important part of writing. Without them everything is a jumble!

Let's write

Background

You have been emailing a friend who lives abroad that you met on holiday. Your friend's last email to you asked about sport in Jamaica.

Task

Use all you have studied on Jamaica's sporting success, what you have read about Jamaican sports stars and the vocabulary you have learned to write a reply to your friend.

> **Special instructions**
> - Try to use as many of the words from the "Word builder" lesson as you can, plus any other special sports vocabulary you know.
> - Use adjectives, conjunctions, transitional phrases and correct sentence punctuation.
> - Show that you can use these parts of grammar in your work.

Plan

Use these questions to get you started. You may write a few sentences for each answer or one or two paragraphs to include these ideas.

- How will you begin your email?
- There are many great Jamaican athletes, but who is your favourite and why?
- Is there an athlete that inspires you? What have they achieved? How do you feel when you watch them?
- What do you know about sport in your friend's country? Think of some questions to ask your friend.

Using correct grammar means that I can write better, even in informal situations like writing to a friend!

Editor's checklist

Proofread your email when you finish.

- Have you used transitional phrases to help with meaning?
- Does the email sound interesting? Have you given information, your opinion and asked questions, too?
- Do all sentences have a full stop, exclamation mark or question mark?
- Do all proper nouns have capital letters?
- Are all words spelt correctly?

Project 6

Speaking and listening

Song of the Banana Man

Touris, white man, wipin his face,
Met me in Golden Grove market place.
He looked at m'ol' clothes brown wid stain,
An soaked right through wid de Portlan rain,
He cas his eye, turn up his nose,
He says, "You're a beggar man, I suppose?"
He says, "Boy, get some occupation,
Be of some value to your nation."
I said, "By God and dis big right han
You mus recognise a banana man."

"Up in de hills, where de streams are cool,
An mullet an janga swim in de pool,
I have ten acres of mountain side,
An a dainty-foot donkey dat I ride,
Four Gros Michel, an four Lacatan,
Some coconut trees, and some hills of yam,
An I pasture on dat very same lan
Five she-goats an a big black ram,
Dat, by God an dis big right han
Is de property of a banana man."

"I leave m'yard early-mornin time
An set m'foot to de mountain climb,
I ben m'back to de hot-sun toil,
An m'cutlass rings on de stony soil,
Ploughin an weedin, diggin an plantin
Till Massa Sun drop back o John Crow mountain,
Den home again in cool evenin time,
Perhaps whistling dis likkle rhyme,
(Sung) Praise God an m'big right han
I will live an die a banana man."

"Banana day is my special day,
I cut my stems an I'm on m'way,
Load up de donkey, leave de lan
Head down de hill to banana stan,
When de truck comes roun I take a ride
All de way down to de harbour side-
Dat is de night, when you, touris man,
Would change your place wid a banana man.
Yes, by God, an m'big right han
I will live an die a banana man."

"So when you see dese ol clothes brown wid stain,
An soaked right through wid de Portlan rain,
Don't cas your eye nor turn your nose,
Don't judge a man by his patchy clothes,
I'm a strong man, a proud man, an I'm free,
Free as dese mountains, free as dis sea,
I know myself, an I know my ways,
An will sing wid pride to de end o my days
(Sung) Praise God an m'big right han
I will live an die a banana man."

by Evan Jones

1. Listen to your teacher read the poem aloud. Listen for parts of the poem that are repeated like a chorus of a song. Why does the poet, Evan Jones, do this? What effect does it have on you?

2. With your partner, discuss these questions. Find evidence in the poem to back up your answers:

    1. What mistake has the tourist made?

    2. Why do you think he made this mistake?

    3. How do you think the banana man feels about the job he does? How do you know?

    4. Do you believe that banana men are "of some value to your nation"?

3. Share your ideas with the class. Listen to the responses from others.

4. Make five groups in the class so each group works on one stanza (a verse).

    1. Work on the stanza your teacher gives your group. Each group member reads the stanza out loud, taking it in turns to speak. Discuss any tricky words or pronunciations. Make sure the meaning is clear in your group.

    2. Decide how to share the reading of the stanza. How will you read the words that are repeated in each group's stanza?

    3. Decide how to enhance the words. Will you add actions? Music? Sound effects? Practise the group performance over time if you can.

    4. When each group is ready, watch and review each group. Identify two positive things and one thing to improve for each group.

    5. Finally, come together and make a class performance of the poem. Try to find a real audience to appreciate your work!

Word builder

Tourism is when people take a vacation in a place that they do not live. This vocabulary is about tourism:

Vocabulary box

tourist	excursion	aeroplane	different
journey	travel	visit	sunshine
resort	hotel	experience	problem
beach	vacation	luggage	

1. Read the words slowly and clearly to a partner. Listen to your partner read the words to you. Help each other with the pronunciation of the words.

2. Work with a partner to test each other on spelling the words from the vocabulary box. Listen as your partner reads the words aloud while you write the words in your notebook. Then swap over.

Look and learn

Compound words are formed when two or more words are joined together to make a new word with a new meaning. For example, the word *toothpaste* is made up of two words: *tooth* and *paste*.

3. Match two words to make a compound word and write it under the last column. The first one is done for you.

Word 1	Word 2	New word
~~sand~~	ground	sandcastle
sun	bow	
rain	end	
play	glasses	
week	~~castle~~	

Term 1 Unit 1

4   These sentences are from brochures aimed at tourists. Find a word from the list to complete each sentence.

   1   The most luxurious __ __ __ __ __ on the island!

   2   Relax and enjoy the __ __ __ __ __ __ __ __ whilst on the beautiful __ __ __ __ __ __.

   3   An unforgettable __ __ __ __ __ __ __ __ __ __.

   4   Free __ __ __ __ __ __ __ storage in the lobby.

> **Extra challenge**
>
> Some of the sentences could be completed by more than one word from the vocabulary box. Write those sentences out again using alternative words to complete them.

5   Describe your last vacation to a partner and try to use some of the words from the vocabulary box. Listen to your partner describe their vacation to you and make sure that they use some of the words from the vocabulary box, too.

6   Write two sentences about your partner's vacation. Use at least one of the words from the vocabulary box in each sentence.

> **What's your view?**
> Why do people choose to go on vacation? Discuss your ideas with your partner, using the words in the Vocabulary box to help you.

Let's read

Tourism in Jamaica

Read this travel magazine article about visitors to Jamaica.

Tourism in Jamaica

Visitors

In the 1950s, Jamaica welcomed around 122,000 visitors a year. In 2015, Jamaica welcomed over 3,500,000. It is believed that there are around 30,000 hotel rooms on the island with more due to be built in the future.

Travelling to Jamaica

Visitors travel to Jamaica by air or by sea as large cruise ships dock in ports such as Ocho Rios and Kingston. Visitors are attracted to Jamaica because of the beauty of the natural landscape, the sunshine and the culture.

Tourism Services

In Jamaica, approximately 200,000 people are employed in tourism in jobs including hotel workers, tour guides, cooks and drivers.

TEF

Tourism has a lot of positives, but some negatives as well. Places can get overcrowded and noisy and more people means more waste, so there is a lot more pollution on the island. However, the Tourism Enhancement Fund (TEF) invested $10,000,000 on a coastal clean-up in 2018. TEF are determined to raise awareness and reduce pollution on the island.

Ocho Rios, Jamaica

Project 6 – Tourism in Jamaica

1. Find these numbers in the text and write what they refer to. The first one has been done for you.

   three and a half million visitors to Jamaica in 2015

   ten million _____

   thirty thousand _____

   one hundred and twenty two thousand _____

   two hundred thousand _____

2. In pairs, draw a table like the one shown to describe positive and negative points about tourism:

   - Complete the table with examples from the article. Add your own opinions as well.
   - With your partner, think of ways to make the bad things about tourism better.
   - Use the table to explain to another pair of students why you are in favour of or against tourism.

The positive points are…	The negative points are…

Research and study skills

1. Revise the use of text features in the "Research and study skills" section in the "Let's read" lesson of Project 4. Your teacher may also go over the use of text features with you using various articles and newspapers, or you could work with a partner and do your own independent study using the internet to do some revision on text features.

> **Remember** ☆ ☆ ☆
>
> Make sure you are safe online!
> - Never tell anyone your address or phone number.
> - Never send pictures to strangers.
> - Never download anything without asking for permission from your teacher or parents.
> - Tell an adult you trust if you receive a strange message that makes you feel uncomfortable.

2. In pairs, read different informational texts and create a graphic organiser to identify and explain the importance of text features. Point out how the features help you understand the information.

3. In pairs, present your graphic organiser to the class. Ensure that you both explain the uses of various text features in the articles and information you have researched.

    Example of a graphic organiser:

Sections	Purpose
Title	
Headings	
Subheadings	
Captions	
Highlighted words / Bold words	
Tables and graphs	

Grammar builder

End of unit grammar check

1. With your partner, or in a small group, discuss the questions and tasks in each box together before writing down your answers.

My writing is getting better because my grammar skills are improving.

Adjectives
- What job do adjectives do in sentences?
- Write a sentence that compares two things using adjectives.

Extra challenge

Write a sentence that compares three or more things using adjectives.

Transitional words
- What is sentence punctuation and how is it helpful?
- Give some examples.

Extra challenge

what sentence punctuation is missing in this sentence

My grammar skills

Conjunctions
- What job do conjunctions do?
- Give some examples.
- Write a sentence that contains a conjunction.

Extra challenge

Write a sentence that contains two conjunctions.

Nouns
- What are the differences between common nouns and proper nouns?
- Give some examples.

Extra challenge

Write a sentence that contains both a proper noun and a common noun.

2. As a class, look at the questions and tasks for the four grammar skills again with your teacher. Be ready to share the responses and examples from your group.

ICT opportunity

Choose one of the four grammar skills from the chart on the previous page. Use a computer to make a poster about it. Print it out and use it in a classroom display.

Self-check

How confident are you about using each of the grammar skills?

1. List the skills and draw the emoji that matches how you feel about each skill.

2. If you are not completely confident with a skill, write what you can do to improve. If you are confident, say what you would like to learn next.

Grammar	☹	😐	🙂	What I can improve or learn next
nouns				
adjectives				
conjunctions				
sentence signposts				

Project 6 – Tourism in Jamaica

Let's write

Reporting about tourism

Background

A report is a type of non-fiction writing. A report consists of facts and figures that are compiled after a visit or an experience of some kind.

Task

The mayor of your town has just launched a campaign to increase tourism in your area. Your headteacher has decided that everyone should get involved. Your headteacher has organised a committee of five students from Grade 4 to examine how tourism can be introduced into the community.

- Make a list of the things or places in your community that would be interesting to tourists. Explain how each would benefit the community as a tourist attraction. For example: *The parks have a beautiful bird population.*

- Look at the example and draw a map which shows the sequence in which tourists should explore your community in order to get the best experience.

Our community – Interesting places for tourists

- Write a report for the headteacher of your school explaining the plan to introduce tourism in your area.

- After reading your group's report, the headteacher invites your group to a meeting to speak with the mayor. At the meeting you are informed of plans to improve the roads and build a transport centre with links to other tourist areas. How does the news change your view of introducing tourism in your area?

Plan

- Think about the area where you live. Is it a place where you often see tourists? If not, have you visited places which are popular with tourists like Ocho Rios, Montego Bay or Kingston? What do tourists seem to like?

- Use the picture you are imagining to make a mind map. In the centre, you should write *Tourism in…* (insert the name of the place).

- Use your mind map as a guide to help you to complete your task.

- Create your list of the best things for tourists to see and do in your area.

- Create the map to show tourists what to explore in what order.

- Write the main report for the headteacher.

- Add some bullet points to show how the news about the road plan affects your ideas.

A **mind map** is a quick way to jot down words or phrases related to something. This is what a mind map looks like:

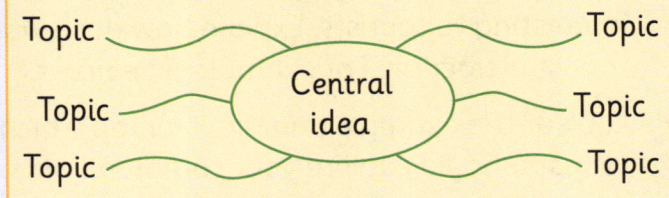

Write

Write up your final report neatly in your best handwriting or type it up on a computer.

Reports are factual pieces of writing, so use the internet or reference books to check any facts or figures that you want to use in your report.

Editor's checklist

Check your work carefully when you finish.

- Does the report have an exciting title and different headings to guide the reader?
- Does the report include accurate facts and figures?
- Does the report include photographs, pictures or graphs?
- Is the report written in the present tense?
- Do all sentences have a full stop, exclamation mark or question mark?
- Do all proper nouns have capital letters?
- Do adjectives add important detail to descriptions?

Term 1 Unit 1 Review and assessment

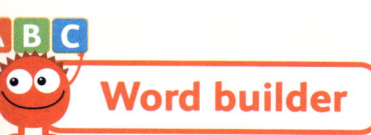

Word builder

1 Complete the words with the missing vowels.

j____ yf ____ l   t____ ____ r____ st

l____ g____ nd   ____ thl____ t____ cs

pl____ nt____ ____ n   f____ m____ ____ s

b____ l____ ____ v____   d____ l____ c____ ____ ____ s

____ xc____ l   f____ nny

d____ ff____ r____ nt   s____ ____ nd

2 Read all the following tasks before you complete them. Think carefully about the words you choose for each one.

1 Choose two words from Activity 1. Give an antonym (opposite) for each word.

_____

2 Choose a word from Activity 1 and use it to write a question.

_____

3 Choose another word from Activity 1 and use it to write a sentence that needs an exclamation mark.

_____

4 Write three words from the list: one that has one syllable, one that has two syllables and one that has three syllables.

_____ _____ _____

5 Choose a word that is related to food. _____

Let's read

1 Read this poem and answer the questions that follow.

> **Anancy**
> Anancy is a spider;
> Anancy is a man;
> Ancy's West Indian
> And West African.
>
> Sometimes, he wears a waistcoat;
> Sometimes, he carries a cane;
> Sometimes, he sports a top hat;
> Sometimes, he's just a plain,
> Ordinary, black, hairy spider.
>
> And always
> Anancy changes
> From a spider into a man
> And from a man into a spider
> And back again
> At the drop of a sleepy eyelid.
>
> *by Andrew Salkey*

1 Describe what Anancy, the man, looks like.

   _____

2 Describe what Anancy, the spider, looks like.

   _____

3 Do you think that Anancy is a strange creature? Quote some lines from the poem to use as evidence for what you think.

   _____

4 What other story book or movie characters do you know that can change from one thing to another?

   _____

5 If you could change from a person into something else "at the drop of a sleepy eyelid", what would you choose and why?

   _____

Review and assessment

Grammar builder

1 Complete the table using comparative adjectives. Be careful with the last word!

small	smaller	smallest
tall	1	2
3	heavier	4
5	6	loudest
clear	7	8
9	faster	10
good	11	12

2 Choose one set of comparative adjectives from the table. Write a sentence that includes all three words.

_____

3 Read this text. Fill the gaps with the words from the vocabulary box.

Vocabulary box

and   hotels   foods   beaches   Kingston   interesting

Firstly, Jamaica has much to be proud of. We have delicious [1] _____,

beautiful places and an [2] _____ history. In addition, the capital,

[3] _____, has many museums to see and [4] _____

for visitors to stay in. Finally, other places like coastal resorts have relaxing

[5] _____ and ocean waters.

4 Find the transitional words and phrases in the text above. In your own words, explain why they are important in writing.

_____

_____

71

5 Choose from the parts of speech to answer the questions.

Vocabulary box

adjective   conjunction   proper noun   common noun

1 What part of speech is *and*?

2 What part of speech is *beaches*?

3 What part of speech is *Kingston*?

4 What part of speech is *interesting*?

Let's write

1 Choose one of the writing prompts and write a paragraph with this title.

1 Food, glorious food!

2 Super sports heroes

3 We can learn from our history

4 Visitors are welcome in Jamaica

5 A freaky folktale

In your writing, demonstrate that you:

- can write in complete sentences with correct punctuation
- can use adjectives for describing and comparing
- can use conjunctions to join sentences together
- understand the difference between common nouns and proper nouns.

Proofread your writing when you finish, in case you spot any errors before submitting your assessment work.

TERM 1

Unit 2

In this unit, you will learn about how your senses keep you safe, bring you pleasure and help you in life. There will also be opportunities to use ICT to research and present your work and regional identity.

Project 7

Speaking and listening

The senses

1 The song "If you're happy and you know it", is a popular tune for children. Now, you are going to learn some new words to sing to the same tune.

   1 With your classmates, discuss what actions could match each verse.

   2 Sing the song together and perform the actions.

> **Remember** ☆☆☆
>
> Human beings have five senses. You can see, smell, hear, taste and feel.

When you look and when you see, use your eyes.
When you look and when you see, use your eyes.
When you look and when you see, all the things there are to see,
When you look and when you see, use your eyes.

When you listen and you hear, use your ears.
When you listen and you hear, use your ears.
When you listen and you hear, all the things there are to hear,
When you listen and you hear, use your ears.

When you touch and when you feel, use your hands.
When you touch and when you feel, use your hands.
When you touch and when you feel, all the things there are to feel,
When you touch and when you feel, use your hands.

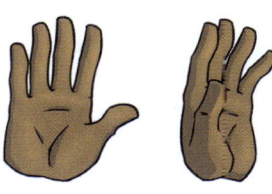

When you eat and when you taste, use your tongue.
When you eat and when you taste, use your tongue.
When you eat and when you taste, all the things there are to taste,
When you eat and when you taste, use your tongue.

When you sniff and when you smell, use your nose.
When you sniff and when you smell, use your nose.
When you sniff and when you smell, all the things there are to smell,
When you sniff and when you smell, use your nose.

2. In pairs, take turns to ask and answer questions about how you used each sense at some time in the past. Show your partner that you are curious by asking interesting questions that continue your conversation.

Example:

Student A: Last weekend, I went to the park and used my eyes to see the different birds in the trees.

Student B: Oh, really. What colours were the birds? What other wildlife did you see?

Project 7 – Introduction to the five senses

Word builder

This vocabulary is about sense organs:

Vocabulary box

sense	organ	smell	hands
tongue	hear	touch	eyes
skin	feel	living	ears
nose	sight	brain	

1 Take turns to read the words with a partner.

    1 Discuss the word meanings. Which words refer to your head?

    2 Only two words have two syllables. What are they?

    3 Can you think of any more sense words with two syllables? Make a list with your partner.

2 Draw a stick person in your notebook. Write out the vocabulary words all around the stick person. If they are parts of the body, draw an arrow to point to the right place on the stick person. Be careful with the words; make sure that they are all spelt correctly.

3 Draw three more stick people and give each one a speech bubble. In each speech bubble, write one short sentence that includes one word from the vocabulary box. For example: *My eyes are brown. I have big ears. I use my nose to smell.*

4   Draw two more stick people, each with a speech bubble. Write a conversation that they are having about the senses. Use at least one vocabulary word in each speech bubble. Here is an example:

5   With your partner, perform your conversation from Activity 4 for the class. Then perform your partner's conversation, too. Listen to the conversations from the other pairs in your class.

6   Write out the words from the vocabulary box again in alphabetical order. Check spelling carefully to make sure they are all correct.

Project 7 – Introduction to the five senses

Let's read

Research and study skills

Skim reading is a quick way to discover what a text is about and how it is organised. You then decide whether you need to read all the text or only some sections. You should read or look at:

- the title, the introduction, any headings and subheadings, and the conclusion
- the first sentence of each paragraph (the topic sentence)
- the concluding sentence of each paragraph
- any words in bold.

Remember

Skimming gives the general idea. **Scanning** locates a specific fact. Skimming is like snorkelling and scanning is more like lobster diving.

Scan reading is when you have learned what the text is about and how it is organised. Perhaps you already know a lot about the topic and do not need to read all the text, just some specific details it contains. In order to find this specific information, you need to **scan** the text.

You should only highlight a few words or key ideas. Scanning is not about understanding every detail, but getting a general **overview** of the **core ideas** in each paragraph. Paragraphs usually focus on one main point. They may include examples, but it is the main point that you need to identify first.

Body matters

1 On the next page, there is an extract from an article in *Live Life* magazine.

  1 Before reading the whole extract, read the heading and subheadings only and discuss them with a partner. What do you think the article will be about, based on only the heading and subheadings?

  2 Then read the article to see if you were right. What does this tell you about the use of headings and subheadings?

2 Describe one way that the senses keep us safe according to the article. Add another idea of your own.

3 Describe one way that the senses give us pleasure according to the article. Add another idea of your own.

Body matters

Welcome to our special on body matters. This month we are looking at the senses. Humans have five senses: sight, touch, smell, taste and hearing. Every moment of every day, the senses work to help us understand the world around us.

Senses mean safety

The senses play a big role in keeping people safe from harm. When you smell smoke from a fire, you know you should find a safe place. When you taste food that is sour or bad, you know not to eat it. When you hear traffic, you know not to cross the street. The human senses are our own built-in security system.

Senses mean pleasure

Some of the most special moments we experience come from using our senses: when a great song makes you happy, when you enjoy your mom's home cooking, when you smell a beautiful flower or gently stroke a pet. These moments are possible thanks to the senses.

4 Now you know some reasons why we have senses.

1. In a group, discuss some other ways that our senses are useful. Make a mind map of your ideas.

2. Join your group with another group. Make a combined mind map of both groups' ideas.

3. Join groups together and combine ideas until you have one big class mind map. Keep adding to it throughout this project and see how useful the senses really are!

5 Ask yourself the following questions about the reading text in this lesson:

- Does the text make sense?
- What am I supposed to be learning?
- How does this relate to what I already know?
- What am I learning?

Project 7 – Introduction to the five senses

Grammar builder

The apostrophe

Look and learn

Read these sentences:

Laura's eyes are green.

Hank's hands are big.

The rabbit's ears are long.

The cat's fur is soft.

These sentences give us information; they tell us who or what something belongs to. The soft fur belongs to the cat and the big hands belong to Hank.

When you want to show who or what something belongs to, you can use an **apostrophe**. By using an apostrophe, you can say "the cat's fur is soft" instead of "the soft fur of the cat".

The apostrophe has other uses too that you will see later, but here it is used to show **possession** or **ownership**.

1. Rewrite these phrases using an apostrophe and *s* in each one.
   For example: *The jacket belongs to the boy = the boy's jacket.*

   1. The bright red collar belongs to the dog.
   2. The old hat belongs to my dad.
   3. The homework belongs to Jack.
   4. The beautiful dress belongs to Mom.

2. Rewrite the story titled *Lucky Dip*. Use an apostrophe and *s* in each underlined phrase.

   I looked in <u>the old, teak wardrobe that belonged to Grandpa</u>. It was dark and warm. What would I find? I touched something soft and pulled out <u>a feather scarf that had belonged to Gran</u>. In went my hand. I felt something prickly. It was <u>the beautiful, sequined dress of my mom</u>. I dipped my hand in again, but this time lower. What can those be that feel so hard and rubbery? They are <u>the smelly, rubber boots of my grandpa</u>! And then I heard the stamp, stamp of <u>the footsteps of my grandpa</u> on the stairs. So, I quickly shut the wardrobe door.

3   Use the story on the previous page as a model to write a similar mini story of your own.

- Use at least three examples of an apostrophe and *s* to show ownership.
- Change the setting and change what you find.
- Include the senses.

4   Read and share your mini story. You could make a class book of *Lucky Dip* stories.

Project 7 – Introduction to the five senses

Let's write

The RAFT strategy

You can use different strategies to help you to plan, draft and compose your writing. One of these strategies is called the **RAFT** strategy.

A raft helps you to stay afloat!

R	Role	What is your role as a writer?
A	Audience	Who will be reading your writing?
F	Format	What type of writing is it?
T	Topic	What is the writing about?

Task

You have been asked to write a short introduction or presentation about the senses for students in Grade 2 in your school.

- What difference does their age make?
- How will you change your writing to suit their needs?

Plan

- Use the RAFT strategy to copy and complete the planning chart for this task.

R	Role	What is your role as a writer?	
A	Audience	Who will be reading your writing?	
F	Format	What type of writing is it?	informative with different points clearly separated under headings or in paragraphs
T	Topic	What is the writing about?	

- Write a list of three key questions the Grade 2 students might ask about the senses. Use these as a content guide to your writing.

Write

- When you are writing, make sure that you stay on the raft!
- Don't start writing a poem if you should be writing information.
- Don't start writing about another topic that is not important.

Editor's checklist

Check your work carefully when you finish.

- Does the introduction have a title?
- Does the introduction include facts suitable for the audience?
- Does the introduction include photographs or pictures?
- Did you use any apostrophes to show ownership?
- Do all sentences have a full stop, exclamation mark or question mark?
- Do all proper nouns and sentence beginnings have capital letters?
- Did you stay focused on the topic?

Reflect and review
When you finish, reflect upon (think about) the **RAFT** strategy. Write a short paragraph as a journal entry to describe your experience. Did you find it helpful? Did it make the writing task easier for you?

ICT opportunity

Type up your writing on the computer. Copy and paste some pictures into the report as well. How do pictures or photographs enrich the introduction? Check the spelling, subjects and predicates, tenses and punctuation. Print it out to be used in the Grade 2 classroom.

Project 8

Speaking and listening

In pairs, take turns to read out loud this story.

Achoo!

Two friends, Tara and Jay, were walking through the park when Jay let out a bellowing sneeze: "Achoo!" Tara explained that there must have been something tickling inside Jay's nostrils and she offered him a tissue. Jay let out another very loud sneeze: "Achoo!". This time his eyes watered a little, too, so he took the tissue and blew his runny nose. Suddenly, again, two really huge sneezes exploded: "Achoo! Achoo!" Tara looked around and realised there were lots of beautiful flowers in bloom in the park. "Of course," she thought, "flowers have pollen in them and this can make some people sneeze when they breathe it in. Even though their scent is lovely, having hay fever is no fun." Tara and Jay decided to leave the park and go to the café instead to avoid any more whiffs and sniffs.

1 Discuss the story. Share experiences of hay fever and how it feels.

   1 How many different words are used to describe Jay's sneezes or how he sneezed?

   2 How else could you describe a sneeze?

2 With your partner, role play this story using Jamaican Creole.

   1 Perform your role play for the class. Remember to speak clearly.

   2 Watch other students' role plays. Remember to listen attentively.

3 As a group, discuss why it is likely that the friends speak to each other in Jamaican Creole.

   1 What other situations can you think of where it is appropriate to speak in Jamaican Creole?

   2 Can you think of situations when it is not appropriate to speak in Jamaican Creole?

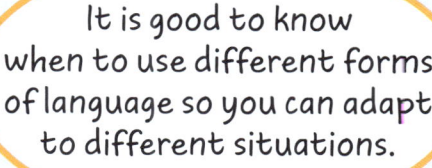

It is good to know when to use different forms of language so you can adapt to different situations.

Word builder

This vocabulary is about the nose and sense of smell:

Vocabulary box

odour	sniff	face	nosebleed
scent	whiff	tissue	beak
nostrils	hair	runny	snout
breathe	sneeze	snotty	

1 Take turns to read the words with a partner.

  1. Discuss the word meanings. Which two words are only used to describe the noses of animals?

  2. Discuss any tricky spellings. For example: words with letters that cannot be sounded out easily: /o/ /d/ /our/ = odour.

  3. Seven words have double letters. What are they? Circle them.

  4. Think of three more words that can be used to describe our sense of smell. How are they spelt?

  _____

2 Play *Codebreakers*. In this game, the letters of each word are worth points.

The letter a = 1 point, b = 2 points and so on, as you can see in the key. For example: the word *face* is worth 6 + 1 + 3 + 5 = 15 points.

  1. Which vocabulary word will score highest? Is there a quick way to work this out?

  2. Which of the words from the list are these?
     - 19-14-15-21-20
     - 2-5-1-11
     - 14-15-19-20-18-9-12-19
     - 18-21-14-14-25
     - 23-8-9-6-6

a	b	c	d	e	f	g	h	i	j
1	2	3	4	5	6	7	8	9	10
k	l	m	n	o	p	q	r	s	t
11	12	13	14	15	16	17	18	19	20
u	v	w	x	y	z				
21	22	23	24	25	26				

  3. Use the same code for three more vocabulary words that have not been used. What are the codes for your words?

Project 8 – About the nose and sense of smell

4 Find the vocabulary words to complete each sentence. Be careful though. This time the numbers are given backwards!

- When you 5-26-5-5-14-19, you need a 5-21-19-19-9-20.

  _____

- We 5-8-20-1-5-18-2 through our 19-12-9-18-20-19-15-14.

  _____

- Some animals have a 20-21-15-14-19 for a nose.

  _____

3 Fill the gaps with a word from the vocabulary box.

Vocabulary box

| nostrils | sniffs | breathe | tissue |
| whiffs | scent | runny | |

1 Tara explained that there must have been something tickling inside Jay's _____ and she offered him a _____.

2 Jay took the tissue and blew his _____ nose.

3 Some people sneeze when they _____ in pollen. Even though the _____ from flowers smells lovely, having hay fever is no fun.

4 Tara and Jay decided to leave the park and go to the café instead to avoid any more _____ and _____.

4 Imagine that a creature from outer space visits you. The creature has no nose and has never seen one before. The creature stares at your nose as if it is the most unusual and interesting thing in the universe. Write a short paragraph to tell it all about the nose. You should use at least five of the words from the list.

Extra challenge

Odour, *scent* and *whiff* are synonyms. They have the same or similar meaning. What other words are synonyms for these three words? Try the same with *nose*, *beak* and *snout*.

> I never knew there were so many words to do with the nose and smells!

Let's read

1. Skim read the story about a boy named Martin to a partner. Which of the headings best describes the topic of the whole text?

    - Martin's mom's cookies are the best
    - Martin's sense of smell
    - Martin's journey to school

Martin woke at six thirty that morning to the scent of home baked cookies wafting from the kitchen. He stretched, yawned and made his way through to his mom. "Don't forget your schoolbag again today!" she said, "Your teacher won't be impressed!" Martin took a last long whiff of the cookies before grabbing a handful of them and heading out for the walk to school. He loved his mom's cookies so much! He walked slowly past a local café and the strong aroma of Blue Mountain coffee beans drifted through the air. It made him think of the day he spent hiking in the Blue Mountains last summer with his brother. That was a great day!

As he got nearer to school it was busier; there was more traffic and he could smell fuel from cars and the odour of rotting fruit in the bins that hadn't been emptied. It was disgusting! Martin covered his mouth and nose with his hand and crossed the street. He pulled the last cookie out of his pocket, smelled it one last time and then gobbled it up in one go as he entered the schoolyard just when the bell started ringing. He had a Science test and he hadn't prepared. He wished he was still at home in the kitchen, surrounded by cookies.

2. Scan read the story and find the answers to the following questions.

    1. What time does Martin get up on a school day?

    2. What had Martin forgotten to take to school the day before?

    3. What did Martin do one day last summer? Who was he with and where did they go?

    4. Name something that is sold at the local café.

    5. Why could Martin smell rotting fruit?

    6. How did Martin feel about the test that day? How do you know how he feels?

Project 8 – About the nose and sense of smell

> **Remember** ☆ ☆ ☆
>
> **Apostrophes** showing possession tell you who or what something belongs to or where it came from. For example: *This is Martin's bag.*

3. Read the story again. Find an example of an apostrophe being used to show possession.

4. Do you think Martin wanted to go to school? Find evidence in the story to support what you think.

5. Smells can bring back memories and trigger feelings and emotions.

   1. Describe two ways that a smell affected Martin.

   2. Do you have a smell that is special to you or a favourite smell? Describe the smell and say why it is special to you.

   3. What smells do you think are disgusting? Describe some of the things that you don't like to smell and say why.

Extra challenge

Think about what you have done today from the moment you woke up to right now. What smells have you experienced today? Create a Smell Trail. Include the time, location and smell. Say if it was + (positive) or – (negative).

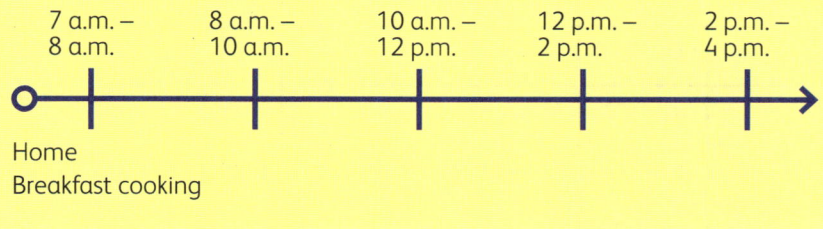

7 a.m. – 8 a.m.
Home
Breakfast cooking

8 a.m. – 10 a.m.

10 a.m. – 12 p.m.

12 p.m. – 2 p.m.

2 p.m. – 4 p.m.

Term 1 Unit 2

Grammar builder

More about the apostrophe

Remember ☆☆☆

An **apostrophe** can be used to show possession.
For example: *Dad's car.*

Look and learn

Apostrophes can also be used to combine two words to make one shorter word. Some letters are removed and replaced by the apostrophe. The new word is called a **contraction**. Here are some examples of contractions:

can + not = can't

where + is = where's

they + had = they'd

1 Here are two lists. Write them out and match the contractions to the original words. For example: *can't = cannot*.

don't	will not
didn't	does not
isn't	is not
doesn't	did not
won't	were not
aren't	do not
shan't	could not
haven't	are not
couldn't	have not
weren't	shall not

88

2 Here is a table of pronoun contractions.

1 Complete the table.

	to be	will	have
I	I'm		I've
You			
He		He'll	
She	She's		She's
It		It'll	
We			We've
They	They're		

2 Copy the table in your notebook and rewrite the contractions as two words without an apostrophe.

3 Here are some sentences that could be shortened by using contractions. Rewrite them with contractions wherever you think there should be one.

1 I do not want to go to cricket practice because I have lots to do today.

2 Where is my phone? I have not seen it since yesterday.

3 Kelvin did not get to see his aunty because he was not on time for the bus.

Extra challenge

Find some everyday examples of contractions that you might see or use. Look at shop signs and advertisements, for example, *pick 'n' mix* or *ma'am*. Begin a class list and add to it. Include cut-outs from magazines or even photos. Make some up.

Let's write

Stories about the senses

Background

In this project, you have read two short stories. The first was about friends in the park and the second was about Martin's journey to school. Both stories involved the senses, especially the sense of smell.

> **Remember** ☆☆☆
>
> Human beings have **five senses**. You can see, smell, hear, taste and feel.

Task

Write your own story about the senses. Choose one sense to focus on in your story.

- Stories have **characters**: the people that we meet in the tale.
- Stories have a **setting**: the time and place that they happen.
- A story is a tale. It needs to have a beginning, a middle and an end.
- Stories have a **title**. You don't need to think of a title straight away. Sometimes it is easier to decide the title after you finish writing.

Plan

Plan your story by copying out and completing this story plan to help you put your story together. You do not need to use complete sentences in your story plan.

- Characters:
- Setting:
- Senses: What will be smelled, seen, heard, tasted or felt?
- Where the story starts:
- Events of the story:
- How the story ends:
- Story title:

Project 8 – About the nose and sense of smell

> It's easier to think of a good title after you have planned your writing.

Write

- Write your story.
- Check it carefully when you finish.
- Refer to the "Editor's checklist" in the "Let's write" lesson in Project 7. Then write up your final version neatly in your best handwriting.

Reflect and review
Write a short paragraph as a journal entry to describe your experience with the story plan. Did you find it helpful? Did it make the writing task easier for you? How would you use it differently next time?

Project 9

Speaking and listening

Caribbean languages

Around the world, over 6000 different languages are written and spoken by people. Humans use the tongue and mouth to make different sounds which together form words. The tongue is an important part of the body because we use it to communicate with others no matter what language we speak.

What languages can you speak? How many languages are spoken in your family? Collate this information in your class to make a language tree to celebrate your talents!

1 Here are some phrases in other Caribbean languages. In a small group, try to say each of them out loud. Record yourselves, if possible, so you can hear how you sound and what you need to improve. Try to notice how differently you need to use the tongue each time.

Me gusta hablar Español. (I like speaking Spanish.)
Spanish is spoken in Cuba.

J'aime parle Français. (I like speaking French.)
French is spoken in Haiti.

Ik hou van de Nederlandse taal. (I like speaking Dutch.)
Dutch is spoken in Aruba.

2 Discuss these questions with your group:

1 In what other ways could we communicate if we could not use our tongue?

2 Is it easier or harder to communicate without using the tongue?

3 What might daily life be like if we could not communicate by speaking?

ICT opportunity

Use technology to record your group's pronunciations of the activity above. Go online and type in the phrases above into a search engine such as Google, Bing or Yahoo. Press the 🔊 speaker sign, listen to the pronunciation online and compare your pronunciation with the one online.

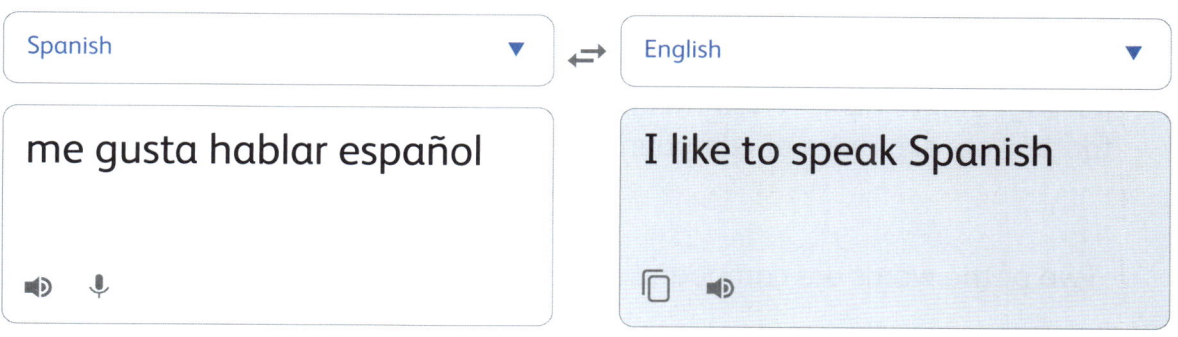

A person who can speak several languages is called a **polyglot**. A person who can speak many languages is a **hyper-polyglot**. The Guinness World Record for being able to speak the most languages is held by Ziad Fazah who claims he can speak 59 languages!

Word builder

This vocabulary is about the tongue and mouth:

Vocabulary box

taste	flavour	often	toothbrush
mouth	clean	dirty	speak
chew	toothpaste	eat	speech
taste buds	regularly	breath	

1 With your partner, take turns to read the words. Discuss the word meanings as you go.

Remember ☆☆☆

Compound words are made up of two or more words, put together to make a new meaning. Earache and football are examples of compound words.

1. Two of the words are compound words. What are they?
   _____

2. List three more words about the tongue and mouth.
   _____

2 Antonyms are opposites. For example, *light* is the antonym of *dark*. Read the vocabulary words. Can you find a pair of antonyms?

3 Synonyms are words that have the same or almost the same meaning. For example, *yell* and *shout* are synonyms. Read the vocabulary words. Can you find a pair of synonyms?

Extra challenge

- Add three more pairs of antonyms to the vocabulary box.
- Add three more pairs of synonyms to the vocabulary box.

4. Copy and label this mouth using the scientific name words from the box. Can you add an extra label?

Specialist words
Sharp front tooth (incisor)
Chewing back tooth (molar)
Tongue
Gum
Middle tooth (canine)

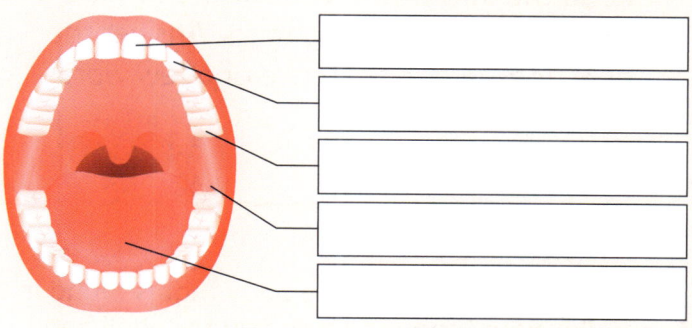

5. Make a poster about oral hygiene. Oral hygiene means keeping your mouth and everything inside it healthy. Choose the best messages from the list below, but be careful as some are not good advice. Add some of your own, too. Use some of the vocabulary words.

- Use toothpaste every day!
- Drink lots of sodas!
- Brush gently and carefully for two minutes!
- Brush your teeth at least twice a day!
- Scrub your teeth really hard!
- Visit your dentist every six months!
- Gently brush your tongue, too!
- Drink water with your meal!

ICT opportunity

Use a computer to find out more about oral hygiene. Check out some videos, too. Research *plaque* and what you can do to get rid of it. Create a word document and insert a table for your information. Use the example information below to help you:

Plaque research	
Action	When? Why?
Brush at least twice a day.	After eating…
Take your time while brushing.	Brush each tooth for at least three seconds because…

Let's read

Scientific facts

1. Read the information about the tongue and complete the following tasks. Answer the questions in one sentence or a few words.

> The first language that you learn to speak at home as a child is called your **mother tongue**.

The terrific tongue

The tongue is a part of the body that is found in the mouth. It is a muscle. You can move and flex your tongue to help you to speak and to help you to eat.

When you speak, different sounds are made when the tongue is in different positions in your mouth. Say the words "risk", "run" and "rise". What happens to your tongue when you say the letter "r"? Try to say them again without moving your tongue from the bottom of your mouth. Can it be done?

The tongue is where the taste buds are found. Taste buds send signals to your brain to help you to recognise different flavours of food. The bumps all over your tongue are where the taste buds are found. Taste buds are what help you to tell if food is sweet, salty, bitter or sour.

You probably already know that the tongue is also associated with pulling funny faces and sometimes with being rude. If you stick your tongue out at another person, this is an insult in most western countries. What you probably don't know is that this is not the case all over the world. In some places, like Tibet in Asia, when you meet somebody it is a tradition to stick out your tongue to them! This is a greeting and is actually a sign of respect.

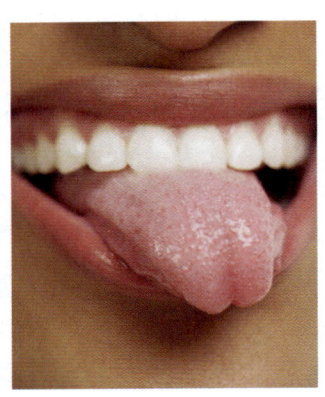

My mom scolds me when I stick out my tongue at people.

1.
    1. What kind of body part is the tongue? Name another body part like this.
    2. Where in the body is the tongue located? What else is in the same place?
    3. What sense does the tongue help with?
    4. Name one other way that the tongue is useful on a daily basis.
    5. What kinds of flavours do your taste buds help you to taste? Draw and label an example of a food with each flavour.

2. A tongue twister is a type of short poem or rhyme that has alliteration (many words beginning with the same sound). They can be difficult to say quickly! For example: *A proper cup of coffee in a copper coffee pot.*
    1. Try saying this tongue twister. How quickly can you say it without making a mistake?
    2. Think of another tongue twister that you know or write one of your own. Write it down and challenge a partner to say it as fast as they can.
    3. Make a class book of tongue twisters to share with classroom visitors or other classes.

3. Read the section of the text that describes sticking out your tongue again.
    1. Do you think it is really wrong to stick out your tongue?
    2. Write a short paragraph about how sticking out your tongue has different meanings in different places.

I never knew that the tongue was so interesting and had so many functions. I can't wait to tell my family all about what I have learned.

Grammar builder

Adverbs of manner

Remember

Adverbs have different functions. One of them is to tell us more about verbs. For example: *She brushed her teeth* **carefully**. *How did she brush her teeth? Carefully!* So *carefully* is the **adverb**.

1 Read these sentences. Circle the adverb in each sentence.

  1 She called loudly across the waiting room.

  2 They waited patiently for their appointment.

  3 He brushed his teeth thoroughly for four minutes.

  4 A bug landed suddenly in the soup!

  5 The rain fell heavily for several days.

2 Is the adverb before or after the verb? Work with a partner to play an adverb game.

- Write each sentence in Activity 1 on a long strip of paper with large gaps between each word.
- Cut up one sentence at a time and muddle up the words.
- Then resequence the sentence putting the adverb in the right place. Check it! How fast did you do it?
- Try the next sentence until you have sorted them all.
- Rewrite each sentence with a different adverb. For example: *She called quietly across the waiting room.*

Extra challenge

Homophones are words that sound the same, but have different meanings. Can you spot a pair of homophones in the sentences above?

Project 9 – About the tongue and sense of taste

> **Look and learn**
>
> Some adverbs are called **adverbs of manner**. These are the adverbs that tell you how something is done or how someone does something.
>
> Adverbs of manner usually end in **-ly**. For example: *loudly, patiently, heavily* and *suddenly*. They usually come after the verb they describe, but this is not always the case as you will see in the next activity.

3 Choose one of the following adverbs to complete each sentence.

Vocabulary box

closely   beautifully   regularly   fiercely   quickly

1 Leah sang her solo _____ at the concert.

2 The wind blew _____ through the night.

3 As they listened, they watched _____.

4 People gathered _____ in the street after the fire alarm rang.

5 Brushing your teeth _____ helps to keep your mouth healthy.

4 Look at these sentences. How does the adverb change the atmosphere?

1 He looked suspiciously at the man in the shop.

2 He looked kindly at the man in the shop.

Let's write

Adverbs improve your writing by providing more detail about what is happening.

Read the paragraph below and complete the following tasks.

The runaway rabbit

Amara skipped out to the yard to feed her bunny, Ralph, his usual breakfast of green leaves, carrots and broccoli. She knelt down to release the catch on the hutch when Ralph leapt out. She dropped the food and tried to catch him, but instead Ralph nibbled her finger and then jumped away before Amara could grab him. Ralph scurried across the yard and snuck underneath the wire fence. Amara began to cry and started calling his name. She went inside to tell her dad about Ralph's escape. Her dad called the neighbour to see if they had seen Ralph and, luckily, Ralph was still in their backyard. Amara went around to the neighbours to collect Ralph. She picked him up and cuddled him. "Naughty Ralph!", she exclaimed, "Don't ever run anyway again!"

1. Copy and complete the table with a list of all the verbs in the story. For each verb, ask "How?" and write an adverb. For example: *verb = skipped; How? happily*.

Verb	How?
skipped	happily
feed	

2. Use the list of verbs and adverbs to rewrite the story. Use your adverbs to make it more detailed and vibrant. Not every verb needs an adverb so choose the ones you want to use for greatest effect.

3 In class, read your new story with adverbs out loud. Listen to the stories that others have written. Which are the most powerful adverbs? Which are less useful and why?

Copy the table and make notes while your classmates are reading their stories.

Student's story	Suitable adverbs	Less useful and why
Anna	Amara skipped **excitedly**. A good adverb, because skipping and excitement go together.	She **fiercely** knelt down. Not a good adverb because kneeling is not something you do with force.

4 After listening to everybody's stories, discuss the ways in which they are similar and different. Although you all began with the same tale, how did the choice of adverbs change it? Did Amara or Ralph seem like a different character in some stories?

5 As a class, take votes on the most powerful and effective adverbs used to create the best version of the story.

Editor's checklist

Check your work carefully when you finish.

- Do the adverbs add detail about the characters?
- Do the adverbs follow the verbs?
- Does the story have a beginning, a middle and an end?
- Are all the speech marks when Amara is talking copied correctly?
- Is the handwriting neat and easy to read?
- Do all sentences have a full stop, exclamation mark or question mark?
- Do all proper nouns and sentence beginnings have capital letters?

Reflect and review
Write a short paragraph as a journal entry to describe your experience with using adverbs to improve a piece of writing. Did you find it helpful?

Project 10

Speaking and listening

At the doctor's

When you visit the doctor, it is important to use descriptive words to help the doctor to understand what your problem is (symptoms) so they know what is wrong and how they can help (diagnosis). The doctor must listen carefully to the symptoms that the patient has experienced and then make a diagnosis.

1 With your partner, perform a role play about a visit to the doctor.

   1 Choose one of the situations from the options below.

   2 Decide who will be the doctor and who will be the patient.

   3 Discuss what you might say to each other. What sort of language will you use? Why?

   > **Symptoms:** red, itchy rash for longer than two weeks
   > **Doctor's diagnosis:** eczema
   > **Advice:** Use this cream.

   > **Symptoms:** hard and very itchy raised bump for about two days
   > **Doctor's diagnosis:** insect bite
   > **Advice:** Use this antihistamine cream.

   > **Symptoms:** sore, discoloured skin around the ankle; very tender to touch since falling off a bike yesterday
   > **Doctor's diagnosis:** bruise
   > **Advice:** Rest. Raise the leg. Apply a cold compress.

   4 Record or make notes of your ideas.

   5 Write the conversation script.

- How will the appointment begin?
- What questions will the doctor ask?
- How will the patient answer the questions?
- How will the appointment end?
- Will there be any surprises during the appointment? For example, will the phone ring or will someone pop in?

6 Practise several times. Do you need any props?

7 Perform it for the class when you are ready.

2 Watch the role plays that your classmates perform. Listen carefully for:

- descriptive language such as *It's so itchy and sore.*
- specialist language such as *medicine* and *antibiotics.*
- language formality. Did they use Standard Jamaican English (SJE) or Jamaican Creole (JC) in the role play? Why did they make this choice?

  _____

- anything that made the performance seem realistic. For example, *They stayed in character.*

  _____

Use many adverbs and adjectives in your conversation for a more vivid description.

3 As a class, make a working wall of all the different adjectives and adverbs that were used to describe the symptoms and diagnoses and keep adding to it.

Term 1 Unit 2

Word builder

This vocabulary is about the skin:

Vocabulary box

layer	pimple	cover	wrinkles
rash	freckle	scratch	soft
sensitive	spots	dark	eczema
light	bruise	cut	

1. In pairs, take turns to practise segmenting the following words. Student A ticks (✓) the box after Student B segments the word into sounds, then swap roles.

Word	Sounds	Student A ✓	Student B ✓
cut	/c/ /u/ /t/		
soft	/s/ /o/ /f/ /t/		
spots	/s/ /p/ /o/ /t/ /s/		
dark	/d/ /ar/ /k/		
rash	/r/ /a/ /sh/		
light	/l/ /igh/ /t/		
wrinkles	/r/ /i/ /n/ /k/ /l/ /es/		

1. Discuss the meaning of the words or any tricky pronunciations and spellings.

Wrinkles begins with **wr-**, but we do not pronounce the **w** because the **w** is silent.

The word **dark** has four letters but only three sounds.

2. Use a dictionary or online tool to look up the meaning of any words you do not know in the vocabulary box.

Look and learn

Consonant blends or clusters

- It can be confusing to count the number of sounds in some words especially when a sound has two or more letters, but only one sound!

    For example: (/ck/, /ll/, /tch/, /ng/) so**ck**, do**ll**, ca**tch**, to**ng**ue

With your partner, practise saying these words and stress the consonant cluster as loud as you can.

/s/ /o/ /ck/

- Things get tricky when multiple consonant sounds are pronounced quickly together.

These are also called **consonant clusters**, but the cluster has individual sounds which are blended together.

- These consonant clusters blend letters such as /dr/, /pl/, /st/, /spl/, /nk/ together.

    For example: **dr**op, **pl**um, **st**op, **spl**ash, **dr**ink.

/d/ /r/ /o/ /p/

With your partner, practise saying these words and stress the consonant clusters as loud as you can.

Remember ☆☆☆

Synonyms are different words that mean the same thing.
Antonyms are opposites.

2. Find a pair of words in the vocabulary box that are antonyms. Write them in a sentence.

3. Find a pair of words in the vocabulary box that are synonyms. Write them in a sentence.

4 Match the description to each person.

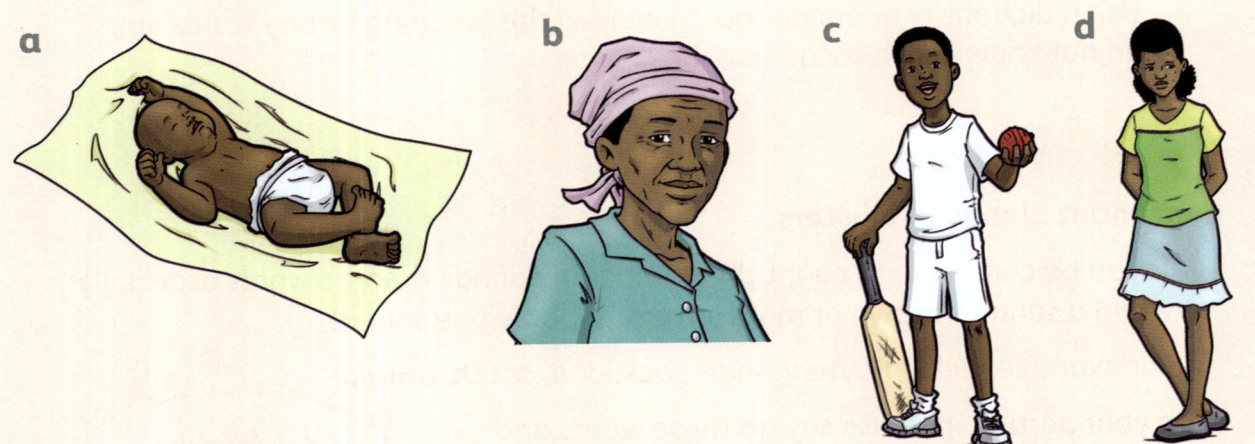

1. She is old and her skin has wrinkles.
2. He fell over playing cricket and has a bruise on his knee.
3. She is a teenager and gets spots.
4. The newborn's skin is so soft to touch.

5 Here are some slogans from advertisements. What word from the vocabulary box is missing from each one? Use a vocabulary word to write your own advertising slogan.

A
Soapy Suds detergent – perfect for _____ skin!

B
Healthy Healing cream soothes all types of _____.

C
_____ your _____ with *True You* make-up for a perfect look.

6 Look at your face in a mirror and focus on your skin. Look also at the skin on your arms and legs. How would you describe your skin? Write three or four sentences about your skin. Use some of the vocabulary words and underline them.

7 Compare your description of your skin with a partner's description. Discuss how they are similar and different. What words did you each use?

Project 10 – About the skin and the sense of touch

Let's read

Spot out!

1 Read the advertisement and answer the questions below.

> Fed up with spot breakouts? Don't want to leave your bedroom because of your pimples?
> The solution is here: **Spot Out** cream!
>
>
>
> Guaranteed to halve your number of spots after just one week!
> Apply directly to spots morning and night for best results.
> Find it in your local pharmacy.
> No more hiding away. Buy **Spot Out** today!

1 What is the name of the product being advertised?

2 What type of product is it? Pick the most appropriate choice from the vocabulary box below.

Vocabulary box

food   ointment   detergent   clothing

3 Advertisements use words and punctuation to persuade people to buy a product. What examples of persuasive words or punctuation can you see in this advertisement?

4 Why do you think this advertisement shows a picture of the product? What can you notice about the picture?

5 How do you think this advertisement tries to make people feel about having spots? Explain your ideas.

107

2   What do you think?

1   What words make this advertisement appealing or not appealing?

2   Do you think it is all true?

3   Should you always believe what you read? Do you?

Extra challenge

Task

In a small group of five, imagine that you have been asked to create a television advertisement for a cream. Work on the advertisement together to create a scene and write a short script based on the advertisement model below. It should be between 45 seconds and one minute long.

Perform your advertisement for the class and then have a vote on which advertisement should be the one used on TV.

> Fed up with _____? Don't want to/Worried about _____?
>
> The solution is here: _____ cream!
>
> Guaranteed to _____ after/in _____.
>
> Apply directly to _____ for best results.
>
> Find it in _____. No more _____. Buy _____ today!

Plan

1   What roles do you need to work well together?
    - team lead
    - ideas manager
    - script manager
    - technology manager
    - visuals and props manager

2   What sort of product is this?
    - Who is the cream for?
    - What does it do?
    - What is its name?
    - How is it packaged?
    - How will you persuade people to buy your product?

3   Use the advertisement for *Spot Out* as a model for your script, but add your own ideas, too.

Project 10 – About the skin and the sense of touch

4. As a class, create an agreed list of things you will judge. Use that list to fairly judge each performance.
5. Perform your advertisement for the class. Use the agreed list to judge and decide which advertisement should be the winner.

ICT opportunity

Film your advertisement on a video camera, phone or tablet:
- switch your device to camera/video recording
- press the record button and film your advertisement.

Post the advertisements to your school website. You will need permission from your teacher to do this:
- select the video on your device and follow your teacher's instructions on how to upload it to a website
- ask viewers to pick the advertisement that they think should be used on TV.

Grammar builder

Noun substitutes – Pronouns

Look and learn

The noun in a sentence can sometimes be replaced by another word. It can be **substituted**.

Read this sentence:

The girl whispered her name quietly. Then the girl began to sing in front of everyone and the girl got a huge round of applause.

Now read this version of the same sentence:

The girl whispered her name quietly. Then she began to sing in front of everyone and she got a huge round of applause.

Can you spot the difference? The second sentence uses pronouns to avoid repeating "the girl".

Work with a partner to write an example of two sentences like this.

These words are the **personal subject pronouns**. You probably use them all the time without realising!

| I | you | he | she | it | we | they |

The pronoun "you" is special. "You" can be used to refer to either one single person, or to a group of several people.

You are my friend!

You are my friends!

Project 10 – About the skin and the sense of touch

> **Remember** ☆☆☆
>
> **Nouns** are naming words. There are **common nouns** and **proper nouns**. Can you give an example of each?

1 Write out these sentences and circle the pronouns.

1. The sun was shining when we went to the beach.
2. As she walked away, she slammed the door.
3. The monkey stole the banana and then it scurried up the tree.

2 Copy the table and write the sentence for each pronoun.

I	I am going to the visit the doctor as I have itchy skin.
You (singular)	
He/She/It	
We	
You (plural)	
They	

3 Write out these sentences and shorten them by using pronouns.

1. Mom, Dad and I went to the carnival together. Mom, Dad and I had a great time.
2. Simon caught the ball and then Simon threw it across the pitch to his teammate.
3. The boys were supposed to be in the yard, but the boys were not; the boys were in the park instead.

4 Write one long sentence for a partner to shorten by using pronouns. Then swap over.

111

Let's write

Advertising products

Background

Advertisements are descriptive and persuasive. Sometimes their purpose is to convince people that they need to buy a product.

Task

Work in a small group to create an advertisement for a new product. You can draw on your experience earlier in this unit if you completed the "Extra challenge".

- Remember to think about the different roles you need in your group. Use people's strengths.
- Use the **RAFT** strategy to help you.

R	Role	What role are you playing as a writer?	
A	Audience	Who will be reading your writing?	
F	Format	What type of writing is it?	
T	Topic	What is the writing about?	

Plan

- Choose one of the following three products:
  - *True You* make-up – covers spots and pimples for a beautiful complexion that will last all day
  - *Soapy Suds* detergent – cleans your clothes, but has no chemicals, so is good for sensitive skin and baby clothes
  - *Muscle Recovery* – an ointment to help soothe your muscles after exercise
- Make a mind map of the ideas for your advertisement. Sift the ideas and take votes to create a first draft of your decisions and plan for the advertisement. Use the questions in the "Extra challenge" in the "Let's read" lesson to guide you.

Project 10 – About the skin and the sense of touch

Editor's checklist

Check your work carefully when you finish.

- Does the advertisement say what the product is and who it is for?
- Does the advertisement include the right language for the audience?
- Does the advertisement persuade? How?
- Are apostrophes used correctly to show possession and/or contractions?
- Do all sentences have a full stop, exclamation mark or question mark?
- Do all proper nouns and sentence beginnings have capital letters?
- Are all words spelt correctly, especially your product name?
- Are personal subject pronouns used appropriately to replace nouns?

Reflect and review
Write a short paragraph as a journal entry to describe your experience with RAFT this time. Did you find it helpful? Did it make the writing task easier for you? How would you use it differently next time? Would you adapt it?

ICT opportunity

Use the computer to design and type up your advertisement. You can use different types of fonts and different sizes of text for parts of the advertisement.

What images have you included? Why?

Outcome

Share your advertisement with the class. Explain how you think it sells the product you have chosen and exchange feedback. Create a display in the classroom for all the different advertisements that you and your classmates have produced.

Pronouns prevent the unnecessary repetition of nouns!

Project 11 – Symptoms and treatments

Project 11

Speaking and listening

Fun with homophones

> **Remember** ☆☆☆
>
> **Homophones** are words that sound the same, but have different meanings.
> Victor **ate eight** mangoes!
> The **four** kids are waiting **for** the bus.

1. Sort and write these words into ten homophone sets. Some groups may have three spellings.

   1. Check the meanings. How will you do that? Dictionaries give examples of the different meanings of homophones. You need to choose the correct context (situation) the word is representing.

   2. Choose three sets of homophones. Write a sentence for each set using both words in the same sentence. Look at the "Remember" box for examples.

115

2. You are going to play games involving homophones. Follow the instructions carefully.

Charades

Play this with a small group.
1. Write up to ten homophone pairs on pieces of paper. Put them in a box or bag.
2. Ask one person to stand up and pull out one word from the bag.
3. They must silently act out the word while the others must guess what the word is.
4. The guessers need to work out the word and give at least two meanings for it.
5. Play several times more.

Pass the whisper

Play this with the whole class sitting in a circle.
1. One person starts by whispering a sentence containing a homophone into the ear of the person on their left.
2. They pass this on to the next person and so on until it has gone all the way around the circle. It needs silence and careful listening.
3. The last person then says the message out loud. Has the sentence changed from the original? What is or was the homophone?

3. What language games do you know? Share your ideas and think carefully about giving clear, numbered instructions for others to follow.

Playing games is a really fun way to learn about language!

Project 11 – Symptoms and treatments

Word builder

This vocabulary is about symptoms and treatments:

Vocabulary box

disease	health	cure	hygiene	sore
symptom	healthy	swollen	antifungal	antihistamine
treatment	infection	antibiotic	medicine	allergy

Look and learn

Many words for treatments start with "anti". This tells you that these medicines will fight against different diseases. Antibiotics fight infection, antifungals fight bacteria in the skin and antihistamines fight allergies.

1. With your partner, take turns to read the words and circle any unknown words. Use a dictionary or online tool to look up their meanings. Join another pair of students and discuss the word meanings.
   - Which three words have just one syllable?
   - Which is the homophone in the vocabulary box?

Remember ☆☆☆

A **syllable** is a unit of sound. Count the syllables in a word by gently tapping your hand under your chin to feel how often it moves.

2. Margaret has written a letter of complaint to the maker of a foot cream she has used because she is not happy. The sentences in the letter are jumbled up. Put the letter back together and write it out in full.
   Tip: It may help you to write and cut out each section so you can move the pieces around to assemble the letter before you write it.

Dear Sir,

Your cream has caused this; it has not cured anything!

I demand a full refund immediately.

You should also put a warning on the pack about allergies.

I am writing to complain about *Fresh Foot* cream. It is an antifungal cream for athlete's foot.

My doctor has given me antihistamines for an allergic reaction.

When I opened it, the smell was horrendous! I used it anyway because it said it would cure the infection in a week.

I have been putting the treatment on my toes for ten days and now they are sore and swollen.

Sincerely,
Mrs M Goodall

ICT opportunity

In pairs, type up your own letter, print it, then cut it up into sections. Make sure the sentence strips contain complete sentences. Give it to another pair of students to piece together. Then ask those students to identify the verbs and any adverbs in the sentences.

3 With your partner, complete table A, then complete table B with example sentences that use root words with prefixes and suffixes related to the skin, nose and tongue. Use a dictionary or online tool to help you. The first one is done for you. Compare your example sentences with other pairs of students.

A

Prefix / Suffix	Meaning	Example word
pan-	across all	pandemic
anti-	against	
-gist	an expert in scientific study	

B

Example sentences
The coronavirus is a pandemic that spread all over the world in 2020.

Project 11 – Symptoms and treatments

Let's read

Research and study skills

How to search

Dictionaries are organised **alphabetically**, so you need to start with the first letter of the word you are searching for, then look at the second letter of the word, and then the third, and so on, in order to find it. You need to scan the dictionary page to find the word you need.

> **Remember** ☆☆☆
>
> **Scanning** is reading quickly to find specific words and information.

> **L👀k and learn**
>
> An **abbreviation** is a shortened form of a word or phrase, such as *Dec.* for *December*.

Word type

In a dictionary there are many abbreviations, but the most common are **vb.** for verb, **n.** for noun and **adj.** for adjective.

Different meanings

It's tricky when words sound similar but have different meanings such as *homographs* that have the same spelling and pronunciation, but different meanings. However, many dictionaries number the different meanings and give examples of the word in a sentence. For example: 1) *I uploaded my video clip to the website.* 2) *My mom clips my hair when it gets too long.*

Other information

Dictionaries may also list synonyms (alternative words with similar meanings) and antonyms (words with opposite meanings).

Self-assessment

- How are dictionaries organised? _____
- What is the abbreviation for *adjective*? _____
- A synonym is a word that is spelled the same as another. True or false? _____
- Homographs may be numbered in some dictionaries. True or false? _____

Some words have more than one meaning! Make sure to give the definition that matches the situation.

1. Work in pairs. Copy the example table into your notebook and complete the table for the following words. The first one is done for you.

Vocabulary box

~~antibiotic~~   exhausted   tonsillitis   operation   prevent

Elements	Purpose
Spelling	antibiotic
Parts of Speech	noun
Meaning	A medicine that kills bacteria (germs) or stops them for spreading.
Syllables	an·ti·bi·ot·ic

Get well, Jean!

Melvin sent a get-well card to his cousin Jean who has been very sick and has received this reply from his aunt:

1. In pairs, read the letter together. Some words are missing. Fill the gaps with a word from the vocabulary box.

Vocabulary box

prevent   exhausted   antibiotics   tonsillitis   operation

120

Project 11 – Symptoms and treatments

Hello Melvin,

Thank you for the lovely card with the animals on that you sent to Jean. She has had a sore throat and been given [1]_____ fourteen times this year!

When she has [2]_____, her throat is swollen, painful and sometimes she can't speak. She has a raised temperature and finds it hard to sleep so she becomes [3]_____ all the time. This means that she can't keep up with schoolwork or join in with sports which makes Jean very sad. You know how she loves to play cricket! The doctor said that antibiotics are not good enough anymore so she has gone to hospital to have her tonsils removed.

She is there now, in Saint Hilda's hospital, but we expect her to be allowed to come home in a week. The staff are taking care of her very well. She had her [4]_____ yesterday and there were no problems. She must rest and gargle with saltwater to [5]_____ infection in the wound whilst it heals. Hopefully, this will stop poor Jean from being so ill all the time in future.

I will pass on your card. I'm sure she will adore it!

Love,

Aunt Brenda

Extra challenge

Discuss what else Melvin could have done to send his best wishes to his cousin. How are you kind to people who are unwell?

2   1   What do you think that Jean is most upset about? Find a sentence from the text to support your answer.

  2   What do you think Aunt Brenda is most upset about? Find a sentence from the text to support your answer.

  3   Copy and complete this doctor's summary sheet about Jean and her symptoms:

  Name and surname of patient: Jean Porter
  Age: 11
  Main symptoms: _____
  Other effects on patient's daily life: _____
  Treatments tried: _____
  Number of attempts with treatment: _____
  New treatment: _____
  Hospitalisation needed? Yes / No
  Hospital to attend: _____

4   Imagine that you are Jean and you are writing in your journal. Choose one of the following activities to complete:

  • Write a short diary entry on a day when Jean was very unwell with tonsillitis.

  • Write a short diary entry for a month after Jean has had her tonsils out, when she is happy and healthy.

Grammar builder

More about pronouns

Remember ☆☆☆

Pronouns can be used as substitutes for nouns. If you need a reminder, look at Project 10 in the "Grammar builder" lesson.

Pronoun game

Play this game with a partner. You will need: a watch, clock or timer to do a 30-second count down.

Step 1: Write out these pronouns on small pieces of paper, twice each. Then fold them up so that you cannot see the words and put them into a small box.

> I   you   he   she   it   we   they

Step 2: Both write out five sentences of your own on separate pieces of paper. Each sentence must contain a different pronoun. **Do not** write out the pronoun. Put a star in the pronoun's place in the sentence. For example: * *went to their party*.

Step 3: When you have both finished writing your sentences, put them face up on the table.

Step 4: Agree who will go first. That student pulls a pronoun out of the box. They then have 30 seconds to find a sentence where that pronoun will fit. They have to read the completed sentence aloud.

Step 5: If they get it right, they can remove the sentence from the table and keep it in their own pile. If not, the sentence remains where it is on the table and the pronoun goes back into the box.

Step 6: Continue to take turns matching pronouns to sentences until all the sentences have been claimed by the players. The winner is the student who has collected the most sentences at the end of the game.

Let's write

Making complaints

Background

Remember the letter of complaint that Margaret wrote about *Fresh Foot* cream? She wrote that letter to request a refund because the product did not do what it promised to do.

> A **refund** is when the money you paid for an item is returned to you in full.

Task

Choose one of these situations and write a letter to the manufacturer requesting a refund.

- You bought a box of plasters to go in your first aid kit, but when you cut your finger, you realised that:
  - they were not sticky
  - they were all one tiny size.

  Add your own idea for what is wrong with the plasters.

- You bought toothpaste that promised extra white sparkling teeth after just one week, however:
  - it tastes horrible and your teeth are turning green
  - it smells horrible and it made you sick.

  Add your own idea about what is wrong with the toothpaste.

Plan

- When you are writing a letter, you have to set it out in a particular way. Make sure you include:

```
Company address                    Your address
                                   Date

Dear (their name),

(heading that states what the letter is about)

• when and where you bought the product
• why you bought it
• how or why the product did not work
• if anything else happened
• state what you want them to do about it

(a finishing statement)

Yours sincerely,
(your name and signature)
```

- What would be different if you thought it was a funny situation and you were writing a text or email to a friend telling them what had happened?
- Share your ideas with the class. Together, write the plan and the message.

Editor's checklist

Check your letter carefully when you finish.

- Is the letter set out in a formal way?
- Does the letter begin with a suitable greeting and end with a suitable phrase?
- Does the letter include the address of the sender at the top of the letter? Why?
- Are facts used to make the message clear?
- Do all sentences have a full stop, exclamation mark or question mark?
- Do all proper nouns and sentence beginnings have capital letters?

Reflect and review

Write a short paragraph as a journal entry to describe your letter writing experience using the guide. Did you find it helpful? What would you do differently next time?

Project 12

Speaking and listening

1. Listen to your teacher read the poem. Answer this question: Where do you think this poem is set?

Sometimes I Am Afraid

Sometimes I am afraid
Of the shadows late at night
And often unfamiliar sounds
They give me quite a fright
But always I am cheered
By the hands of love so soft
They lift me up
They hold me strong
They place me where I safely belong
So always I am cheered
No matter the time of night
For hands so soft that love me
They always make it right.

by K-Eleanor Earle

2. Read the poem quietly to yourself. Stop and think about how you connect with the poem: memories, feelings, questions.

3. Read the poem out loud to a partner.
   - Change your voice so sometimes you whisper and sometimes you speak more loudly.
   - How could you read the poem differently? For example, vary your tone of voice, pause between the title and the poem.
   - Does it change the poem if you read it differently? How?

4. With your partner, or as a small group, discuss the following questions and make notes. Then share your ideas with the class.
   1. Did you change your voice in different parts of the poem? Which words did you say more quietly and which louder? Why?

2   How is the sense of hearing explored through the poem? Are there specific words?
    For example, the word *shadows* may convey (give) a scary emotion or mood that supports the meaning of the poem.

3   How is the sense of touch explored through the poem? Are there specific words?

4   What kind of "unfamiliar sounds" might be heard at night time?

5   Who or what might the "hands of love so soft" belong to?

6   What things sometimes make you afraid?

7   What things always cheer you up?

ICT opportunity

In groups, use the computer to research emojis which we use to communicate different emotions on-screen. Create an A-Z list of emotions. Find or create an emoji for each one.

Our A-Z list of Emoji Emotions	Emotion	Emoji
A	angry	😠
B	brave	
C	confused	
D		

Word builder

Here is some vocabulary. You will come across many of these words when reading the poetry in this project:

Vocabulary box

afraid	tale	love	try
listen	flake	strong	tail
fright	edible	always	seafood
cheer	explore	almost	

1. With your partner, take turns to read the words in the vocabulary box. Discuss the word meanings as you go.

> **Example:**
> When you watch a scary movie, you might get afraid.

L👀k and learn

Consonant clusters can be a combination of **two letters** representing **one sound**, as in /th/ or /wh/

or

two or three consonants which are blended together, as in /fr/. They sound like one sound, but the sounds are separate.

1. Discuss any consonant clusters in the vocabulary box.

> **Example:**
> The consonant cluster /fr/ is in the word *afraid*.

2. Can you find a pair of homophones? Explain their different meanings.

Project 12 – Poetry to stimulate the senses

2 Look at the poem *Sometimes I Am Afraid* in the "Speaking and listening" lesson and *Seafood's Off* in the following "Let's read" lesson. Search in each poem for words from the vocabulary box.

1. Make lists in a table, like the one below.

2. Which words are left over that do not appear in either poem?

3. Add a word from each poem that you think is particularly important. Why did you choose this word?

Sometimes I Am Afraid	Seafood's Off

Extra challenge

Find and count the contractions in these poems and then say the full words.

3 Play a spelling challenge. With your partner, take turns to call out one of the words while the other has to spell it out loud letter-by-letter. Cover over the list of words and try to get the spelling right using phonics and word knowledge. Swap over so that you both have a chance to be the speller and the caller.

4 The words have been mixed up. Unscramble them and write them out with the correct spellings.

1. dfraia
2. alwasy
3. eaklf
4. voel
5. rhece
6. tali
7. nstile
8. somatl
9. ldeibe
10. trgnso
11. atel
12. edosofa
13. ritghf
14. tyr
15. xrleepo

5 How would you create a similar scramble word quiz using the words below? Think about where best to cut each word so it makes sense. Don't just cut letter-by-letter.

Vocabulary box

shadow   twinkling   sparkle   shimmering   frightening   emotional

Let's read

1 Read this poem to yourself.

    1 What are your first impressions of the poem?

    2 Do you like it or not? Why?

    3 Ask a partner about their opinion.

Seafood's Off

Once I ate a <u>starfish</u>,
It tasted worse than tripe,
It gave me <u>indigestion</u>,
Bellyache and gripe.

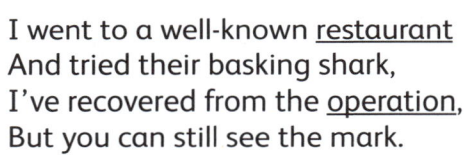

Another time I thought that I
Would try a small <u>sea</u> snake,
My face and hands broke out in <u>spots</u>,
My skin began to flake.

"Have some <u>pufferfish</u>," they said,
"You'll love it." I almost died.
It contracted my <u>skin</u> all over,
And expanded my inside.

I went to a well-known <u>restaurant</u>
And tried their basking shark,
I've recovered from the <u>operation</u>,
But you can still see the mark.

I've had sea urchin, <u>barracuda</u>,
Seahorse, stingray and whale,
And I count myself real <u>lucky</u>
That I've lived to tell the tale.

by Valerie Bloom

2 In a small group, read the poem out loud. Take turns so that each person reads a stanza. Read it together again and ask each person to change their voice, facial expressions and hand actions to convey the meaning of the poem.

3 In your group, discuss these questions. Share your group's ideas with the class. Do all the groups in your class have the same ideas?

1   How did you perform the poem?

> **Example:**
> "We performed in the corner of the classroom. We each acted out a stanza and used different tones and volumes to express the meaning. Bob made funny noises in his stanza but he insisted it was just his tone of voice. We all laughed, it was fun…"

2   What actions and facial expressions did you use?

3   Does the poem have rhythm? Describe it.

4   Which words needed emphasis?

5   If you had to illustrate the poem using emojis, which ones would you choose and why?

6   Try to replace the underlined words in the poem. What did you change them to, and why?

4 Answer these questions about the poem in one or two complete sentences. Use your own words.

1   What sense is mentioned in stanza one?

2   Find and list five items that the poet claims to have eaten.

3   Find and list three words that are illnesses or symptoms of them.

4   Find and list five common nouns that you have not used to answer questions 2 or 3.

> **Never** eat anything that is not edible. *Edible* means safe to eat. If you are not sure if something is edible, always ask an adult before trying to eat it!

Term 1 Unit 2

Remember ☆☆☆

Nouns are naming words. There are **common nouns** and **proper nouns**. Proper nouns start with a capital letter.

5 What effect did eating a small sea snake have on the poet?

6 Look at the title of the poem again. Why do you think the poet chose this title?

7 Find and list pairs of words that rhyme with each other. Add one more rhyme to each pair in the final row.

tripe gripe type				

8 Do you know other poets who write funny poems? Research some online or in the library.

What's your view?
Would you have tried as many different kinds of seafood as the poet? Explain why.

Project 12 – Poetry to stimulate the senses

G Grammar builder

1. With your partner, or in a small group, discuss the questions and tasks in each box together before writing down your answers.

2. Look at the questions and tasks for the four grammar skills again with your teacher. Be ready to share the responses and examples from your group.

I can use grammar to make my writing even better.

Apostrophes for possession
- How are apostrophes used to show possession in sentences?
- Give some examples.
- What other functions can apostrophes have in sentences?

Extra challenge
Write a sentence that describes who or what an item belongs to.

Apostrophes for contractions
- What do contractions do?
- Give some examples.
- Write a sentence that contains a contraction.

Extra challenge
Write a sentence that contains two or more contractions.

My grammar skills

Noun substitutes
- What do noun substitutes do?
- What are noun substitutes called?
- Give some examples.

Extra challenge
Write a sentence about the senses that contains a noun substitute.

Adverbs of manner
- What are adverbs of manner?
- How are they helpful?
- Give some examples.

Extra challenge
Write a sentence about the senses that contains at least one adverb of manner.

ICT opportunity

Choose one of the four grammar skills from the chart on the previous page. Use a computer to make a poster about it. Print it out and use it in a classroom display.

Self-check

How confident are you about using each of the grammar skills?

1. List the skills and draw the emoji that matches how you feel about each skill.

2. If you are not completely confident about a skill, say how you would like to improve. If you are confident about a skill, say what you would like to learn next.

Grammar	☹	😐	🙂	What I can improve or learn next
Apostrophe – possession				
Apostrophe – contractions				
Noun substitutes				
Adverbs of manner				

Project 12 – Poetry to stimulate the senses

Let's write

Poems that describe through the senses

Read this short poem which describes the season of spring through the senses.

Springtime

Springtime smells like fresh morning dew
And feels like cool, wet grass between my toes.
Springtime is the warm sun against my face
And the gentle chirp of crickets in the fields.
Springtime is Mom's ginger biscuits,
Hot and sweet with cold milk to dip.
Springtime is always green and bright;
It promises summer is almost here
And I dream of those long hot days to come.

Task

It's time for you to become a poet!
Write a poem that involves your senses.

Poems do not always have to rhyme you know!

Plan

- Choose one of these themes.

Dinner time   Carnival   Christmas   Summer   Night time

- Draw a mind map like this to gather your ideas. In each box, write down words related to your chosen theme that match each sense. For example, the foods you will taste, the sounds you will hear and what you might see.

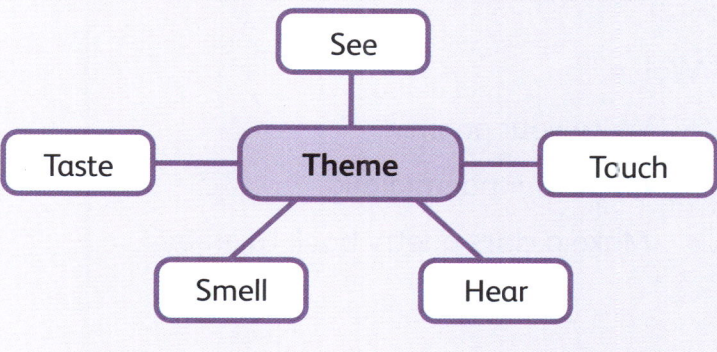

- Your poem should describe things that you can smell, feel, hear, taste and see as well as imagine. Choose how you want to write it. Work in rough as you write down your ideas.

> **Remember** ☆☆☆
> **Adverbs** and **adjectives** bring your writing to life by making it more vibrant and detailed.

- You can use the poem *Springtime* as a model if it helps you.

> **(Theme) by (your name)**
> (Theme) _____ smells like _____
> And feels like _____
> (Theme) _____ is (how it feels) _____
> And I love the sounds of _____
> (Theme) _____ is the taste of _____
> _____
> (Theme) _____ is always (how it looks) _____
> It promises _____
> And I dream of _____

- You may prefer to write your theme down the page letter-by-letter and make an acrostic poem like this.

> **S** is for the sights and sounds of twittering birds
> **P** is for the pretty flowers bursting from the earth
> **R** _____
> **I** _____
> **N** _____
> **G** _____

Write

- Write your poem.
- Read your poem aloud.
- Make a class poetry book to enjoy.

ICT opportunity

Make some audio recordings of your poems to show how you want your poem read.

Editor's checklist

Check your poem carefully when you finish.

- Does the poem include ideas for each sense?
- Does the poem rhyme?
- Does the poem use rhythm or repeated lines?
- Do all sentences have a full stop, exclamation mark or question mark?
- Does each line of the poem begin with a capital letter?
- Does the poem use lots of descriptive language?

Reflect and review
Write a short paragraph as a journal entry to describe your mind map as a planning guide to writing your own poem. What do you think of your poem? How would you mark yourself out of 10? What would you improve?

Term 1 Unit 2 Review and assessment

Word builder

1 Each of these words can have the same prefix.

Vocabulary box

fungal   histamine   biotic

1 Which of these prefixes is missing from the beginning of these words?
   anti-   ex-   pan-

2 Where would you buy the items in the vocabulary box?
   a a food shop   b a pharmacy   c a bookstore

3 Add the same prefix to the word *freeze*. What do you think this word means with its prefix? Write your answer in a sentence.

_____

2 1 *Super* is also a prefix. Complete this table.

Word	power	nova	natural	man
Prefix *super-*				

2 Choose one of the new words with a prefix. Write a sentence using your chosen word.

3 Copy and complete the table to give information about the other four senses. You can put as many words as you wish in each column.

Sense	Touch	Sight	Smell	Taste	Sound
Body part	skin, hands, feet				
Verbs	feel, touch, stroke, finger, grab				

4 Write the correct vocabulary word next to each definition.

Vocabulary box

antibiotics   bruise   disease   scent   taste buds   toothpaste

Review and assessment

1 an ailment or illness _____
2 discoloured skin usually after an injury _____
3 use daily to clean teeth _____
4 a sense organ for taste _____
5 perfume or smell _____
6 a medicine _____

Let's read

Around the world, over six thousand different languages are written and spoken by people. Humans use the tongue and mouth to make different sounds which together form words. The tongue is an important part of the body because we use it to communicate with others no matter what language we speak.

1 Read the text, choose the correct response and write the answers in complete sentences.

   1 Approximately, how many languages are spoken on Earth?
   - over six thousand
   - over sixty
   - over six hundred

   _____

   2 How do humans make sounds?
   - using their tongue and ears
   - using their nose and eyes
   - using their tongue and mouth

   _____

2 What do you think?

   1 What other body parts are used to communicate?

   _____

   2 Why is communication important? Give your own opinion.

   _____

Grammar builder

1 Here are some sentences with missing apostrophes. Rewrite the sentences with the missing apostrophes. Some are missing more than one.

1 It wont get better unless you rest.
_____

2 Mrs Peterson asked me to bring her dogs ball.
_____

3 The dentist said Lauras teeth were the healthiest he had ever seen.
_____

4 You cant jump that far; dont be so silly!
_____

5 Its Dads socks that stink.
_____

2 Rewrite the sentences. Include an adverb of manner to give more detail in each case.

1 The girls played in the schoolyard.
_____

2 Stephen ran to the bus stop.
_____

3 The trees swayed in the wind.
_____

4 I looked before I crossed the street.
_____

3 Briefly explain why adverbs are used.
_____

Let's write

Task

Choose what type of writing you want to complete.

- Write a letter to complain about an empty box of cookies and ask for a refund.
- Write a poem that involves smells.
- Write an advertisement for a new type of soda.

Plan

Write a plan for your chosen project using bullet points or a concept map to show what questions or points you will cover in your writing. Think about the kind of planning you want to use.

- RAFT
- story map
- mind map
- questions
- set layout

Remember to show that you know how to use:

- complete sentences with correct punctuation
- apostrophes to show possession and to make contractions
- adverbs of manner to give details.

Write

- Write your short text on your chosen title.
- Write your own "Editor's checklist" to show what you reviewed in your writing. Look at the "Editor's checklist" you have used before to get ideas.

TERM 2

Unit 1

Project 13

In this unit, you will learn how we communicate information about the Jamaican landscape. You will look at the beautiful natural environment and landscape, whilst using skills such as RAFT writing strategies to communicate effectively on this topic.

Speaking and listening

Look at the comic strip and complete the task below.

A stroll in the forest

That morning | Three hours later | Even later | Later still | Night fall | Dinner time

Project 13 – Natural places of Jamaica

Describe

1. In a small group, take turns to describe each scene in the comic strip.

   For example:

   Student A, scene 1:

   There are two tourists outside a hotel. One is holding a map and is asking a local outside the hotel for directions. The tourists are wearing hats, have rucksacks on their backs and binoculars around their necks. It looks like they are going hiking.

   Student B, scene 2:

   Three hours later, the two tourists are now in a village area. One of them is talking to a fruit seller. They may be lost because the other tourist is asking another local for directions.

Make notes

2. Plan a role play.

   1. In a group, make a list of all the characters in the comic strip and decide which person will play each character. Be respectful to all group members and their ideas.

   2. Make notes for each scene. Decide which characters will speak in Standard Jamaican English (SJE) and who will use Jamaican Creole (JC).

   For example:

Scene	Notes
Scene 1	tourists set out / dressed for hiking / asks passer-by for directions (SJE)
Scene 2	Jamaicans happy to talk to tourists / answer their questions / give directions (JC) Tourist 1 asks fruit seller questions. / Tourist 2 asks another local questions. (SJC)
Scene 3	

Use visuals

3 Create signs on paper to show your audience the settings for the play. For example, for scene 1, write the sign HOTEL on the board or create a paper sign. Place the sign wherever you are doing the role play.

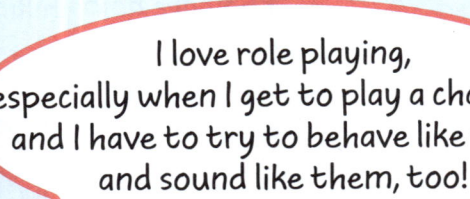

I love role playing, especially when I get to play a character and I have to try to behave like them and sound like them, too!

Dialogue refers to words spoken by the characters in a play, television show or movie. It can also refer to conversation between people. Look up the word *dialogue* in the dictionary or online for more examples.

Role play

4 Perform your role play in front of the class. Remember to face the audience and speak clearly. The dialogue between the characters should be clear and your body language should contribute to the performance.

Listen and evaluate

5 Watch and listen to the role plays of other classmates, using the presentation checklist to evaluate their presentations. Note down how good the presentations are or where they could be improved.

Presentation checklist	Appropriate Why?	Not appropriate Why?	Unsure
Use of language appropriate to the task.			
Appropriate use of SJE / JC.			
Eye contact – characters look at each other and the audience when necessary.			
Voice is audible (loud and clear).			
Body language – character's facial expression and body movements contributed to the presentation.			
Use of visuals to improve the presentation.			

Vote

6 Refer to your evaluation in Activity 5 and decide as a class which presentation was the most convincing and why.

Project 13 – Natural places of Jamaica

Word builder

This vocabulary is about the natural landscape:

Vocabulary box

mountain	waterfall	reef	shore
ocean	sea	sky	rainforest
beach	stream	coast	natural
river	feature	cloud	

1 1 In pairs, take turns to practise segmenting the following words. Student A ticks (✓) the box after Student B segments the word into sounds, then swap roles.

Word	Sounds	Student A ✓	Student B ✓
beach	/b/ /ea/ /ch/		
reef	/r/ /ee/ /f/		
sea	/s/ /ea/		
sky	/s/ /k/ /y/		
stream	/s/ /t/ /r/ /ea/ /m/		
coast	/c/ /oa/ /s/ /t/		
cloud	/c/ /l/ /ou/ /d/		
shore	/sh/ /ore/		

2 Discuss any tricky pronunciations and spellings.

For example:

The words **stream** and **cloud** begin with the consonant clusters /st/ and /cl/.

The word **shore** has five letters, but only two sounds.

145

2 The words in Activity 1 are all one-syllable words.

1 Look at the vocabulary box on the previous page. Find the words with two and three syllables and complete the table.
Tip: As you read the words, count the number of syllables in each word by gently tapping your hand under your chin.

Two syllables	Three syllables

2 Two words in the vocabulary box are compound words. What are they?

_____   _____

3 Look at the words in the vocabulary box again. Can you make them all plural just by adding an -s to the end? Write any words that cannot be made plural in this way, and explain why they are different.

> ### L👀k and learn
>
> A **plural noun** describes more than one person, place or thing. For most nouns, add -s, but if a noun ends in:
>
> - -s, -z, -x, -sh, or -ch, add **-es** (beach – beach**es**)
> - a consonant (b, c, d, f, g, etc.) + o, add **-es** (tomato – tomato**es**)
> - consonant + -y, change the -y to **-ies** (sky - sk**ies**)
>
> When you add an ending that changes the original noun to plural, it is called an **inflectional ending**.

4 Copy and complete this Venn diagram by placing each word from the vocabulary box in the right place. Words in the middle can be both wet or dry. If you think a word does not fit either category, write it outside of the diagram.

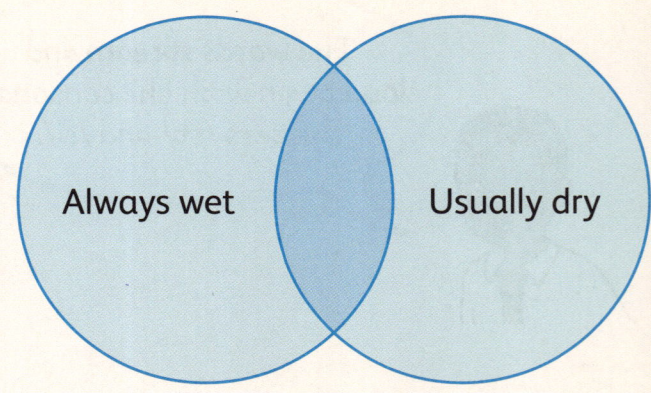

5 Think about the area where you live. Do you live near a river, a beach or a mountain? What does the sky look like? Write two short sentences to describe the area. Use at least one word from the vocabulary box in each sentence.

> **Extra challenge**
>
> Try to use two or more words from the vocabulary box in each sentence.

6 Challenge a partner to a *Spelling Bee* game. Spell a word out loud letter-by-letter. Get a point for each word that you spell correctly. Make a note in your notebook of any words you get wrong and remember to practise those again. Do not let the Spelling Bee beat you!

Term 2 Unit 1

Let's read

Research and study skills

Graphs and charts are drawings that show information called **data**. Data can be presented as lines, shapes or pictures.

Look and learn

- Useful words to know when reading a graph:

A **vertical** line rises straight up from bottom to top.
A **horizontal** line runs from left to right.

- A graph has two axes called *x* and *y*:

The *x*-axis is horizontal and the *y*-axis is vertical.

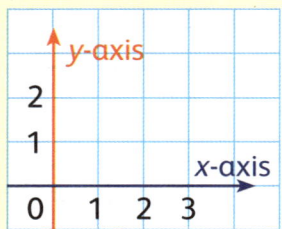

A bar graph shows the data in bar shapes of different sizes and colours. Longer bars have a higher value than shorter bars. For example, the green bar shows one hotel has 100 guests and the red bar shows that another hotel has 50 guests. Two bars represent the different hotels. The bar for the hotel with 100 guests is twice as long as the bar for the hotel with 50 guests.

1 In pairs, look at the bar graph and ask and answer questions together about the data. For example: *What is the title of the graph? What is the unit of measure? How many guests stayed at the… ?*

Title: Hotel guests Jan 2020

Unit of measure: Multiples of 50

Label: Hotels

148

2   In pairs, answer the following questions about the bar graph below.

1   What is the title of the bar graph? _____

2   Which day are students absent the most? _____

3   Which day are students absent the least? _____

4   How many more students are absent on Monday than on Tuesday?

_____

(Tip: Find the bar for Monday on the **horizontal** line (*x*-axis) and its value on the **vertical** line (*y*-axis). Do the same for Tuesday. Then take the smaller value away from the bigger value).

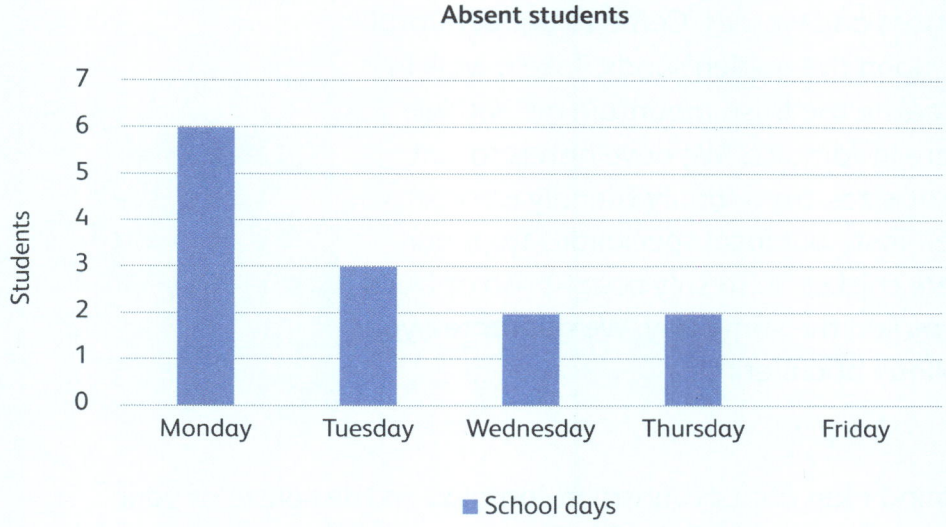

3   In small groups, discuss the data and report back to the class with your findings and recommendations.

1   Why do you think more students are absent on Monday than the other days?

2   Why do you think there are no absent students on Friday?

3   What do you suggest the school should do about the high absence rates on Mondays?

1. Read this tourist information leaflet about Jamaica and then complete the tasks below.

Visit Jamaica

Let go of your stress and worries. Come to our beautiful island and relax upon the golden sands. Take a walk in the forests or breathe the fresh mountain air. You will find paradise here in Jamaica. We have hotels to suit all budgets and all sizes, from family-friendly resorts to couples' retreats. Taste our local specialities from our world-famous jerk chicken to freshly caught fish or fruits that have been picked the same day. We guarantee you will have the holiday of a lifetime.

1. Create a mind map about tourism in Jamaica. In the centre of your mind map, write the word *Jamaica*. Around the mind map, write some facts and details about tourism in Jamaica based on what you have read in the leaflet.

2. Complete the RAFT strategy for this leaflet.

R	Role	What is the writer's role?	
A	Audience	Who is the writer writing for?	
F	Format	What type of writing is it? What is its purpose?	
T	Topic	What is the writing about?	

> **Remember** ☆☆☆
>
> A **summary** is a short version of a story or piece of text containing only the essential facts. It does not have many extra details or specific information.

3   Write a summary of the information in the leaflet.

Extra challenge

Plan your own leaflet online to promote tourism for Jamaica.
- Use the RAFT strategy to help you. What type of language should you use: formal, descriptive, SJE or JC?
- Use text boxes to separate different parts of the leaflet. You can copy and paste photos and diagrams from the internet or do some independent study and learn how to create a simple bar graph of your own to present data on tourism.
- Use the leaflet above and the template below to guide you. Copy it out in your notebook and build the content for your online leaflet.

Topic sentence:	Let go of… / Think of the beautiful… / Why not…
Places to go and things to do: Forest Mountains / Fresh air Hotels / Beaches (sand, sea, sun, swimming) Food (delicious/unique to Jamaica) Music / Dance	
Concluding sentence: final persuading comment	We guarantee… / What are you waiting for…? / You will not regret it!

Term 2 Unit 1

Grammar builder

Collective nouns

You already know a lot about nouns:
- There are **proper nouns**, like *Jamaica*, and **common nouns**, like *island*.
- Nouns can be **singular**, like *island*, or **plural**, like *islands*.

> **Look and learn**
> Some nouns are called **collective nouns**. Collective nouns refer to a group.
> For example:
> For one lion we say *a lion*.
> For a group of lions we say *a pride of lions*.
> Some words can have more than one collective noun.
> For example, a group of people could be *a crowd*, *a mob* or *a gathering*.

Some collective nouns for groups of animals are very unusual words. Often, they reflect the character, appearance or ability of the animal. A group of flamingos is called a *flamboyance*. *Flamboyant* means "showy" or "fancy" and flamingos are certainly fancy birds! What else could you describe as *flamboyant*?

Vocabulary box

flock   den   ~~clowder~~   colony   herd

1 Complete the table with a collective noun from the vocabulary box.

Animals that live in Jamaica

Animals	Collective nouns
cats	clowder
ducks	
snakes	
cattle	
bats	

152

Project 13 – Natural places of Jamaica

"I do not recognise some of these words. I will go online or find a dictionary to look them up."

Extra challenge

Name three more animals that live in Jamaica and find out what their collective nouns are.

2   What is your favourite animal and what is its collective noun?

3   It is not only animals that have collective nouns. Here are some words and their collective nouns.

  1   Match them without looking them up online or in a dictionary.

  - robbers
  - soldiers
  - flowers

  - bouquet
  - army
  - gang

  2   Write a sentence for each collective noun.

  _____

  _____

  _____

153

Let's write

Natural places of Jamaica

Background

You are lucky enough to live in a beautiful country with a rich natural landscape. The landscape ranges from beautiful blue waters to lush green forests filled with animals and plants of all colours, shapes and sizes. Everywhere in Jamaica there is much to see and wonder about.

> **ICT opportunity**
>
> Use an online search tool to zoom in to see the natural features of places in Jamaica. For example:
> 1. Open Google Earth.
> 2. Search for a location.
> 3. Zoom in to see the area in more detail.
> 4. Click the Pegman on the bottom right of the screen.
> 5. Drag the Pegman into the area to see Street View.

Task

Write a journal entry entitled *Natural places of Jamaica* as a gift for your grandparents. Reflect upon how you feel about the landscape of your country.

In your journal, you should write about some of the natural features of Jamaica. You should write a minimum of one paragraph.

Plan

- Look at the photographs on the next page.
- Jot down some notes and key words that you want to include in your journal. Add your own ideas, too.
- Copy the table on the next page with columns to organise your notes.

The natural feature	What I see	Adjectives to describe it	How it makes me feel
a beach	sand, sky, water	brilliant white sand	
deep green and blue water	calm, relaxed, happy, peaceful		

Ocho Rios Beach • Looking towards the Nassau Mountains • The Dunn's River Falls

Write

- Use the information in your table to write a first draft. How will you organise your paragraphs?
- Write your final draft out neatly in your best joined handwriting in your journal.

My writing must be very detailed so that someone who has never seen Jamaica can imagine what it is truly like.

Term 2 Unit 1

Editor's checklist

Check your work carefully when you finish.

- Does the journal entry include any collective nouns?
- Does the journal entry include photographs or pictures?
- Are adjectives and adverbs used to make the writing vibrant and detailed?
- Are all apostrophes and commas used correctly?
- Are all spellings correct, especially of place names?
- Do all sentences have a full stop, exclamation mark or question mark?
- Do all proper nouns and sentence beginnings have capital letters?

Reflect and review
Write a short paragraph as a journal entry to describe your experience using a column approach. Did you find it helpful? Did it make the writing task easier for you? How? How would you use it differently next time? Would you adapt it?

Project 14

Speaking and listening

It is important to listen attentively. This means listening carefully, especially when you are listening for facts or information.

Show that you can listen attentively by doing these things:

- Sit still.
- Do not whisper or talk.
- Do not play with anything.

An **acronym** is made when we use the first letter of each word in a phrase. Together, these letters create a new word that becomes easy to remember and speeds up communication. For example:
LOL – Laughing Out Loud
BTW – By The Way
What acronyms do you know?

What else can you add to this list?

1 Follow this text as it is read aloud to you. Listen for answers to these questions.

1. What does JPAT stand for?

2. Name one place JPAT looks after.

3. Name one thing in that area that makes it special.

The work of JPAT

The acronym JPAT stands for Jamaica Protected Areas Trust. This organisation helps to look after and protect natural places in Jamaica. One of the places that they look after is the Blue and John Crow Mountains National Park which covers an area of approximately 780 square kilometres. In this area, there is a lot of rainforest covering the mountain slopes. Many hundreds of species of trees, plants and animals can be found there and some are very rare or endangered. This is why it is important that there are organisations like JPAT helping to preserve the natural landscape.

2. In pairs, share your answers. How different are they?
3. What do you do to listen well? Share your listening strategies. For example:

I make eye contact, so the speaker can see I am listening attentively.

I always try and relate to the topic. Without thinking for too long, I connect to my own experience.

If ever I drift off or daydream, I move my head to one side and back again. This makes me focus again.

4. Make a class poster about active listening for display so you all remember how to do it.

ICT opportunity

Visit the JPAT website (https://www.efj.org.jm/jpat-fcf-protected-areas/) to find out more about their work in protecting the beautiful landscape of Jamaica. Report back to the class with an example of how JPAT protects the natural landscape. Listen to your classmates' examples attentively.

Project 14 – Our mountains

Word builder

This vocabulary is to do with mountains:

Vocabulary box

peak	Mountains	coffee
temperature	landform	National Park
Blue Mountains	Juan de Bolas	range
decrease	Mountain	increase
kilometre	steep	summit
John Crow	Mocho Mountains	

Remember ☆☆☆

Synonyms are different words for the same thing.
Antonyms are opposites.

1 Take turns to read the words in the vocabulary box with a partner.

1 Discuss the word meanings.

Example:
You find the **temperature** of something to measure how hot or cold it is.

2 With your partner, have a spelling challenge. One of you calls out one of the words or phrases and your partner has to spell it out loud letter-by-letter. You must cover over the list of words and try to get the spelling correct using your knowledge of phonics (word sounds). Swap over so that you both have a chance to be the caller and the speller.

3 With your partner, explore different ways to sort the words. For example, you can sort them by word length, by meaning or by word class (noun, verb, adjective). Add some more words about the landscape to this group. Share your ideas with a group or the class.

Remember ☆☆☆

Homophones are words that sound the same but are spelled differently and have different meanings.

4   The words *peek* and *peak* are homophones. Write a definition for both of these words.

peek _____

peak _____

2   Look at the vocabulary words.

1   Find a pair of synonyms. _____ _____

2   Find a pair of antonyms. _____ _____

3   Complete the following sentences.

1   The four major mountains in Jamaica are _____.

2   _____ is a crop that is grown in the mountains.

ICT opportunity

Find an outline map of the island of Jamaica online. Paste the image into a document. Label it with the locations of the four major mountain ranges as well as any other natural features that you think are important.

Alternatively, find a map in an atlas to copy, then draw your own island and label it.

Project 14 – Our mountains

Let's read

1 Read the text and answer the following questions.

I never knew that the collective noun for a group of mountains or hills is a range!

The Island of Jamaica

The island of Jamaica is located south of Cuba and belongs to the North American continent. The island is inside the Atlantic Ocean's hurricane belt. Hurricane season usually lasts from June to November.

Jamaica is the third largest island in the Caribbean Sea, after Cuba and Hispaniola. This large mountainous island is home to a population of over 2,900,000 people. Kingston is the capital city and the largest English-speaking city in the Caribbean.

The longest river in Jamaica is Rio Minho which is 92 km / 57 miles. The longest mountain range in Jamaica is the Blue Mountains. The island's highest point is Blue Mountain Peak at 2256 metres / 7402 feet, but this is not the highest peak in the Caribbean.

1 What is the main purpose of this text?

    a to provide information about Jamaica

    b to persuade people to visit Jamaica

    c to sell holidays to Jamaica

2 Which of these facts is not mentioned in the text?

    a Jamaica's position in the Atlantic Ocean.

    b The population of the capital city, Kingston.

    c The size of Jamaica compared to other Caribbean islands.

3 Which of these statements about the text is false?

    a Over 2.9 million people live in Jamaica.

    b Rio Minho is the longest river in Jamaica.

    c Jamaica has the highest mountain peak in the Caribean.

4 Which definition is the word *belt* closest in meaning to?

  a A strip of cloth or leather worn around the waist.

  b An area of land that gets storms with strong wind.

5 Write true (T) or false (F).

  The words *point* and *peak* in the text are synonyms. _____

2 In pairs, think of two more geographical facts that you could add to the text.

> **Extra challenge**
>
> Write two statements based on your facts to ask another pair of students to answer. Use the statements above to guide you.

Research and study skills

This table shows data about the height of the four major mountain ranges of Jamaica.

Mountain range	Peak height (m)
Juan de Bolas Mountains	836
John Crow Mountains	1,140
Mocho Mountains	436
Blue Mountains	2,256

The same data about the height of the four mountain ranges of Jamaica can also be shown in a graph. In the following bar graph, you can see that the data is the same as in the table. It is just shown in a different way.

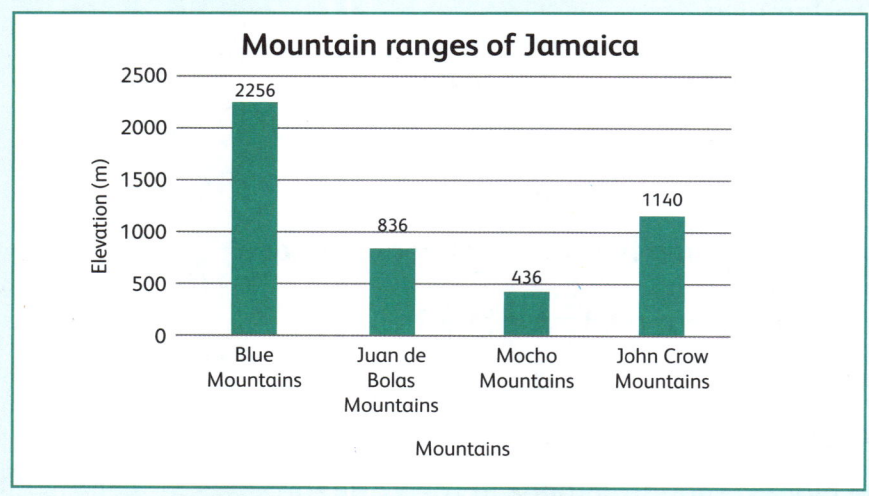

Project 14 – Our mountains

Remember ☆☆☆

- A graph has two axes called *x* and *y*.
- The *x*-axis is horizontal and the *y*-axis is vertical.

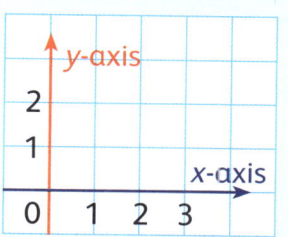

1. What unit of measurement is used for the height of the mountains?
2. What is the highest mountain range in Jamaica?
3. What is the lowest mountain range in Jamaica?
4. The label is missing from the *x*-axis. Where should the label be written? What should the label be? Look back at the "Research and study skills" lesson in Project 13 for guidance.

*Why is the y-axis labelled **elevation**? I'm not sure what that word means, what should I do?*

5. Write a sentence to give the peak height of each mountain range as a figure in words.

   Here is an imaginary example:

   The peak height of the Magic Mountains is eight hundred and forty-two metres.

6. Write three sentences that compare different Jamaican mountains using the following words:

Vocabulary box

tall   taller   tallest   small   smaller   smallest

Here are some imaginary examples:

Sunny Mountain is taller than Cloudy Mountain but smaller than Magic Mountain.

Sunny Mountain is tall, but Magic Mountain is the tallest.

Extra challenge

Use a ruler and a pencil to carefully and accurately copy out the graph about the mountains of Jamaica. Do not forget to include all the labels and numbers.

Grammar builder

Commas

Look and learn

A **comma** is a punctuation mark that has several uses:

- to pause between items in a list
- to show where two sentences have been joined together by a conjunction
- after an introductory word or phrase. For example: *firstly, next, finally, in addition*, etc.

When you see a comma in a sentence or a list, it is telling you to take a short pause in your reading.

Remember ☆☆☆

A coordinating conjunction joins two complete sentences to make a compound sentence.

There is always **a comma before** a coordinating conjunction.

For example: *I was hungry, but I forgot my lunch.*

Look back at Project 3 in the "Grammar builder" lesson to review coordinating conjunctions and where to place the comma.

1. Read these sentences with a partner and answer the questions.

   1. Jamaica has four main mountain ranges. They are the Blue Mountains **and** the John Crow Mountains **and** the Juan de Bolas Mountains **and** the Mocho Mountains.

      Jamaica has four main mountain ranges. They are the Blue Mountains, the John Crow Mountains, the Juan de Bolas Mountains **and** the Mocho Mountains.

   - What are the differences?

Project 14 – Our mountains

2. I want to climb to Blue Mountain Peak – but it is too high.

   I want to climb to Blue Mountain Peak, but it is too high.

   - What is the difference in punctuation?
   - Which sounds better and why?
   - What did the comma tell you?

   > Be careful with your spelling. **A comma** and **a coma** are very different things!

3. In the morning the mist settles around the mountain peaks.

   In the morning, the mist settles around the mountain peaks.

   - What is the difference in punctuation?
   - Which sounds better and why?
   - What did the comma tell you?

ICT opportunity

Listen to *The Comma Song* on YouTube or any song about commas to hear all about the many uses of this little punctuation mark. Write bullet points to summarise the main points made in the song.

You could make up your own comma song and record it.

Remember, we must be sensible when we are online. Only search for information about your lesson. If you see anything that makes you feel uncomfortable, you should tell your teacher.

2. In a small group, read the paragraph about mountains in Jamaica on the next page. Discuss each sentence and decide if there are any commas missing. Write the paragraph with all the commas in place. There may not be a missing comma in every sentence.

The island of Jamaica is well known for its beautiful beaches lush forests and hilly mountains. The highest of all the mountains in Jamaica is Blue Mountain Peak and it stands at over 2000 metres high! The soil on the mountain sides is full of nutrients vitamins minerals and water that plants love. This is why coffee bananas potatoes and yams grow so widely in this area. Not as many people live in the mountains as in cities like Kingston but there are some small farming communities. There is also a lot of wildlife in the mountains. You can see animals including butterflies birds snakes frogs and the Jamaican Coney.

Extra challenge

In your group, write a paragraph about the natural landscape of Jamaica. Leave out the commas. Give your paragraph to another group and challenge them to put the commas in. Make sure you have only left out the commas. There should be no spelling mistakes, capital letters or full stops missing.

> Commas are very useful. I can use them to punctuate my writing, to separate information in lists and to break long sentences into parts.

You can find out information by looking in reference books. At the back of the reference book there is usually an **index**. The index lists the topics of the book in alphabetical order and tells you what page you need to go to. Find a book that has an index in your class or town library.

Let's write

Non-fiction writing

> **Remember** ☆☆☆
>
> **Fiction writing** is when you write stories or poems that are not real, even if they are about real-life events. Some fiction is make-believe or fantasy and these things are not true.
>
> **Non-fiction writing** is when you write about real and true things. Non-fiction writing is usually factual.

Task

Work in pairs to design a short, factual leaflet for tourists about one of the mountain ranges in Jamaica. Choose one of the four main mountain ranges: Blue Mountains, Juan de Bolas Mountains, Mocho Mountains or John Crow Mountains.

Plan

Use RAFT if you find it useful. Work through these points with your partner. Decide what you want to tell the tourists:

- the name of the range
- where it is in Jamaica
- the height of the mountains
- wildlife that can be found there
- plants or trees that can be found there
- the farming that happens there
- how to get there
- what parishes are nearby
- where to stay
- where they can get further information
- organised trips
- dangers and where to get help.

Think about what else they might need to know.

Search

- Use books or go online to find any information or pictures you need.
- Record your findings using a graphic organiser such as a mind map. Use your mind map to begin to draft your leaflet.
- Decide on the layout of your leaflet.
- Will your leaflet be one whole piece of paper or will it be folded?
- Will it be black and white or in colour?
- Will it use different fonts and sizes of font?
- Will it have headings? Why?
- Sketch a visual plan of how your leaflet will look before you begin so all the information fits.

Do not forget to use adjectives and adverbs to give details about what you are describing.

Editor's checklist

Check your work carefully when you finish.

- Does the leaflet give facts and helpful information?
- Does the leaflet use the right language for the audience?
- Does the leaflet include photographs or pictures?
- Is all sentence punctuation correct like capital letters and full stops?
- Is all spelling correct, especially for proper nouns?
- Are commas and apostrophes used in the right places?

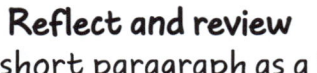

Reflect and review

Write a short paragraph as a journal entry to describe your experience of writing a leaflet. What went well? What would you change?

Project 15

Speaking and listening

Debate about rivers

You are going to hold a debate about rivers with your classmates. A debate is a discussion where different views are shared and it can end in a vote to see which side has won.

Maps showing the locations of the rivers Nile and Amazon

The debate challenge

The Nile and the Amazon are both huge rivers, but which is bigger? There will be two teams for the debate. Each team must try to prove that this statement is true for their river.

Debate statement: _____ is the biggest river in the world.

Team tips

Work together to present the team's evidence during the debate. Decide on team roles.

- Who will be team leader?
- Who will be the script writers?
- What area will each person research about the river?

Who will research:
- the rivers length, depth and width?
- the source (beginning) of the river?
- the mouth (end) of the river?

Content

The speech needs to convince everybody listening that your team is right. It needs to be persuasive. How? Graphs, tables, illustrations and sourced information make your argument more convincing. Speak clearly and confidently.

Debate

1. The first person in Team A and then Team B will have one minute to present their argument.

   Example:
   The _____ river is the biggest river in the world because a website states that it is… long and has…

2. The second person in both teams will now have one minute to defend the argument of their first speaker and present more information and facts.

   Example:
   It is clear that what my team member says is correct because… . In addition,…

3. The third person in both teams will now have one minute to present final information and sum up the team's argument.

   Example:
   As we can see from all the evidence presented such as…, …, and…, there can be no doubt that the … river is the biggest.

4. Both teams will have five minutes to discuss how to respond to the argument of the other team. Each team must think of what they can say to argue against all the points made by the opposite team.

Project 15 – Famous rivers

5. As above, the first person in Team A and Team B will now respond to each other's points and **refute** (say why that information is false or not accurate) the information of the opposite team member.

For example:

Team A says..., but the internet is not always accurate and they did not mention their source.

Well, Team B states..., but we disagree because the government report says.... A report from the government is a reliable source which means we can trust this information.

- Invite a wider audience such as another class or parents.
- Listen carefully to each argument made. Make notes so you remember.
- When a person makes an excellent point, the people who are listening can clap or cheer.
- Often, when people listening to a debate agree with a point, they call out "Hear, hear!" to show their support.

Debates are great fun, but you must express yourself clearly and remember that the people on the other team are still your friends!

Vote

After both teams have given their speeches, everybody who has been listening will cast their vote. The team with the most votes wins the debate.

ICT opportunity

Use technology for any part of your debate where you think it will make a difference. For example, you may wish to produce charts or diagrams that have facts and figures to illustrate what the speakers are saying. You may wish to use handouts for your audience, too.

Word builder

This vocabulary is about rivers:

Vocabulary box

spring	Rio Minho	tributary	bend
fish	depth	dock	flow
Black River	Amazon	lake	bridge
water sports	gush	Nile	

1. Take turns to read the words aloud to a partner.
2. Copy and complete the table.

1 Copy	2 Practise	3 Write
spring fish	spring fish	

1. Copy the words from the vocabulary box into column 1.

2. Practise writing each word in column 2.

3. In pairs, cover the first two columns and listen as your partner reads the words aloud while you write the words in column 3. Then swap.

3 1. Four words are proper nouns. What are they? How do you know? Check your answers with your partner.

2. In pairs, add at least two more words to this group. Use an online tool to help you search for information on rivers.

Project 15 – Famous rivers

> **L👀k and learn**
>
> **Homograph** comes from the Greek word *homos* which means *same* and *grapho* which means *to write*. So, homographs are words that are written the same but have different meanings. For example, *park* can either be a noun for a place where you go to relax and have fun or it can be a verb: to *park* a car or vehicle.

4 Look at these sentences. Underline the correct meaning of the homograph in bold in each sentence.

1. It is hard to believe that a tiny **spring** can become a huge river.

    a source of water / the season that follows winter.

2. Sam put his phone in the speaker **dock**.

    a port or harbour for ships / something that can hold and connect to a smaller item.

3. The old man loved to **fish** in the early mornings.

    animals that live in water / a sport or hobby using nets or rods to catch water creatures

5 Write a homograph challenge like the ones above for your partner to solve. Swap so you can solve theirs, too.

6 Write a sentence for each meaning of these homographs. Use a dictionary or online tool to check the different meanings.

1. row   2. refuse   3. wind   4. present

7 There are four names of rivers in the vocabulary box.

1. What are they?

2. Find three more famous rivers to add to the list from around the world. Write their names carefully, starting with capital letters.

Extra challenge

Use the internet or reference books to find out more about the Jamaican rivers.
- List them in order from longest to shortest.
- State the distance for each river.

Let's read

1. This story has two parts. In a small reading group, read and discuss Part 1 together.

The story of a river – Part 1

A tiny spring burst out of the ground. "Plop, plop, plop", it said. As it ran down the hillside, it whispered, "Pitter, patter, pitter, patter." It had become a stream.

The stream passed through a field and a girl jumped over it. "Ha, ha!" laughed the stream. "You can jump over me now, but I am growing bigger and bigger."

On it went, and soon it was joined by another stream, and another, and another. These other streams are called tributaries. Soon the stream became quite big.

It came to a bridge; only a small wooden bridge, but the stream felt proud. "I am too big to be jumped over now!" It danced on and on, until it reached some children. "We can fish here!" shouted one little boy. "I must be a river now." said the stream. "I am quite big, and children can fish and even bathe in me."

Look and learn

Alliteration is the repetition of consonant sounds at the beginning of several words.
Personification is when a non-living thing is portrayed as if it were living.

1. The story involves alliteration. For example: *Plop, plop, plop*. Find another example in the story.

2. The story features personification. Decide which non-living thing is personified in the story. Why might the author have chosen to personify this thing?

3. Do you like the effects of alliteration and personification? Do they improve the story? Explain why you think so.

4. What do you think will happen in Part 2 of the story? Share your ideas and predictions with the class.

Finish reading the story in your group. Were your predictions about Part 2 of the story correct? Tell your group.

Project 15 – Famous rivers

The story of a river – Part 2

The river began to run more slowly. The land was flatter with fields on each side. The river became stronger. It tore off rock and soil where the bank was not wide enough and dropped them later at a wider place.

Suddenly, it ran into a village. "A real bridge of stone!" it cried. "Now I am so big that people must build a bridge to cross me!" The river found itself carrying hundreds of little boats, all full of happy, cheerful people. "I wish I could stay here always, but I cannot. I must go on. I do not know why but I must go on." On it went, past more trees and green fields until it came to a huge city.

The river flowed on and became wider and wider. On went the river until it reached the docks. It was a grand sight to see so many cargo ships and liners. "I shall never be able to carry such huge ships. I am not strong enough!" it thought. Then a wonderful thing happened. Suddenly, the river met the sea and flowed into it. The river shouted with joy "This is where I belong! This is why I could never stop! Now I am perfectly happy!"

2 Work on your own to answer these questions about the story. Share your answers with your group when everyone is ready.

   1 Why did the river slow down?

   2 Why did the river feel happy in the village?

   3 Why did the river feel worried at the docks?

   4 How did the river feel at the end of the story?

3 Write the key events of the story in the correct order from 1 to 6. The first one is done for you.

   It met the sea. _____

   A tiny spring burst out of the ground. _1_

   It became a river. _____

   It flowed under a small wooden bridge and then under a bigger stone bridge. _____

   It carried small boats and flowed to the city docks with bigger ships. _____

   It became a stream and then other streams joined it. _____

Grammar builder

Adverbs of time

Remember

Adverbs describe verbs. **Adverbs of manner** tell you *how* something is done or how someone does something and usually end in **-ly**. For example: *The Black River flows quick**ly** in many places.*

Look and learn

Some adverbs are called **adverbs of time**. These are the adverbs that tell you *when* something is, was or will be done. They are usually written or said at the end of a sentence. Some common adverbs of time are:

today   yesterday   tomorrow
now   later   before   after

Say a sentence for each adverb of time.

There are other types of adverbs including adverbs of place that you will learn about later.

1 Circle the correct adverb to complete each sentence.

1 I'm going to cricket practice today / yesterday.

2 The rain was heavy tomorrow / yesterday.

3 Strong wind is forecast for tomorrow / yesterday.

4 I need my dinner yesterday / now!

5 Mom said I can tidy my room later / yesterday.

2 Look at these sentences.

The hurricane warning has been issued. Residents should evacuate now.

The hurricane warning has been issued. Residents should evacuate later.

1 Which sentence is more urgent? How do you know?

2 What could you do to make the urgent sentence sound even more urgent?

Look and learn

Sometimes, **adverbs of time** can be moved to the front of a sentence. When they are moved, they are followed by a comma. For example: ***Tomorrow**, I will see Grandma.*

3 Match the time expressions to the most suitable sentence and punctuate it correctly. Check your answers with a partner and explain your choice for each sentence.

1 Every year   a I get my books from my locker.

2 After a while   b my mom always serves us a delicious pudding.

3 Before class,   c we visit Trinidad and Tobago for the carnival.

4 In the evening   d I watch TV after I have done my homework.

5 After dinner   e it stopped raining.

Let's write

Fiction writing

> **Remember** ☆☆☆
>
> **Fiction** writing is when you write stories or poems that are not real even if they are about real-life events. Some fiction is make-believe or fantasy and these things are not true.
>
> **Non-fiction** writing is when you write about real and true things. Non-fiction writing is usually factual.

Task

Remember the story of the river? Now it is your turn to write a short story using alliteration and personification.

Plan

- Choose your story focus. Here are some suggestions to give you a few ideas:
    - You are the boat on a dangerous fishing trip. How can you help the fishermen?
    - You are the river watching a family enjoy their day, but then something happens. How can you help?
    - You are a river on a journey to the sea. What do you see and hear? Who do you meet?
    - You are the Nile or the Amazon – king of the rivers. What do you say to passers-by on the riverbanks and afloat in the river?
- Use a planning strategy to help organise your ideas. Choose the one you like best:
    - RAFT
    - Mind map
    - Story planning chart

Write

- Use your plans to write a first draft and review it. How will you do that?
- Write your story.

Project 15 – Famous rivers

Remember ☆☆☆

- **Alliteration** is the repetition of consonant sounds at the beginning of several words.
- **Personification** is when a non-living thing is portrayed as if it were living.

Remember ☆☆☆

A story needs:
- characters and a setting
- a beginning, a middle and an end
- a series of interesting events
- a problem that has to be solved by the end of the story.

Editor's checklist

Check your work carefully when you finish.

- Do characters' names (proper nouns) have capital letters?
- Have you used some special features such as alliteration or personification?
- Does the story have a beginning, a middle and an end?
- Do all sentences begin with a capital letter and end with a full stop, question mark or exclamation mark?
- Are commas and apostrophes used in the correct places?
- Are there adverbs of time that have been used correctly?

Reflect and review
Write a short paragraph as a journal entry to describe your experience of planning and writing this story. What went well? What would you change?

Project 16

Speaking and listening

Rain poems

1 Listen to your teacher read these two poems and compare them.

The Rain

The rain is falling heavily
The breeze is blowing hard
And once where there were roses
Flows a river in the yard
The barking dogs are silent
The birds are out of sight
The tallest trees and all their leaves
Have made the earth their bed tonight.

by K-Eleanor Earle

Rain

She makes the trees sway with delight.
She tells the long grass, "Shiver".
She puts laughter in the stream
And the gurgle in the river.

She drives the thunder grumbling off,
Orders the wind to sing,
Snuffs the lightning's fire out,
Takes the roof tap dancing.

She pours a drink for the thirsty earth,
Washes the face of the sky,
Puts a sparkle on the leaves
And a glint in the ocean's eye.

She plays a tattoo on the windowpanes,
Paints doors a darker brown,
And creates a brand new swimming pool
In the centre of town.

In anger, she will pound the ground
With the force of a cannonball,
But happy, she sings a lullaby,
This celestial waterfall.

by Valerie Bloom

2 Now read the poems aloud with a partner or small group.

3 Discuss these questions in a group and share your ideas with the class.

1 One of the poems uses personification. Find a line from the poem to demonstrate the use of personification.

2 Rivers must be important. Both poems mention them. Why do you think this is? Discuss food, energy, recreation, transportation and your own ideas.

3 Which poem did you prefer to read out loud? Is it because of the rhythm or the way that you could change your voice?

ICT opportunity

Use technology to make some audio recordings of these poems. Make the recordings using different voices and different ways of reading. Make this available in a listening corner so you can listen at other times. You may add other poems and stories, too.

Word builder

This vocabulary is about the landscape:

Vocabulary box

breeze	sway	swimming	bleak
hills	trickle	windowpane	shimmer
earth	fire	meander	lullaby
sparkle	crag	babbling	

1. With your partner, take turns to read the words aloud.

Remember ☆☆☆

Consonant clusters can be a combination of **two letters** representing **one sound**, as in /th/ or /wh/, or **two or three consonants** which are blended together, as in /br/, but the sounds are separate.

1. In pairs, write the words that begin with a consonant cluster with one sound. Check your answers with your teacher.

2. In pairs, write the words that begin with a consonant cluster with two or three sounds. Check your answers with your teacher.

3. How could you say any of the words to sound like their meaning?

Example:

2 Write the words in alphabetical order. Be careful and make sure that you spell them correctly.

3 Write the words that begin with the letter *s*. Two of them are synonyms. Which two?

_____ _____

4 Write the words that begin with the letter *b*.

   1 One of them is a common noun. Which one? _____

   2 One of them is a verb. Which one? _____

   3 One of them is an adjective. Which one? _____

5 Which vocabulary word matches each definition?

   1 part of a house   _____

   2 hot and dangerous   _____

   3 a bend in a river   _____

   4 a planet in the solar system   _____

   5 a gentle song   _____

   6 a rocky landform   _____

Term 2 Unit 1

Let's read

1 Listen to your teacher read this poem aloud.

1 How is it similar to or different from *The story of a river* in the last unit?

2 Make a class table to show this comparison and use these headings:

Ideas	Language	Type of text
non-fiction, fiction. narrative, descriptive	stanzas, paragraphs	rhyming, story

Song of a Blue Mountain Stream

In a cleft remote
Where white mists float
Around Blue Mountain's peak,
I rise unseen
Beneath the screen
Of fog clouds dank and bleak;
I trickle, I flow
To the hills below
and vales that lie far under,
From babblings low
I louder grow,
I shout, I roar, I thunder.

I fall with a rush
In the morning hush
While the mountain sleeping lies,
There swift I sleep –
Here slow I creep,
Till the sound of my motion dies:
Oh! I rejoice
In the night wind's voices
As soft it kisses my stream,
And dance and glimmer
And glance and shimmer
Where moonlit reaches gleam.

With ice cold wave
I gently lave
The flowers as I wander,
I gleam and glide
'Neath mountain pride,
I murmur and meander
Thro' fern arched dells
Where fairy bells
And violets scent the air,
While calls above
The soft blue dove
Or lone voice solitaire.

And here I crash
With silver flash
Over a mighty crag,
And the echoes ring
As I headlong fling
The trees I downward drag –
Till last I pour
With deafening roar,
A mountain stream no longer,
O'er plains below,
And seawards flow
A river broad and stronger.

by Reginald M Murray

2   Now read the poem to yourself. Draw a large thought bubble. Draw in it anything that this poem makes you see or feel as you read.

ICT opportunity

Use technology to make some audio recordings of this poem. Make the recordings using different voices and different ways of reading. Make this available in a listening corner so you can listen at other times. You may add other poems and stories, too.

3   Find any words in the poem that you do not know the meaning of. Read the lines around them carefully and try to predict what they might mean. Then, use a dictionary or online tool to find the correct definition. Record your work in a table like this:

Word	Prediction	Definition
Cleft		

4   Find and list five words in the poem that help you to imagine:
   • the sounds made by the river
   • the movement of the river.

This poem uses so much vivid language. I can see and hear the river clearly in my imagination!

5   The poet has written the poem as if she were the stream.

   1   Why do you think she did this?

   2   How well does she do it?

   3   Give some examples of personification from the poem.

6   Compare this poem with *Rain* by Valerie Bloom, which also uses personification.

   1   What do you like about each poem?

   2   Do you have a favourite from the two? What makes it a better poem in your opinion?

   3   Use a Venn diagram to structure your thoughts.

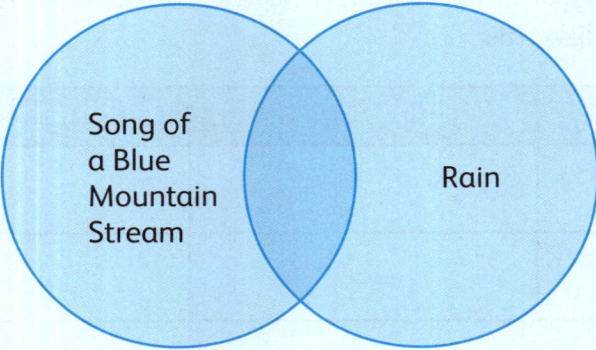

7   Which line of the poem is your favourite? Write the line and why it is your favourite in a speech bubble. Share it with others in the class.

Extra challenge

In a small group, perform the poem as a piece of drama for the rest of the class. Role play the movement of the stream during its journey down the mountain towards the sea. Alternatively, you could perform the poem as a class in a show or assembly.

Project 16 – The natural world in stories and poems

Grammar builder

Prepositions of time

Look and learn

Adverbs of time like *today* and *tomorrow* can be used to tell you when something happens. Another way to describe when something is happening is to use *in*, *at* or *on*.

Here are some examples:

- I am going fishing **at** eleven.
- Uncle Clark will visit **in** January.
- Mom always goes to church **on** Sundays.

The words *in*, *at* and *on* are **prepositions**.

- The preposition *in* is used to refer to a general point in time, such as a part of a day, month or season.
- The preposition *at* is used to refer to a specific point in time, such as a time of the day.
- The preposition *on* is used to refer to days of the week, dates and special occasions, such as Christmas.

1 Write out these sentences and fill the gaps with *in*, *at* or *on*.

1. Flowers blossom _____ summer.
2. Keisha will arrive _____ eight o'clock.
3. I'm going to the beach _____ my birthday.
4. We are going on holiday _____ June.
5. We do not go to school _____ Saturdays.
6. Lunch is served _____ noon.
7. My birthday is next week, _____ 14 May.
8. What time do you get up _____ the morning?
9. What time do you go to bed _____ night?
10. She will be back _____ an hour.

Extra challenge

Write three sentences of your own to say when something:
- happened
- is happening
- will happen.

In each sentence, use a different preposition. Find an example in your own notebook or journal where you have used a preposition.

Project 16 – The natural world in stories and poems

Let's write

Poetry

Background

Look at the three photographs of the landscape in different parts of Jamaica.

Jamaica has over 100 km of coastline and more than 50 beaches open to the public.

Rafting on the Martha Brea river.

A view across the vast Blue Mountain range.

Task

Write a poem about our Jamaican landscape for a class celebration and a display of Jamaican landscapes. Choose one of the landscapes to focus on: beaches, rivers or mountains.

Plan

- Look again at the photograph of the landscape you have chosen.
- Jot down some notes and key words that you want to include in your poem.
- Add your own ideas, too.
- Make columns like this to organise your notes.

The natural feature	What I see / hear	Words to describe it (try to use alliteration)	How it makes me feel

What shape will your poem be? Could the shape reflect your choice of landscape?

Write

- Use your columns to write sentences.
- Put those sentences together and make your poem come to life.
- You may need several drafts. How could you improve your work as you write each draft? What might help you?
- Write your final draft out neatly in your best joined handwriting for a class celebration of Jamaican landscapes.

Remember

- **Alliteration** is the repetition of consonant sounds at the beginning of several words.
- **Personification** is when a non-living thing is portrayed as if it were living. Will the beach, the river or the mountain be speaking in your poem?

ICT opportunity

Use technology to make an audio recording of your poem as part of a class audio collection of Jamaican landscape poetry. Make this available in the listening corner so you can listen again at a later time. You may add other poems and stories, too.

Editor's checklist

Check your work carefully when you finish.

- Does your poem use special features like alliteration or personification?
- Does your poem rhyme or not?
- Does your poem make use of shape for special effect?
- Is the punctuation correct at the end of sentences?
- Is there a capital letter for each new line of the poem?
- Are prepositions used correctly?

Reflect and review

Write a short paragraph as a journal entry to describe the process of planning your own poem. What do you think of your poem? Mark yourself out of 10. What could you improve?

Project 17

Speaking and listening

What do you know about pollution?

Research and study skills

When you are surfing the internet, you can use a search engine to find what you are looking for. Google, Bing and Yahoo are all search engines. If you type in some key words about what you are looking for, the search engine will generate a list of websites for you to visit. For example, if you type in *Pollution Jamaica*, you will see a list of suggested websites to visit in a dropdown list.

Online searching

1 Which search engine do you use?

2 If you are researching beach pollution in Jamaica, what key words would you use? Make a quick list of words to share with a partner. Did you choose the same words? If you can, test them to see if they are the best key words for your search.

3 What should you do if your key words take you to something that is not suitable for children?

In a search engine, you can click to choose images, videos or news and it will show you those rather than just websites. This is very handy to know!

Task

Work in a group to make a short presentation to the class about one aspect of pollution: air, litter or water. Make sure you know which aspect your group is researching before you start.

Term 2 Unit 1

Plan

Read the text together. Make notes on:
- how the pollution is caused
- why it is a problem
- any ideas to improve it.

Pollution stinks!

Pollution is a big problem. It is a problem that has been created by humans and only humans can help to reduce it. Pollution makes the environment and the landscape around us dirty and smelly. Some pollution you can see, like smoke in the air, litter on the streets and pollution in our waters or washed up on beaches. Pollution in the environment can harm animals and plants, or even kill them.

Smoke from vehicles, factories and power stations fills the air and this makes it harder not only for animals to breathe, but also for humans. Humans drop their rubbish or dump it in in open spaces. This can be harmful to animals and creates a stink when it rots away. Waste from huge factories is dumped into the oceans. Sometimes, this contains nasty chemicals or oils which can kill fishes and birds.

Pollution is not just a problem in Jamaica, but in all parts of the world. It is one of the biggest issues that we have to start to tackle before things become much worse.

Remember ☆☆☆

Each group must work together to research the topic.

Decide on team roles:
- Who will be team leader? Choose someone who has not had this role before.
- Who will be your script writers?
- Every team member must speak, so how will you divide the presentation between you?
- Practise at least twice before you present. Support and encourage each other.

Presentation

- Listen carefully to each argument made. Make notes so you can remember.
- Give quality feedback. Try to say two things that were good and one thing that could be improved. At all times demonstrate respect for others in your feedback.
- Receive feedback with grace and dignity.

Remember, listening is an important skill. Do not talk when other people are speaking. Wait for your turn to talk.

Word builder

This vocabulary is about our environment:

Vocabulary box

environment	harm	waste	chemicals
pollution	smelly	issue	data
dump	vehicles	stink	factor
smoke	charity	litter	

1 Take turns to read the words with a partner.

2 **1** Here are some segmented words from the vocabulary box. In pairs, practise saying the sounds that make up these words and complete the table. The first one is done for you.

Word / letters	Sounds
smelly (6 letters)	/s/ /m/ /e/ /ll/ /y/ (5 sounds)
issue (_____ letters)	/i/ /ss/ /ue/ (_____ sounds)
litter (_____ letters)	/l/ /i/ /tt/ /er/ (_____ sounds)
data (_____ letters)	/d/ /a/ /t/ /a/ (_____ sounds)
factory (_____ letters)	/f/ /a/ /c/ /t/ /or/ /y/ (_____ sounds)

2 Now blend the letter sounds together.

Example:
Segment: Blend:
/s/ /m/ /e/ /ll/ /y/ → smelly

3   One word has four syllables. Which one? _____

4   One word ends in *-ment*. Do you know other words that end with that suffix?
    _____

3 Which vocabulary word matches each of these definitions?
    1   a place where something is made or manufactured _____
    2   rubbish that is thrown away by people _____
    3   an overpowering or horrible smell _____
    4   facts and figures _____

> **Extra challenge**
>
> Write your own definitions for another two of the words from the vocabulary box.

4   1   Look at the vocabulary words again. Some of them can be changed into new words by adding the suffix -ing. Copy the table below and add the correct words. You might need to remove some letters from the starting word.

Word	With -ing
Pollution	Polluting

2   Use your table to help you choose the correct words in these sentences:

The words in the first column are **nouns/verbs**. The words in the second column are **adjectives/verbs** in the **present/past** tense.

5 Imagine you could have a talking bin in your school.

1. What would it look like? Copy the mind map and draw it in the middle.

2. Complete the speech bubbles for:
   - what it would say when litter is dropped in it
   - what it would say when litter is dropped near it.

3. Do you think it would make any difference to those who normally drop litter? Why?

Project 17 – The environment and pollution

Let's read

Beach pollution

Beach pollution – how are we helping to fix it?

The International Coastal Clean-up Day is held every year and is organised by the Ocean Conservancy, which is a global charity that helps to look after the oceans and seas. Jamaica takes part in the International Coastal Clean-up Day each year, usually in September, and this is arranged by the Jamaica Environment Trust (JET). Jamaica has been involved in this since the mid-1990s. Many people, including children, walk along areas of beach and collect all of the litter that they can see on the clean-up day. They use a phone app to record the amount and type of litter that is collected. The data can be used to identify what the biggest problems are and then ways to tackle those problems can be put in place.

In 2017, there was an amazing total of 149 clean-ups on the beaches of Jamaica, all carried out by volunteers who wanted to help to make their communities a safer, cleaner place to be. According to the Ocean Conservancy, over 12 million people around the world have taken part in the clean-up day since it began. Their data shows that over one and a half million plastic bottles have been collected from beaches around the world!

The Ocean Conservancy and JET both have their own websites as well as YouTube channels and social media pages that you can visit to find out more information about them and their work.

1. Read the statements and decide whether they are true (T) or false (F). If the statement is false (F), write a new sentence to correct it.

    1. The International Coastal Clean-up Day is organised by a global charity. ____

    2. The JET arranges the Clean-up Day yearly in September. ____

    3. Only children collect the litter from the beach. ____

    4. Different kinds of litter is collected from the beach. ____

    5. Over 20 million people take part in the Coastal Clean-up Day every year. ____

    6. The Ocean Conservancy found that more than one and a half million tin cans have been collected from beaches around the world.. ____

ICT opportunity

If you have a computer room or homework centre, go online to find out more about how big the problem of rubbish on beaches is in Jamaica. Find out why it is a serious issue, how it harms the environment and what is being done to help solve the problem.

2 Research beach pollution in books or online.

   1 Find three interesting facts to share with the class. Find pictures or photographs to share, too.

   2 As a class, combine all the research findings by making a display or planning a presentation for your next assembly. Make it a working wall so you can continue to add to it.

   3 If your class could make three pledges to help to look after the beaches, what would those pledges be? Have a class vote on what the most important issues are.

What's your view?
Why is it important to keep our beaches clean?

Project 17 – The environment and pollution

Grammar builder

More about collective nouns

Remember ☆☆☆

Collective nouns are the words for groups. For example: *a **range** of mountains*, *a **flamboyance** of flamingos* and *a **pride** of lions*.

1 Match the phrases and words to make collective nouns.

1	a range of		a	cattle
2	a school of		b	crocodiles
3	a colony of		c	mountains
4	a bask of		d	hummingbirds
5	a herd of		e	bats
6	a charm of		f	fish

2 Make up two collective nouns of your own on the theme of conservation. For example: *a mess of plastic bottles*.

3 Look at these three pictures.

　1　Discuss them with a partner. How would you describe the landscape?

　2　What collective nouns could you use to describe what you can see?

　3　Make up a collective noun for each picture that you think works well. Made-up words like this may be useful in poetry writing.

199

4 Read this text written by a tourist about Jamaica. Identify any collective nouns and write them down.

> Take a look at any postcard and you will not be disappointed by the beauty of Jamaica. The Blue Mountain range looks down over lush forests of tall trees. The trees and countryside are home to a variety of animals and other plants. Take a wander and you may see a flight of beautiful butterflies in the sky or hear a charm of hummingbirds as they sing in the sunshine. Be careful though! Watch your step to make sure you do not disturb a den of snakes! In the city, there are rows of hotels and restaurants. You will see crowds of people gathering for celebrations. You can smell a freshly baked batch of bread in the air and you can grab a hand of bananas in local stores.

Project 17 – The environment and pollution

Let's write

Community issues

Background

Think about your own local community or region.

- Is it a city area that is very built up?
- Is it a rural area in the countryside?
- Is it coastal, near the sea?
- Is it inland, not near the sea?
- What problems are there in the environment in your community?
- Are you involved in any conservation groups? If not, what would you like to help with?

Task

Write a letter to a government minister about an environmental problem in your area.

Your writing should be polite and formal and should include facts and reasons as well.

It should be positive and include some ideas to help with the problem.

Plan

You could use the RAFT strategy to help you.

R	Role	What is your role as a writer?	to inform them about a problem
A	Audience	Who will be reading your writing? What does that mean for the language you use?	the government official
F	Format	What type of writing is it? What does that mean for the way you set out your writing?	a letter
T	Topic	What is the writing about? Be specific.	an environmental problem in your community

201

Write

- Write a first draft and then read it over.
- Swap with a partner and ask them to give you some feedback. Do the same for your partner.
- After getting some feedback, write up a final version.

ICT opportunity

Instead of writing a letter, write an email.
- Emails do not include an address like letters do.
- Emails have a subject box at the top. In the subject box, you write what your email is about. This is like a title. The person who receives the email will get to see the subject before they decide to open it or not. Make sure that your subject clearly identifies what the email is about or it might just not be read!

Editor's checklist

Check your work carefully when you finish.

- Did you begin and end with a suitable greeting?
- Did you include your full name and address at the top of the letter or at the end of the email? Why?
- Did you include some suggestions about how you could help to solve the problem?
- Are all sentences punctuated correctly?
- Did you set out the letter or email in a formal way?
- Did you use facts to make your message clear?

Reflect and review
Write a short paragraph as a journal entry to describe your formal letter writing experience. What would you do differently next time?

Project 18

Speaking and listening

Other islands

1 Which Caribbean islands do you already know? How do you know them? Have you visited or do you have family there?

> There are over 7000 islands in the Caribbean area. They belong to thirteen island nations, including Jamaica, and twelve dependencies.
> A **dependency** is an island that belongs to another, bigger country. For example, Aruba belongs to the Netherlands.

1. Find them on a globe or map.
2. In small groups, list some other islands and find them on the globe or map.
3. Share your findings. Practise reading and saying them.

ICT opportunity

Use an online search tool to locate other Caribbean islands. If you can, zoom in to see the natural features of the landscape such as beaches, rivers and mountains.

2 Play a game about other countries. Follow the instructions carefully.

Game
How many Caribbean island nations or dependencies can your class name?

What you need
- a beanbag or soft toy
- a volunteer to keep a list of the names (someone good at writing quickly)

What you do
- Stand in a circle with your classmates. You will play games about other islands.
- Your teacher will call out "Jamaica" and throw the beanbag to one person.
- That person must call out the name of another nation and then throw the beanbag to another person in the circle. This continues until no more names are known and everyone is sitting.

Rules
- If you repeat a name that has already been said, then you have to sit out.
- If you can't think of any places to say, then you must also sit out.
- You cannot keep throwing to the same people or person.

Variation
Repeat the game, but name towns and cities in Caribbean countries instead of other islands.

Word builder

This vocabulary is about Caribbean places:

Vocabulary box

Caribbean	flag	Bahamas	between
republic	neighbour	Trinidad	official
nationality	independent	Atlantic	climate
language	Cuba	population	

1. Take turns to read the words aloud with a partner.

   1. In each speech bubble, write one short sentence that includes one word from the vocabulary box. For example: *I have family all over the* **Caribbean**. *My aunty comes from Cuba. I am proud to be Jamaican.*

   2. What are the five proper nouns in the vocabulary box? How do you know?

      _____

   3. Think of three more words that you could add to the vocabulary box.

      _____

ICT opportunity

Did you know that most printed dictionaries have online versions as well? You can search for the meanings of words in an online dictionary or a paper one.

Project 18 – Other Caribbean countries

2 Look up the word *flag* in a dictionary.

1 It is a homograph, so it has several meanings. Write two sentences where the word *flag* is used differently.

_____

_____

_____

> **Remember** ☆☆☆
>
> Homographs are words that are spelled the same way, but have different meanings. For example, the word **bat** can mean an animal, or a piece of sporting equipment.

2 If you could add a picture to the Jamaican flag, what would the picture be? Draw your own version of the Jamaican flag. Explain what you have included and why.

3 Some of the words in the vocabulary box can have a suffix added to them. Write the words with the suffixes shown in the table. Then write a sentence using the new word you have made. Use a dictionary to help you if you do not know the new word's meaning.

Watch out! You will have to change the ending of one word to add the suffix.

Word	Suffix	New word	Sentence
republic	-s		
neighbour	-ing		
independent	-ly		
population	-ing		
official	-ly		
climate	-s		

I'm looking forward to using these new words in my writing to help me to describe my Caribbean neighbours!

Let's read

1. Read the information about Cuba in the fact file below:

Cuba fact file

Cuba is the biggest island in the Caribbean.

The country of Cuba also includes more than 4000 smaller islands.

Cuba is officially named the Republic of Cuba.

The population of Cuba today is about 11 million people.

Christopher Columbus landed on Cuba in 1492 and claimed it for Spain.

The official language of Cuba is Spanish because of its history.

Cuba became an independent country, or republic, in 1902.

The capital city of Cuba is Havana, *La Habana* in Spanish.

People say that the map of Cuba looks like a crocodile, so it is sometimes called *el cocodrilo*, which is Spanish for *crocodile*.

Famous Cuban people include baseball player Jose Canseco, singer Gloria Estefan and rapper Pitbull.

Christopher Columbus was a famous explorer and he is said to have "discovered" the Americas in 1492.

1. Copy and complete the table with the correct information from the fact file. Read the fact file first, then try to complete the table without looking. How good is your memory and comprehension?

Official name:	Republic of Cuba
Said to have been discovered by:	
Population:	
Size in relation to other Caribbean islands:	
Number of smaller islands:	
Official language(s):	
Capital city:	
Shape of island:	
Independence day:	
Some famous citizens:	

2. Create a fact file like this for Jamaica.

ICT opportunity

Choose a famous person, such as Christopher Columbus, and look on the internet to read more about them. When you search, type the name of the person and *biography* in the search box.

Project 18 – Other Caribbean countries

Grammar builder

1. With your partner or in a small group, discuss the questions and tasks in each box together before writing down your answers.
2. Look at the questions and tasks for the four grammar skills again with your teacher. Be ready to share the responses and examples from your group.

I have learned so much about nouns, commas and prepositions. It is good to review my progress!

Commas
- Do they have more than one function?
- Write a sentence that shows one correct use of the comma.

Extra challenge

Write another sentence that shows a comma being used for a different purpose.

Prepositions of time
- What are the three prepositions of time? How are they helpful?

Extra challenge

Write a sentence to demonstrate one of the prepositions of time.

My grammar skills

Collective nouns
- What are the differences between collective nouns and other nouns?
- Give some examples of collective nouns.

Extra challenge

Write a sentence that contains at least one collective noun.

Adverbs of time
- Give some examples of adverbs of time.
- Write a sentence that contains an adverb of time.

Extra challenge

Write a sentence that contains two or more adverbs of time.

ICT opportunity

Choose two of the grammar skills from the chart on the previous page. Use a computer to make a poster about them that can be printed out and used in a classroom display.

Make it a hanging poster so both sides can be seen. Where and how will you hang it to be most useful?

Self-check

How confident are you about using each of the grammar skills?

1. List the skills and draw the emoji that matches how you feel about each skill.

2. If you are not completely confident about a skill, say how you would like to improve. If you are confident about a skill, say what you would like to learn next.

Grammar	☹	😐	☺	What I can improve or learn next
Collective nouns				
Prepositions of time				
Adverbs of time				
Commas				

Project 18 – Other Caribbean countries

Let's write

Islands of the Caribbean

Background

Study the map of the Caribbean below. There are so many beautiful islands in the Caribbean Sea from large ones like Cuba to smaller ones like St Kitts. Large islands have been named and smaller islands are numbered. Use the key to identify them.

There are many languages spoken in the Caribbean, but the four most common are English, Spanish, French and Dutch. In how many Caribbean languages can you say "please" and "thank you"?

209

Task

Complete two writing tasks which involve describing another Caribbean island in different ways for different audiences.

Task 1

Your headteacher has asked your class for a series of posters to decorate the school corridors for a special school celebration for Carnival. There is little time, so she has asked you to research other Caribbean islands and make fact files. They need to be accurate, but should be fun and displayed as posters.

Task 2

The next day the plan changes! Your headteacher has heard that there is a local Carnival competition. There is a chance to win a box of beautiful reference books for the library. Fact files and posters will not work! She needs a written piece that is rich in description, but still includes some useful information. It needs to show the personality of the island!

Plan

- Choose an island you want to research.
- Use the internet or reference books to research facts and ideas about your chosen island.

Plan for Task 1

- Use the information you discover to write a fact file about the island. Look at the fact file in the "Let's read" lesson on Cuba to guide you. You may use the table about Cuba as a guide for your own research.
- You should include only basic information such as facts, figures and dates.
- Think about headings and subheadings.
- You may include a small informative picture, such as a flag, if you wish.

Plan for Task 2

- Use the same and new information to write a minimum of one paragraph about the same island.
- Use conjunctions to link sentences.
- Make the language vivid and descriptive. Try to describe things that you can see, hear, taste or smell to help the reader understand a little about what the island you have chosen is like. You can still provide some facts, but use them to persuade or describe.
- You may use some of the poetic language from the poems in previous units, if it works for your chosen island.

- Think about headings and subheadings.
- Show your personality as a writer!

Write

Write both texts and keep the differences clear.

Review

Which text do you prefer? Why?

If the plan changed again, what other text type could you use to present the same or similar information?

ICT opportunity

Type up your fact file and/or descriptive paragraph on a word processing program to create a digital text. You may include pictures or photographs that you can copy and paste into the text. Your teacher could put it on a school blog or print it out for a display on Caribbean nations.

Editor's checklist

Check your work carefully when you finish.

- Do both texts have an exciting title and different headings to guide the reader?
- Do both texts include accurate facts and figures?
- Do both texts include photographs, pictures or charts?
- Have you used capital letters where you need them?
- Have you used commas where they are needed?
- Have you used adjectives to give descriptions and to make comparisons?

Reflect and review
Write a short paragraph as a journal entry to describe your research process and ability to write for different audiences.

Term 2 Unit 1 Review and assessment

Word builder

1 Copy and complete this Venn diagram by placing each word from the vocabulary box in the right place. Words in the middle should be both in *land* and *sea*.

Vocabulary box

mountain	river	reef	shore
ocean	waterfall	coast	rainforest
beach	stream	cloud	

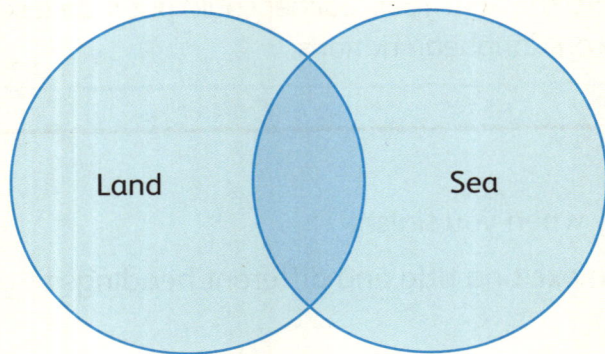

2 Look at the vocabulary box. Write each word in the correct column in the table below.

One syllable	Two syllables	Three syllables

Review and assessment

Let's read

1 Read the text and complete the fact file.

> Jamaica is the third largest island in the Caribbean. It is the largest land mass of 28 islands. The capital city of Jamaica is Kingston. The population of Jamaica in 2020 was over 2,900,000 people which included 590,000 who live in Kingston. Whilst the official language is English, most islanders speak Jamaican Creole. The island's highest point is Blue Mountain Peak at 7,402 feet, which is also one of the highest mountains in the Caribbean. The longest river in Jamaica is Rio Minho which is 92 km / 57 miles. Jamaica is famous for reggae music. Many famous people in the music and sports world come from Jamaica, such as the musician Bob Marley and the Olympic Gold medal winner Usain Bolt.

Fact file	
Official name of country:	
Size in relation to other Caribbean islands:	
Number of smaller islands:	
Capital city:	
Population of country:	
Population of capital city:	
Official language:	
Highest mountain's name and size:	
Longest river's name and size:	
Famous Jamaican people:	

G Grammar builder

1 Complete the collective noun phrase with its matching noun from the vocabulary box.

Vocabulary box

lions   birds   flowers   soldiers   thieves   cattle

1 a gang of _____.
2 a flock of _____.
3 an army of _____.
4 a den of _____.
5 a bouquet of _____.
6 a herd of _____.

213

2 Write the missing commas.

1 Jamaica has high mountains forests rivers and a beautiful coastline.

2 Jamaica's land is rich in nutrients vitamins minerals and water.

3 More people live in cities like Kingston but there are some small farming communities in the mountains.

3 Look at the sentences and write the comma in the correct place.

1 Bob got up late so he missed the bus.

2 I wanted more jerk chicken but it was all finished.

3 I study hard for the exams and I always get high grades.

4 You can buy your own reading book or you can borrow it from the library.

5 School is really interesting yet it can also be exhausting.

4 Write these sentences and fill the gaps with the correct preposition.

1 What time do you go to bed _____ night?

2 John and I will meet _____ 6 o'clock.

3 I'm having a party _____ my birthday.

4 We are going to Trinidad and Tobago _____ March.

5 I have football practice _____ Saturdays.

6 What time do you catch the bus _____ the morning?

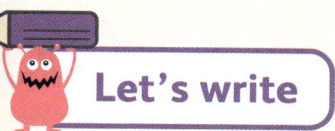

Let's write

Background

In this unit, you have written different text types:

- a journal entry for your grandparents
- a leaflet for tourists
- a story using alliteration and personification
- a poem for a class celebration
- a formal letter to someone in government
- a fact file about a Caribbean country
- a blog post about a Caribbean country.

Task

Reflect on all the writing in this unit. For each piece of writing say:

- what you enjoyed
- what you did not enjoy or found difficult
- what you did well
- what you want to improve.

Look back over your work to answer the questions honestly.

Write

Organise your writing as a chart, a mind map or a paragraph. Whatever you choose, you must include all four feedback points in the task.

Review

- Write your own "Editor's checklist" to show what you reviewed in your writing. Look at the Editor's checklists you have used before to get ideas.
- Why is an "Editor's checklist" important?

TERM 2

Unit 2

In this unit, you will explore the different uses of water and the importance of clean water for communities. You will use ICT opportunities to present your work on the topic of water and the Jamaican environment.

Project 19

Speaking and listening

We use water in many different ways. Water is essential for humans, animals and plants to survive. The body needs water to function. We also use water to stay clean, make our food and drinks and get rid of waste from toilets:

1 Discuss these questions with a partner:

1 How do you use water?

2 How do other people use water? Do different people have different needs?

3 How is water used around you at home or in the community?

216

Project 19 – We all need water

> **Extra challenge**
>
> Make a giant class mind map or working wall to show different ways water is important to people. Keep adding to it over time. You could do this by hand or on a computer. Try to find unusual or interesting facts.

2. Imagine you are one of the following people. Pretend to be the person and explain to the class how you use water and why it is important to you.

- a fisherman
- a farmer
- an athlete
- a busy mom
- a grandmother
- a chef

When others are talking, it is important to listen and let them have their turn. Other people may not have the same opinion as you, but that is OK.

Word builder

This vocabulary is about water:

Vocabulary box

need	flush	toilet	leisure
wash	thirst	running	hydration
bathe	survive	pipe	dehydration
shower	essential	tap	

1 1 Take turns to read the words with a partner and discuss the word meanings.

Example:
It is really hot today. I **need to** drink more water.

2 With your partner, have a spelling challenge. One of you call out one of the words or phrases and your partner has to spell it out loud letter-by-letter. You must cover the list of words and try to get the spelling correct using your knowledge of phonics (word sounds). Swap over so that you both have a chance to be the caller and the speller.

Remember ☆☆☆

- A **prefix** is the part of a word that comes at the **beginning** and changes its meaning.
- A **suffix** is the part of a word that comes at the **end** and changes the meaning of the word.
- A **root** word is the **original meaning** of any word. It is what is left when the prefix and suffix is removed.

3 One word in the vocabulary box appears with and without the prefix *de-*. What is that word and its meaning? Write some other words that begin with that prefix.

_____

2 Choose four words from the vocabulary box. Draw a picture to represent each word. Swap drawings with your partner and guess which words they chose. Did they guess all of your words correctly?

3 Rewrite each sentence. Replace the word in bold with a word from the vocabulary box that makes sense.

1 I have a **bath** every morning.

_____

2 You will get $500 if you **clean** the car.

_____

3 You **have** to drink water every day.

_____

4 May I go to the **bathroom**, please?

_____

4 Write a vocabulary word to match each definition.

　1 A tap in the kitchen or bathroom. _____

　2 A long tube that is used to transport water. _____

　3 This is caused when a living thing does not have enough water.
　　_____

　4 This means that something is absolutely necessary.
　　_____

> **Remember** ☆☆☆
>
> **Homographs** are two or more words that are spelled the same, but have different meanings.

5 The word *running* is a homograph. Look up the meanings of *running* in a dictionary. Write a sentence where *running* is used in relation to water and a different sentence with at least one other meaning.

_____

> **Extra challenge**
>
> Search for another word that is a homograph and is linked to water. Explain the meanings.

6 What is the difference between *bath* and *bathe*?

　1 Think about this question. It may be helpful to look up the words in a dictionary or online.

　2 Make some notes and then have a discussion with a partner. Use correct language to describe each word.

Project 19 – We all need water

Let's read

The people in these pictures are all characters from plays about water.

A 　B 　C 　D

1 Here are the titles of the four plays. Match the pictures to the titles.

   1 What a stink! _____

   2 It grew and grew and grew! _____

   3 Stuck in the mud! _____

   4 Thirsty work! _____

2 If you could change one title, which would it be? How would you change it? Why is it better, in your opinion?

> I would change title _____ because _____.

3 With your partner, look at the pictures again. Even though you cannot see some of their faces, how do you think the people in the pictures are feeling? Look for clues in what the pictures show and in the titles to help you. Then share your ideas in groups.

4 Here are short summaries of two of the plays:

> Mia and her brother went to the park. Her brother ran after a dog and ended up falling into a stream.
>
> Mike never tidies his bedroom. His mom got a smelly surprise when she tried to tidy it.

   1 Match each summary to its title.

   2 With a partner, think of and write a summary of the other two plays.

5 Now that you know more about each story, think again about how the characters in the pictures are feeling. Imagine you are one of the characters. Draw the character you want to be and explain how you are feeling and why. Use the following format:

My character

Grammar builder

Remember ⭐☆☆

Pronouns can be used as substitutes for nouns. You already know about these pronouns: *I*, *you*, *he*, *she*, *it*, *we* and *they*. They are called **subject pronouns**.

Look and learn

There is another group of pronouns called **object pronouns**. These are the words:

| me | you | him | her | it | us | them |

You can use these words as substitutes for nouns in sentences just like other pronouns.

- Louise gave the water bottle to **Mark**.
- Louise gave the water bottle to **him**.

Mark has been substituted by the pronoun *him*.

Did you notice that some of the object pronoun words are the same as the subject pronoun words? Which ones?

1 Write out these sentences and circle the object pronouns.

1. When they went on a hike, the boys took bottled water with them.
2. The biggest boat on the lake belongs to him.
3. Ask her if the dog needs water.
4. Do you want to come to the swimming pool with us?

2 Rewrite these sentences and replace the words in bold with a pronoun.

    1 I will put **the flowers** in a vase of water.

    2 They wanted to go swimming but **the water** was too cold.

    3 Alex came to **the pool** with my sister and me.

    4 I gave my last one to **Tyler**.

3 Use different colours to write the subject and the object with their pronoun in the correct column. Then write the verb in the middle column. The first one is done for you.

Sentence	Subject	Verb	Object
Bob loves his dog.	Bob (He)	loves	dog (it)
Tom helped his friends.			
Anna's parents drove Anna to school.			
Linda plays with her brother.			

A subject pronoun is often used at the beginning of a sentence. Object pronouns often come after verbs. For example: Bob loves Linda. He loves her.

Project 19 – We all need water

Let's write

Background

What is an interview? Share your experiences of listening to or watching an interview. Which hero of yours would you like to interview? Why?

An **interview** is a conversation between at least two people. The **interviewer** prepares a list of questions to ask. The **interviewee** is the person answering the questions.

Remember ☆☆☆

Common question words are:
When? How? Who? Where? What? Why?

Task

Choose a person you know to interview about how he or she uses water. Find out how the person uses water every day, how water is used by others in their household or community and how important they feel water is to them.

Plan

- Choose and invite your person to the interview.
- Use the RAFT strategy to start your planning.
- Create a mind map to structure your questions. Here are three questions to get you started:
  - Do they use water in their job?
  - Do they use water for everyday chores?
  - Do they use water for their hobby?
- Decide on five questions that you will ask during the interview and write them down. Use the *Wh-* question words in the "Remember" box.

Sentences which are questions are called **interrogatives**.

Example:
What do you use water for before you come to school?

- Do the interview. Make notes of the answers.

ICT opportunity

You could record the interview on a tape recorder or a mobile device so you can listen to the answers later, or you can make notes by hand. What is the benefit of a recording?

You may wish to take a photograph of the person if they give permission.

Write

After the interview, use the answers to your questions to compose a short report about the person you have interviewed and how they use water. Give the report a title. Your report should include:

- facts about the person, such as their name, their relationship to you, their job or something interesting about them
- how the person you interviewed uses water
- a few extra questions you asked and their answers.

Editor's checklist

Check your work carefully when you finish.

- Have you used the answers to your interview questions well in the report?
- Does the report tell you interesting facts about the person and their use of water?
- Does the report reference and thank the person you interviewed?
- Have you used apostrophes and commas correctly where they are needed?
- Have you checked spellings, especially for names?
- Have you kept to the interview focus?

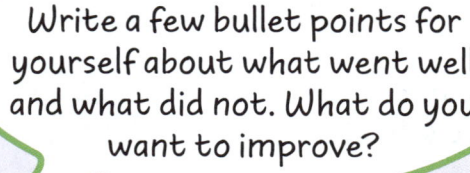

Reflect and review
Write a few bullet points for yourself about what went well and what did not. What do you want to improve?

Project 20

Speaking and listening

1. In pairs, read this report to each other and circle any words you do not fully understand.

> **Water woes**
>
> The town of Milton Hill is located in a remote, rural area. Not all the buildings have running water, but most homes, two farms, the health clinic and the school do. Recently, the colour of the water has changed. It has become murky and yellow. Sometimes it is brown and sludgy and some people have noticed a smell. The residents are worried that the running water is unsafe to drink. The school has decided they will not let the children drink the water. The residents have organised a meeting to discuss the situation and decide what they are going to do about it.

> In Jamaica, a government department called the *Ministry of Water and Housing* is responsible for water supplies. Most of the supplies are looked after and provided by an organisation called the *National Water Commission (NWC)*.

2. With your partner, use a dictionary or online tool to look up the words you circled in Activity 1.

3. In pairs, ask and answer the following questions: What is your water like at home? What is your water like at school? Share any experiences with the class of a time when you have had problems with drinking water.

4. In pairs, summarise the problem in the *Water woes* report in one sentence. Compare your sentence with another pair of students.

5. In a small group, plan and role play the residents' meeting. Each person is a resident of Milton Hill and is worried about the water.

   Suggestions for characters:
   - the headteacher of the local school
   - a farmer
   - moms and dads
   - a nurse or doctor
   - children

"The residents are all friends and the meeting is not formal. I think they would probably speak to each other in Jamaican Creole instead of Standard Jamaican English."

Suggestions for questions to ask and answer:
- What might they be worried about?
- What do they use water for?
- What can they do if they cannot drink or use the water every day?
- What about their pets?
- Who could they complain to?
- How can they help each other in the community?

6 Watch and listen carefully to each role play. Try to give feedback about what was good and what could be improved. Listen to the feedback for your group.

Project 20 – Clean water is safe water

Word builder

This vocabulary is about making water clean and safe:

Vocabulary box

purify	contaminated	unsafe
quality	water-borne	organism
pollute	filter	debris
bacteria	murky	antibacterial
sanitation	equipment	stagnant

1. Take turns to read the words with a partner and write the number of syllables next to each word. If you are unsure how to say a word, use an online tool to check pronunciation.

I thought a filter was something you put on photos in phone apps! What has that got to do with keeping water clean and safe? I will look it up and find out.

Extra challenge

Record yourself saying the words out loud and then listen to yourself. What mistakes did you make?

2. Copy and complete the table. Use the steps on the next page.

1 Copy	2 Practise	3 Write
purify quality	purify quality	

229

1   Copy the words from the vocabulary box into column 1.

2   Practise writing each word in column 2.

3   In pairs, cover the first two columns and listen as your partner reads the words aloud while you write the words in column 3. Then swap.

Remember ☆ ☆ ☆

- A prefix is the part of a word that comes at the **beginning** and changes the word's meaning. For example: *anti-, un-, re-, de-*.

- A suffix is the part of a word that comes at the **end** and changes the word's meaning. For example: *-ed, -ing, -est, -tion, -less*.

- A root word is the **original meaning** of any word. It is what is left when the prefix and suffix is removed.

3   1   *Antibacterial* begins with *anti-*. What words have you seen before that also use this prefix?

_____

2   What can you guess about the meaning of a word that begins with the prefix *-anti*?

_____

3   *Sanitation* ends with *-tion*. Which other vocabulary words can you add this suffix to?

_____

4   Write two sentences about water. Use at least one vocabulary word in each sentence.

5   Form a team with some classmates to take part in a Spellathon. A person from each team will be challenged to spell a vocabulary word out loud letter-by-letter. One point will be given for each word correctly spelt out loud. Which team will win?

Project 20 – Clean water is safe water

Let's read

1. An extract is a small piece taken from a longer text. As you read, use your imagination to visualise what you are reading about.
   - What can you see?
   - What is being described?

Extract 1

> Visit the National Water Commission website (https://www.nwcjamaica.com/water_treatment.php) to find information about what they do to ensure the water is safe for drinking. Look for key phrases, such as "potable water" or "water treatment".

ICT opportunity

Visit the website of the National Water Commission to find out more about what they do.

2. Draw a flow chart to describe, in your own words, the main steps to make water safe. Sketch a small picture of what you visualise at each step.

3. Read Extract 2 and answer the questions on the next page.

Term 2 Unit 2

Extract 2

An interview with the Minister of Health in 2016:

"Normally after heavy rain and flooding, you get a spike in water-borne diseases such as gastroenteritis, and that is a consequence of contaminants when people drink or otherwise interact with the water. So, it is advisable that persons boil water before drinking and avoid, as best as possible, playing in puddles of water, especially children, because that could lead to other ailments."

(From: www.jamaica-gleaner.com)

1. Choose three words from this extract that you do not know the meaning of. Read the sentences around the words and predict what each one means. Record your ideas using a table or sentences.

2. Compare your predictions with your partner. Did they choose the same words? Did you make similar predictions? Discuss whether you agree with their predictions.

4. Read the interview with the Minister of Health again. Replace the words crossed out from the original text with the words and phrases that have similar meanings below.

| as a result of | recommended | an increased risk of |

| torrential | do anything else | problems |

"Normally after ¹ _____ heavy rain and flooding, you get ² _____ a spike in water-borne diseases such as gastroenteritis, and that is ³ _____ a consequence of contaminants when people drink or ⁴ _____ otherwise interact with the water. So, it is ⁵ _____ advisable that persons boil water before drinking and avoid, as best as possible, playing in puddles of water, especially children, because that could lead to other ⁶ _____ ailments."

5 Read Extract 3 and answer the questions. The extract is from a magazine article about clean water.

Extract 3

Untreated water in natural sources such as rivers, springs and aquifers is usually clean enough for a number of purposes such as washing clothes, but definitely not good enough to drink. Although the water may look clean, it is not safe for drinking. Untreated water contains bacteria and a host of other micro-organisms and chemicals. If this waste is used, a number of water-borne diseases such as cholera, typhoid, dysentery and other illnesses may result.

(From: www.jamaica-gleaner.com)

1 Find the first word of the extract that starts with a prefix. Then add this prefix to another word.

   _____

2 What can you do with untreated water?

   _____

3 What is in untreated water?

   _____

4 Why are the things in untreated water not visible to us? Which word gives us a clue about this?

   _____

Extra challenge

Find out more about cholera or typhoid. How else can we prevent these diseases?

Research and study skills

1. Read the information from the different sources in the "Let's read" lesson. Copy and complete the table to summarise the information.

Sources of water	Contents of dirty water	Water-borne diseases	Ways water is treated	Ways water can be purified

L👀k and learn

Often, problems are the result of something else that happened. This is called **cause and effect**. For example, there was a hurricane – *cause* – and there was flooding – *effect*. So, we can say "There was flooding because there was a hurricane."

What cause and effect relationships can you identify in the information you have been reading about?

2. Work in teams.
   - Share the work you did in Activity 1 with your team members.
   - Summarise and organise the information you extracted from the three different sources.
   - Add any examples of untreated water in rivers nearby your area and discuss whether they are a cause of any problems.
   - Create a final table of information. Present the information to the class using a pamphlet or chart. In your presentation, refer to the cause and effect of the problems your team has identified.

Project 20 – Clean water is safe water

Grammar builder

Look and learn

In sentences, there are often words that link different parts of the sentence together. You have already learned about linking words called **conjunctions**. Conjunctions join together two sentences. Although the following words may be classed as conjunctions, they all have a specific purpose because they either join two sentences to make one or they make a connection between two sentences. They signal connections for us, so these conjunctions are called **signal words**.

- Some signal words and phrases signal that you are comparing:

like	in the same way	just as	similarly

- Some signal words signal that you are giving reasons:

since	because	for

*We do not use **for** very much in modern Jamaica.*

- Some signal words and phrases signal that you are sequencing events:

first	next	in addition	another

1 Copy and complete the sentences using these words to compare clean water and lemonade:

Vocabulary box

like   just as   in the same way as   similarly

1 Clean water is clear _____ lemonade.

2 Clean water is clear _____ lemonade is clear.

3 Clean water is clear _____ lemonade is clear.

4 Clean water is clear; _____ lemonade is clear.

2 Now write your own four sentences comparing the colour of dirty water to mud.

235

3 The following examples use *because* or *since* to link sentences with reasons.
   - Clean water is safe to drink *because* it has been treated.
   - Clean water is safe to drink *since* it has been treated.

   Finish this sentence using either *because* or *since*.

   Muddy water is unsafe _____.

4 Fill the gaps using these words to add information to a sentence in a sequence.

   Vocabulary box

   next   another   first   in addition

   1 _____ the water is collected from sources.

   2 _____ it is piped to treatment plants.

   3 _____ to filtering, _____ treatment is the use of chemicals.

   Now that I know more linking words, I can write longer sentences and give even more information!

5 Write your own sequence about water problems.

   First, _____.

   Next, _____.

   In addition to _____, another _____.

Project 20 – Clean water is safe water

Let's write

Background

The following text provides seven top tips for purifying water at home. Unfortunately, the tips are in the wrong order.

- Sort and write the tips in the correct order.
- If you find this difficult, then write them out and cut them up to sequence them on a table first.
- Look out for words such as *Firstly* that help to sequence the tips. They will give you clues.

Firstly, collect water from a stream or puddle. NEVER drink this untreated water. ALWAYS use a clean bucket or container to collect water and rinse it clean with disinfectant or bleach to kill bacteria when you finish.

When the pot is cool enough to touch, filter it a second time through a sieve and leave the water to cool.

Next, look at the water in the bucket. Remove any dirt or stones you can see with a net or by hand. ALWAYS wear gloves.

Now the liquid must be boiled. Heat the water in a large pot on the stove until it bubbles. After it has boiled, you may see a foamy layer appear on top. This is called "scum". Carefully remove the scum using a net or sieve.

Once you have removed the bits of dirt you can see, filter the water by pouring it through a sieve to remove finer bits of dirt.

Finally, you can purchase chemical tablets to add to the water to kill bacteria. Make sure to follow the instructions on the pack.

When cool, filter the water through a sieve for a third time. Then transfer the water from the bucket into another container indoors.

Task

You have been asked to write just three top tips for purifying water at home using some of the ideas on the previous page. The tips are for teenagers, so you will present them as a comic strip.

Plan

- Choose three of the tips.
- Go to the library or online to check the features of a comic strip. Use that as a guide to make your own.
- Draw a comic strip to illustrate your chosen tips.
- Make sure you leave enough room for your speech and thought bubbles.

Here are three examples to help you with the design layout:

 **ICT opportunity**

Check online to find free programmes that provide you with comic strip templates to work on online or to download. This may help with your planning.

Editor's checklist

Check your work carefully when you finish.

- Have you used capital letters for whole words for effect?
- Does the comic strip still make the tips clear?
- Do the comic strip pictures help with the message of the tips?
- Did you use apostrophes and commas correctly?
- Is all spelling correct, especially the spelling of names?
- Did you keep the audience in mind?

Reflect and review
Write a few bullet points for yourself. Say what went well and what did not. What do you want to improve?

Project 21

Speaking and listening

The debate challenge

Remember ☆☆☆

A **debate** is when two teams put forward points or arguments for and against a statement or suggestion. Different views are shared and can end in a vote to see which side has won.

When a speaker makes an excellent point, the people who are listening can clap or cheer. Often, when people listening to a debate agree with a speaker, they call out *Hear, hear!* to show their support.

Your teacher will divide your class into two groups to debate this statement.

> Water should be free in Jamaica.

Team tips

Work together to present the team's evidence during the debate. Decide on team roles.

- Who will be team leader?
- Who will be the script writers?
- What area will each person research about the topic?

One team will argue why water should be free: survival, clean water is a basic human right, etc.

One team will argue why people should pay for water: it will reduce waste, it costs money to clean water, etc.

Content

The speech needs to convince everybody listening that your team is right. It needs to be persuasive. How? Graphs, tables, illustrations and sourced information make your argument seem more convincing. Speak clearly and confidently.

Debate

1. The first person in Team A and then Team B will have one minute to present their argument.

> **Example:**
> **For:** Water should be free as we all need it to survive and should not have to think about how much we use…
> **Against:** People should pay for water because if they are allowed to use as much as they want, they may waste it.

2. The second person in both teams will now have one minute to defend the argument of their first speaker and present more information and facts.

> **Example:**
> It is clear that what my team member says is correct because… . In addition, …

3. The third person in both teams will now have one minute to present final information and sum up the team's argument.

> **Example:**
> As we can see from all the evidence presented such as…, …, and…, there can be no doubt that water…

4. Both teams will have five minutes to discuss how to respond to the argument of the other team. Each team must think of what they can say to argue against all the points made by the opposite team.

5. As above, the first person in Team A and Team B will now respond to each other's points and *refute* (say why that information is false or not accurate) the information of the opposite team member.

ICT opportunity

Use an internet search engine to help you to do research. Remember to type key words into the search box to get the best results.

Use technology where you think it will help to present your debate.

Produce some charts or diagrams with facts and figures to illustrate your argument.

Vote

Hold the debate in your classroom or assembly hall. When both teams have given their speeches, everybody who has been listening will cast a vote for the team that they think has made the best arguments. The team with the most votes wins the debate.

Project 21 – Water in our community

Word builder

This vocabulary is about water in the community:

Vocabulary box

people	community	key	resource
well	source	vital	conserve
pleasure	dam	borehole	adequate
surfing	supply	necessary	

1
1. Take turns to read the words with a partner. Circle the words you are unsure about and look them up in a dictionary or online.

2. Discuss the word meanings.

3. *Source* is a homophone. What is the other spelling for it? What are the different meanings?

> **Example:**
> The National Water Commission (NWC) supplies more than two million people with water.

> Saying a word incorrectly by mistake is called a **miscue**. It is very easy to make miscues, especially with new or long words.

2 Some of the vocabulary words have a suffix (a word ending) and others do not.

1. Make a list of the words in the vocabulary box that can be used as nouns. There might be some homographs that can also be used as verbs; include these in your list, too.

2. Use *-s* or *-es* suffixes to make the nouns on your list plural. Remember that you might have to change the endings of some words to do this.

3 These words have meanings that are the same as, or very similar to, one of the vocabulary words. They are synonyms. Find the word that matches each one:

1 enough

2 essential

3 needed

4 fun

4 Make a word wall on a sheet of paper. Write out the vocabulary words in big letters and at different angles. You could use different colours or styles of writing. Check the words carefully. Make sure the spellings are correct. How will you use this word wall in your work? How will it help you?

5 Look up the meanings of *key* in a dictionary. Write three sentences where *key* is used with three different meanings.

Extra challenge

As a class, make a big word wall on a larger piece of paper and include the word lists from other projects in this unit. How will you organise the words so they are quick to find? Add your own class words to it, too.

Project 21 – Water in our community

Let's read

Research and study skills

This is a map of the major rivers in Jamaica:

ICT opportunity

Use Google Earth™ to zoom in on some of the rivers shown on the map. What adjectives would you use to describe what you can see?

Look and learn

The start of a river in the mountains is called the **source**. The end of a river where it flows into the sea is called the **mouth**.

Research the locations of the source and mouth of one river in Jamaica.

1 Copy and complete this key for the river map by drawing in the symbols in colour.

KEY	SYMBOL
capital	
river	

What else could you add to the key?

245

2. Name four Jamaican rivers that you can see on the map. What do you notice about the way they are written?

3. Which city is the capital of Jamaica? How do you know from the way it is written?

4. Which river flows into Bluefield's Bay?

1. Rivers are important natural sources of water. With your partner or in your group, share what you already know about rivers in Jamaica. You might be surprised!

2. Read the text and complete the tasks in small groups.

> Industries like farming rely on a supply of clean water from rivers for animals to drink and for watering crops. Unfortunately, many industries like mining, tourism, factory plants and even farming itself can pollute rivers by disposing of waste in them. Waste water from hotels, factories and mines, and run off water from fertilisers used in farming all result in chemicals ending up in rivers and streams. Polluted water can be harmful to plants and wildlife and may even kill some species such as fish.

1. Where do you think a river will be cleaner: high on a mountainside near the source or downstream near a busy tourist resort? Give a reason for your answer.

2. How do you think some businesses pollute water supplies?

ICT opportunity

Search online or visit a library if you are unsure and need to find more evidence for your answers.

3. What negative effects does industry have on water supplies? Find some evidence in the paragraph above to back up your answer.

3   Each person in your group should write two questions to ask someone in your group. The first question should require an answer of *yes* or *no*. For example: *Do you think farming relies on clean water from rivers? Is it true that Rio Minho is the longest river in Jamaica?*

The answer to the other question should not be possible to answer with *yes* or *no*. For example: *What does farming use clean water for? Where is the mouth of the river Rio Minho?*

What's your view?
Whose responsibility is it to keep our rivers clean?
Why do you think this?

Grammar builder

Remember ☆☆☆

Verbs tell us if something has happened in the past, if it will happen in the future or if it is happening at this present time. For example:

- I **watched** the waves **yesterday** as they came onto the shore.
- I **will watch** the waves **tomorrow** as they come onto the shore.
- I **am watching** the waves **now** as they come onto the shore.

Look and learn

Let's look more closely at the present tense. Read these sentences:

- I **play** cricket on Tuesdays.
- I **am playing** cricket.

Both of these sentences are present tense. The first sentence is the **present simple** tense. The second sentence is a special type of present tense called the **present continuous**. To form this tense, you take the verb *to be* and then add the verb with the *-ing* ending.

1 Rewrite the sentences. Fill the gaps with the correct form of the verb *to be*.

1. I _____ playing.
2. You _____ swimming.
3. He/She/It _____ racing.
4. We _____ singing.
5. You _____ diving.
6. They _____ hopping.

2 Write sentences in the present simple or present continuous using the words below.

1. I / swim. _____
2. He / surfing. _____

3   They / fishing. _____

4   We / drink. _____

5   Is it / rain? _____

6   It / leak. _____

3 Work with a partner to practise using tenses.

   1 Ask three questions that begin with *Do you* (verb)?

   2 Ask three questions that begin with *Are you* (verb)?

   3 Answer each other's questions to practise using the present simple and the present continuous. Write the questions and your partner's responses. Check each other!

4 Copy and complete the table. For each sentence:
   - decide if each sentence is in present or past tense
   - give a reason for your choice
   - change the tense of the verb and state which new tense you used
   - use a new verb (not a new tense).

Sentence	Tense	How do you know?	New tense – Which?	New verb
It rained constantly.	Past tense	Verb ends -ed	*It is raining now.* Present continuous	*It snowed constantly for nine days.*
1 I am watching the race!				
2 She swims at least three times a week.				
3 Dexter and Mark surf at weekends.				
4 The boys are fishing in the river.				
5 Rivers flow into the sea.				
6 The dog howled all night long.				
7 We go to the pool together.				

Sentence	Tense	How do you know?	New tense – Which?	New verb
8 The man over there is reading a newspaper.				
9 The river burst its banks and flooded the entire town.				

5. Think about the different ways you use water every day, such as washing, brushing teeth, drinking, cooking, playing and swimming. Imagine that yesterday you went for a day without water. How did you manage? What did you do?

   1. Write one paragraph with the title *A day without water*. Describe some of the things that happened on that day. Begin with:

      I woke up…

   2. Swap paragraphs with a partner and read each other's work. Proofread your partner's paragraph. Check carefully that the writing is in the past tense. Be careful with past tense verbs that do not end with *-ed*. These are irregular verbs. For example, the past tense of *wake* is *woke*, not *waked*.

Extra challenge

Rewrite your paragraph, but instead of describing what happened yesterday when there was no water, imagine that there is no water today.

- Change the tense of your verbs so that your paragraph is in the present and not in the past. Begin with: *I wake up…*
- Swap work with a partner and proofread each other's work to check the tenses.

Project 21 – Water in our community

Let's write

Background

Water is important to us for survival, but also for pleasure. We can take part in sports and hobbies such as swimming and surfing. We can go fishing or boating in rivers or on the sea. Water is something that we can enjoy in so many ways. Think about a time when you have had fun with or in water.

- What were you doing? When was this?
- How did the water make you feel? How did it smell or taste? How did it look and sound?

Put your idea in the middle of a planning sheet and then surround it with notes. Use this to structure your ideas:

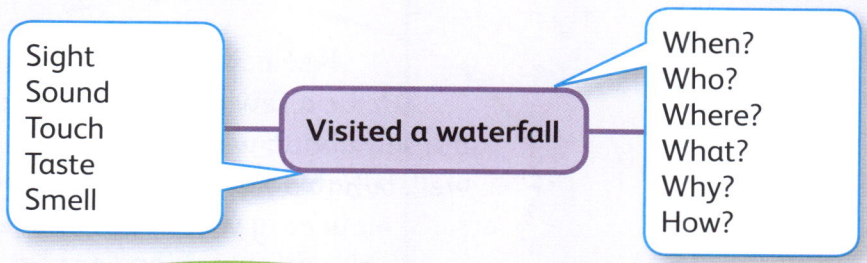

If I am talking about something that I can remember, then this means that it happened in the past. So, I need to make sure that my verbs are in the past tense when I am describing it.

Task

- Imagine that a friend has sent you a message online asking you what you did last week during your holidays.
- Use your notes to write a reply to your friend. The reply should be one paragraph long.
- Then write the same reply as a text. Make the message much shorter without leaving out any of the key information. How will you do that? What will you include? Can you shorten any sentences so they still make sense?

Editor's checklist

Check your work carefully when you finish.

- Did you begin and end with a suitable greeting?
- Did you use sentence signposts in the paragraph (first response)?
- Did you include lots of descriptions to make it interesting?
- Did you punctuate sentences correctly?
- Did you use apostrophes for contractions or to show possession?
- Did you use commas to separate items in a list or parts of sentences?
- Did you use only key information in your text message (second response)?

Reflect and review
Write a few bullet points for yourself about what did and did not go well. What do you want to improve? How easy was it to reduce the information for the text version?

Project 22

Speaking and listening

1. St James Primary School in Milton Hill has 43 students and 7 teachers. They have been doing a whole school project about water. Has your school ever carried out a whole school project? In small groups, discuss what sort of projects you do at your school.

> **Look and learn**
>
> Using water for different purposes is called *water consumption*. A synonym for *consume* is *use*.
>
> | Verb | Noun |
> |---|---|
> | use | usage |
> | consume | consumption |

2. In this project, each student and teacher has recorded how much water they consume every day. The class totals have been added up, then the year group totals and then the whole school totals. They have discovered that they use this many litres of water:

Per day	15,000	fifteen thousand
Per week	105,000	one hundred and five thousand
Per month (28 days)	420,000	four hundred and twenty thousand
Per year (364 days)	5,460,000	five million four hundred and sixty thousand

1. In pairs, decide what title you would give this table to tell people what it is about.

2. Where will you use capital letters in the title?

3. St James Primary School is quite small, so they were very surprised to see the volume of water they use. To give people a better idea of just how much this is, they worked out these facts. In pairs, take turns to read each fact to each other.

- In a day, they could fill six thousand kettles!
- In a week, they use enough water for 1750 showers!
- In a month, they use enough water to fill 5250 average-sized bath tubs!
- In a year, they could fill two Olympic-sized swimming pools which take 2.5 million litres each and still have water left over!

Why do we give examples? What does an example provide?

What other examples could they have given to make the numbers easier to understand?

People have been talking about the school's water project. A local TV news channel wants to focus on the school in a report that will be broadcast live.

They hope that the facts discovered in the project will help people to think more about how they use water and encourage them to use less so that water can be conserved.

Extra challenge

Use the information here to work out how much water is used per person, per day, in litres. Work out the amount and write down the answer in figures and in words.

Task

In a group, perform a role play of the interview for the news channel. One student will be the news reporter and the other members will be students and a teacher from St James School.

- The news reporter will speak formally and should use Standard Jamaican English.
- The children and teacher should try to be formal but can use some elements of Jamaican Creole.
- Make sure to include some of the statistics and interesting facts from the project in the interview.

Remember ☆☆☆

Listening is an important skill. Show respect for others whilst they are performing by being quiet, sitting still and watching them with interest.

> **Remember** ☆☆☆
>
> Each group must work together to research the topic. Decide on team roles.
> - Who will be team leader? Choose someone who has not had this role before.
> - Who will be your script writers?
>
> Practise at least twice before you present. Support and encourage each other.

Plan

- Work out a title and an introduction.
- Work out three questions for the news reporter to ask the teacher.
- Work out three questions for the news reporter to ask the students.
- Plan the answers to the questions.
- Plan a suitable ending: summarise and thank the students and teacher for their comments.

Practise and perform

- Practise several times until your group is happy with the role play.
- Perform your role play for the class and watch the role plays performed by other groups.

Review

After all the groups have performed, discuss the performances as a whole class. Consider these questions:

- Which news report was most informative?
- Which news report would most encourage people to use less water?
- Which news report did you enjoy the most? Can you say why?
- How do you and others in your class now feel about how much water you use?

"Wow! I did not realise just how much water we need every day."

Word builder

You will use this vocabulary when you are looking at a school water project:

Vocabulary box

litre	consume	volume	investigation
domestic	advise	hundred	public
consumption	kettle	measure	million
thousand	reduce	leak	

1 1 Take turns to read the words with a partner and write the number of syllables next to each word. If you are unsure how to say a word, use an online tool to check its pronunciation.

   2 Three of the vocabulary words are measurement terms. What are those three words? Say them in order starting with the smallest.

2 1 Think of a way to sort the words in the vocabulary box into two or more groups. Make tables or lists of the words and check that you have included all of them.

   2 Explain to your partner how you have sorted the words. Listen to how they have sorted theirs. Did you make similar choices?

   3 Together, think of one more way that you could sort the words in the vocabulary box into groups.

3 What is the difference between the words *advise* and *advice*? For each word, write a sentence showing its meaning.

4 Write the vocabulary box words backwards in alphabetical order, starting at *z* and working back to *a*. Will *measure* come before *million*? Why or why not?

5 The word *measure* is in the vocabulary box. How many endings can you think of that could be added to this word? Write down the different words you can form from the word *measure*.

6 Challenge a partner to a Spellathon. Write the words onto small pieces of paper and turn them over. In turn, pick a word and ask your partner to spell it out loud letter-by-letter. Get a point for each word you spell out correctly. Who will win?

Extra challenge

For two of the words you form (from adding endings to *measure*), write sentences to show the different meanings.

Let's read

1 Read this newspaper article about the students from St James Primary School and their water project. Then answer the questions.

> Local school children made the news last night. Children from St James Primary School in Milton Hill appeared on News32 where they were interviewed about a project on water consumption.
>
> Their investigation found that, in an average week, the staff and students use over a hundred thousand litres of water and this rises to a staggering figure of over five million litres per year.
>
> They urged people to help to conserve water by reducing the amount they use for domestic tasks. Examples included taking showers rather than baths and using the washing machine for full loads only instead of more often for half loads or less. In the community, people can also help by not leaving taps running in public buildings and by reporting leaky pipes when they see them.

1 Where is the primary school located? _____

2 Who took part in the project? _____

3 What channel interviewed them? _____

4 True or false? In an average week they use 95,000 litres of water. _____

5 True or false? In an average year they use 5,000,000 litres of water. _____

6 Give some examples of "domestic tasks" that use water which are not mentioned in the report.
_____

7 How does it help to save water if you have a shower instead of a bath?
_____

8 What are three more ways that the children suggest to conserve water?
_____

2 What do you think?

1 How do you think the children and staff measured the water they used?

2 How accurate do you think the measurements would be?

3 What can you do to save water in your school?

4 How can you save water in your home?

Project 22 – A school water project

Grammar builder

Remember ☆☆☆

Sentence **signposts** are used at the beginning and end of sentences.

Start of sentences	End of sentences
Sentences always start with a **capital letter**.	All sentences must end with a **punctuation mark**. A **full stop** (.) is used at the end of a statement or fact. A **question mark** (?) is used at the end of a question. An **exclamation mark** (!) is used at the end of a powerful, funny, or angry word or sentence. It is also used at the end of a sentence or a few words that begin with *What* or *How*. For example: *What fun! How funny you are!*

Look and learn

- A sentence that ends in a full stop is called a **statement**. Statements are used to give facts and to communicate information.

- A sentence that ends in a question mark is called an **interrogative**. Interrogatives are used to find out information by asking questions.

- A sentence that ends in an exclamation mark is called an **exclamation**. Exclamations are used to catch attention, for emphasis and to express emotions such as surprise, strength and anger.

1 Discuss these questions with a partner. Write down your ideas.

1 Look at the following sentences:

   In a day, they could fill six thousand kettles!
   In a week, they use enough water for 1750 showers!

   Why do you think that the sentences end in an exclamation mark? Why do they not end in a question mark or a full stop?

2 Write a phrase beginning with *What* or *How* after each bullet point as if someone is exclaiming. Do not forget the exclamation mark! For example: *In a day, they could fill six thousand kettles! What a lot of kettles!*

3 Think about the role play of the news broadcast that you performed. What type of sentences did the reporter mostly use in the interview? Why was this?

4 Look back at the newspaper article about the St James Primary School water project. Why are all the sentences statements?
Do you think any of them should or could be exclamations? Why do newspapers not generally tend to ask questions?

259

Let's write

Plan your own school water project

Task

Imagine you have been asked by the headteacher to plan a whole school project like the one at St James Primary. Decide on the project (it does not have to be about water) and then present it to the headteacher.

Plan

Work in groups to share ideas about what your project proposal will be to the headteacher.

Here are some ideas:

- using less paper
- not wasting food
- reusing water in school
- capturing more genius ideas!

Think about these points:

- What do you want to find out? What questions will you ask?
- How will you collect your information?
- How can technology help you?
- Will you need any special equipment?
- How will you stay safe?
- What results might you expect?
- How will you tell people about your project?
- How will you know whether your project has been successful?

> Even if it is not possible to actually run such a big project, it is still fun to plan!

Complete an outline plan for the project. First, quickly jot down key ideas, facts or information in a table like this one. You may include pictures if you wish.

The project question (What you want to find out and why)	
Reasons and questions	What we will do
Safety points to remember	Telling people about it

Write

Write out a neat, final plan by hand or you can type it up and print it out. Use the planning guide on the previous page as your headings.

When I write out my work, I always try to use joined handwriting and keep it as neat and clear as I can.

Editor's checklist

Check your work carefully when you finish.

- Do any sentences need linking words to make them flow better?
- Have you used the correct sentence signposts?
- Did you write neatly in joined writing so others can read your proposal?
- Look out for spelling, punctuation and grammar!
- Have you used commas and apostrophes in the right places?
- Are spellings correct?

Reflect and review
Write a few bullet points for yourself to say what did or did not go well in both the planning and writing of your proposal. What do you want to improve? How did you work as a class?

Extra challenge

Make a poster to inform people about the water project and what you hope to achieve.

Project 23

Speaking and listening

> ### Look and learn
> A **drought** happens when there is not enough water for the needs of the people, animals and plants in a place. Rivers and streams may dry up; soil becomes dusty and the earth can crack. Droughts usually happen when there has been little or no precipitation for a few weeks or months.

Discuss your experiences of drought. Have you ever felt really thirsty and had to wait to get a drink? How did it feel? What did you do? Do you remember a time when you tried to grow something and it died? Share your experiences with the class.

1. Read this part of a script from a television news broadcast with a partner.

> Good evening. This is News32 bringing you all the latest news and weather updates. Making the headlines tonight is the announcement that a drought has been officially declared across three parishes in southern Jamaica.
>
> Communities across the south coast are facing the worst drought conditions on record for over a decade. Water supplies to homes and businesses are to be shut off as there is not enough water. Residents will have to collect limited amounts of water from storage facilities until a disaster relief plan is put in place. The government says they are doing all they can to help those affected by the crisis at this time.

1. Discuss its content.
2. Together, check the meaning of these words:

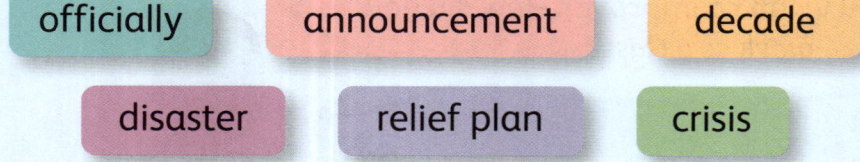

2 Take turns pretending to be the news reporter. Read the news in a serious tone of voice and speak slowly and clearly.

  1 Where will you pause and why?

  2 Which words might be difficult?

  3 Will you stand or sit? What difference might that make?

Practise a couple of times and look out for miscues or errors as you are reading. It is important that the news reader does not make miscues because they could change the information they are providing.

ICT opportunity

Record yourselves reading the broadcast on a video camera or mobile device. Your videos could be uploaded to a school website or class blog, or just shared with the class to review.

Term 2 Unit 2

Word builder

This vocabulary is about times of drought:

Vocabulary box

drought	lack	condensation	existence
scarce	dusty	crisis	moisture
enough	evaporation	dry	precipitation
disaster	temperature	conditions	

1 Take turns to read the words with a partner.

1 Discuss the meanings of the words. Either give each other a definition of the word or use it in a sentence to explain its meaning, like below.

> **Example:**
> Jamaica had a terrible drought 23 years ago. There was very little rain for over one year.

2 Do you pronounce the word *drought* to rhyme with *thought*, *spout* or *enough*?

2 Read the words again. Count the number of syllables by gently tapping your hand under your chin. Copy and complete the following table so that every word is placed in one of the columns.

Think carefully about the word *temperature*.

One syllable	Two syllables	Three syllables	Four syllables	Five syllables

3 Which vocabulary words match these definitions?

1 the antonym of *wet* _____

2 rain, snow or hail are examples of this _____

3 tells you how warm or cold something is _____

4 when there is not enough water for the needs of a community _____

4 In these sentences, there are two vocabulary words that could fill the gaps.

What are the two options in each case?

Which word do you prefer for each and why?

1 During a drought, soil becomes extremely _____.

2 A drought is a type of _____.

5 Complete the text. Use words from the vocabulary box.

> The water cycle tells us about how water moves around the planet.
>
> 1_____ and precipitation are part of the cycle. Whilst
>
> there is 2_____ water on planet Earth for humans,
>
> animals and plants to survive, some places have more than they need
>
> and in other places, water is 3_____. When a place does
>
> not have enough water to meet its needs, a 4_____
>
> occurs and can lead to a 5_____.

6 In teams, challenge each other to spell a word letter-by-letter. The team that spells the most words correctly wins.

Let's read

Read this text about a walk to school in a drought.

Devastating drought

It was another blistering hot day. As Leo began his walk to school, he could feel the dusty soil beneath his feet starting to rub between his toes. He looked around at his father's farm which was normally lush and green with lemons and limes growing aplenty. The leaves on the citrus trees were dry and shrivelled. Some had gone brown and it looked like there had been a fire. It was only seven thirty in the morning and the sun was already scorching the earth below. His usual ten-minute walk to school took nearly double the time because of the heat. By the time he got there, he was thirsty and sweating. His school had a water tank so they were lucky. He knew he would be able to have a drink when he got inside. As the day went on, Leo tried his best to concentrate but could not help thinking about his parents and their farm. The fruit crops were destroyed, so they would have nothing to sell at market. His mom made homemade lemonade with their own lemons. How he wished for an ice cold glass of lemonade now! "Leo Johnson!" a voice boomed. It was his teacher.

"Sorry, Sir", Leo answered. "I am just so worried about my family. We are farmers and our crops are dying." The teacher turned to Leo and said, "Look around. Everyone is going home early today. It is too hot to be here. Go home and be with your family."

When you answer questions about a text, it can be helpful to have a strategy to follow. One of these is the **QAR** strategy.

- **Q** stands for *question*.
- **A** stands for *answer*.
- **R** stands for *relationship*.

This strategy tells us that there are four types of questions to look out for and that each question might need a different kind of answer.

Question-Answer Relationship (QAR)
IN THE TEXT

Right There

These answers are "right there" in the text and are often easy to find.
- Quickly reread and **scan** to find exact information.
- Look for keywords.

Think and Search

These answers are found in different parts of the text.
- Quickly reread and **skim** to find general information.
- Look for important information.
- Link different parts of the text to answer the question.

IN MY HEAD

Author and You

This type of answer is not directly given to you in the text, but you can find clues from what the author says in the text and use these to decide your answer.
- Think about what you know and what is in the text. How does this link together?
- Reread.
- Predict.

On Your Own

These answers are not in the text at all. They are based on your own knowledge and experience.
- Think about your own experience.
- Think about what you have read before.
- Make connections.

1 Complete the table. For each question:
- Say what type of question it is.
- Answer the question.
- Write your own question of the same type based on the text.
- Answer your own question.

Question	Type of question	Answer	My question of the same type	Answer to my question
What time does Leo normally leave for school?	Right There	7:30		
How many minutes did it take Leo to walk to school?				
What sort of boy is Leo?				
What other citrus fruits are there?				

Grammar builder

Parts of speech

Look and learn

When we talk about **parts of speech** we are talking about the jobs that words do in a phrase or sentence. They each have a different job or function.

- Nouns – names of things: common, proper and collective
- Verbs – doing words: past, present or future tense
- Adjectives – describe nouns: positive, comparative and superlative
- Adverbs – describe verbs: adverbs of manner and time
- Pronouns – noun substitutes: subject and object pronouns
- Conjunctions – joining, linking and transitional words
- Prepositions – position of things in time or place
- Interjections – independent words that are not connected to any other part of a sentence and express emotions or make demands

1 Read these sentences. What is the function of each word in bold?

1. The rain fell for five days before the river burst its banks **and** flooded the village.
2. There was a drought because it had **not rained** for **three** weeks, so the river had gone dry.
3. Leroy was running across the school yard when **he** tripped and landed **heavily** in a puddle.
4. The weather will start to improve on Tuesday **until** Thursday with the best weather in the south. **Yay!**
5. The children were jumping **over** the stream **when** one of them fell in.

2 Look back at the story about Leo.

1. Search the text for an example of each of the eight parts of speech.
2. Create a tabletop reminder for yourself listing all the parts of speech and your examples from the story.
3. How will you use it to improve your own writing?

> It is amazing how the different parts of speech have their own functions, yet they work together to form perfect sentences.

Project 23 – Time of drought

Let's write

Drought and the landscape

Look closely at the photographs.

- What is happening and what has happened?
- Choose one of the photographs to write about.
- Make a list of adjectives to describe what you see.

Task

Write a news report for News32 describing the drought and its effects. You should write at least two paragraphs about how drought has affected the landscape you have chosen. Use the adjectives you have listed to make your work vivid and realistic.

Plan

- Use a writing strategy such as **RAFT** to help you to plan your first draft.

R	Role	news reporter
A	Audience	viewers, local people
F	Format	report, minimum two paragraphs
T	Topic	effects of drought

Extra challenge

Include quotes from an interview with a local person whose life has been affected by the drought.

269

- Use these strategies to help you to write your first draft.

Function	Example
Introduction	Good evening. This is News32 bringing you all the latest news and weather updates.
Introducing the topic	Making the headlines tonight is…
Fact 1	Communities across the south coast are facing the worst drought conditions on record for over a decade. (Could include a quote from a weather expert.)
Fact 2	Water supplies to homes and businesses are to be shut off as there is not enough water. (Could include a quote from an affected resident or business.)
Fact 3	Residents will have to collect limited amounts of water from storage facilities until a disaster relief plan is put in place. (Could include a quote from a water supplier.)
Some reassurance and hope	The government says they are doing all they can to help those affected by the crisis at this time.
Exit message	Thank you for watching. Follow News32 for further updates on this crisis.

Write

If you are happy with your draft, write your article neatly or type it up.

ICT opportunity

Research online for further facts about drought linked to the picture you have chosen. Remember to cite any sources even if you find them online. This means you should identify the author who created the content or picture that you use in your work.

Even when I type my work on the computer, I still need to proofread it. I might make spelling mistakes by typing the wrong letters, especially if I type too quickly. Mistakes made by typing the wrong letters on a computer are called **typos**.

Editor's checklist

Check your work carefully when you finish.

- Did you stay focused on the topic?
- Did you use rich adjectives to make it interesting to hear?
- Does it have both facts and personal opinion?
- Have you used apostrophes and commas in the right places?
- Have you checked spelling, punctuation and grammar?
- Did you use formal language?

Reflect and review
Write a few bullet points for yourself about what did and did not go well. What do you want to improve?

Project 24

Speaking and listening

In small groups, discuss what you have already read about water in this unit;

- where water comes from: the sources of water
- the uses of water
- how water is purified
- what happens in a drought.

Now discuss what water is:

- What do you know about water's appearance, smell and taste?
- What do you know about how and why water can change?
- What else do you know about water?

Share your ideas in your group.

Background

You are going to do some research to answer this question:

> What is water?

You can go to a library or homework centre and use reference books or an internet search engine to help you to do your research. You may work alone, in a pair or in a small group.

Plan

Use a graphic organiser for your research. This could be a mind map, thought bubbles or a flow chart. Here are some headings that you could use:

- Appearance: What does water look like?
- Smell and taste
- How and why water changes
- Interesting facts

Select some facts and interesting points from your research and create a presentation. Use photographs, illustrations or diagrams to make some of your points.

> I have always known how important water is for life, but I have never stopped to think about what water actually is!

ICT opportunity

You could use PowerPoint or Prezi to make a slide show for your presentation.

PowerPoint

Step 1: Launch the PowerPoint program.
Step 2: Choose a design.
Step 3: Create a title page.
Step 4: Add extra slides for information.
Step 5: Add pictures and text features to make the presentation clear.

Prezi (You may need permission and help from your teacher to use Prezi.)
Step 1: Start a new Prezi presentation online.
Step 2: Create frames by clicking ADD.
Step 3: Add text and images to as many frames as you need.
Step 4: Click SAVE to update and save your work.

Remember ☆☆☆

When you present, you need to:
- stand tall and face your audience
- introduce your topic
- speak slowly and not rush
- answer questions
- thank your audience for listening
- smile!

Word builder

This vocabulary is about the properties of water:

Vocabulary box

solid	frozen	vapour	properties
colourless	change	ice	gas
steam	clear	state	molecules
tasteless	liquid	odourless	

Remember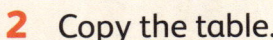

A **suffix** is a letter or group of letters added to the end of a word or root to change the word.

For example: *-less, -ness, -able* in the words *helpless, happiness* and *fixable*.

1. Take turns to read the words with a partner.

   Discuss the word meanings. Either give each other a definition of the word or use it in a sentence to explain its meaning like below.

> I cannot smell anything because it is odourless.

2. Copy the table.

   1. Write the words from the vocabulary box in column 1.
   2. Write the stem of the word in column 2.
   3. Write the suffix (word ending) of the word in column 3.

1 Word	2 Stem	3 Suffix
solid	solid	(none)
colourless	colour	+ less
steam		

3 Look at your table again.

    1   Three words in the vocabulary box have the same suffix. What are they?

    2   What does this suffix mean?

4 Rewrite these sentences using words with the suffix *-less*.

    1   Water usually has no colour or taste.

    2   He does not care and does not think.

    3   She has no fear and her energy has no end.

> **Remember** ☆☆☆
>
> **Synonyms** are different words with the same or very similar meanings. For example, *big* and *large*.

5 Find two pairs of synonyms in the vocabulary box. Write a sentence for each synonym.

6 Challenge a partner to a Spellathon. Write the words onto small pieces of paper and turn them over. In turn, pick a word and ask your partner to spell it out loud, letter-by-letter. Get a point for each word you spell out correctly. Who will win?

Let's read

Water: strange and wonderful facts

Read this report about the science of water.

[1] The scientific name for water is "hydrogen oxide". This is because it is made of two elements; hydrogen and oxygen. The scientific formula for water is H_2O.

[2] Water covers approximately 70 % of the surface of planet Earth. Some of the water on Earth is salt water and some of the water is fresh water. Salt water is found in the oceans and seas. It is an interesting fact that a kilogram of sea water contains around 35 grams of salt. Fresh water is found inland in rivers, lakes and streams and contains very little salt.

[3] Water is found in three states; as a liquid (flowing water), as a gas (water vapour) and as a solid (frozen water).

[4] Water boils at a temperature of 100°C, but if you travel high up a mountain it will boil at a lower temperature. The reason for this is changes in air pressure. The lower the pressure, the lower the boiling point becomes. Water freezes at 0°C, but if it is very salty like sea water, it takes even lower temperatures of around -2°C to freeze. This is because the salt makes the water impure.

[5] The amount of water on planet Earth is constant; this means that it will never change. Water is not going to run out. Instead, water constantly moves around the planet as it changes states in a process called "the water cycle".

I just read that on top of Mount Everest, water will boil at around 68°C. This is over thirty degrees cooler than at ground level!

The water cycle is also called the **hydrological cycle**.

Project 24 – The properties of water

1. Copy and complete the table with facts about water from the texts on the previous page.

Scientific name	
Chemical formula	
Boiling point	
Freezing point	

2. Would it be true to say that half of the planet is covered by water? Explain your answer.

3. Copy and complete the table to summarise some of the differences between fresh water and salt water. Find information in the text, but add your own ideas, too.

Fresh water	Salt water

4   There are three states of water. Look at the pictures and answer.

   1 What are the three states of water?

   2 What state is the water in each picture?

A

B

C

5   Why do you think the water cycle is also known as the "hydrological cycle"?

6   Fill the gaps to explain how the boiling and freezing points of water can change. Use the information in the reading text on the science of water if you need help.

> Water ¹_____ at a temperature of 100°C, but if you travel high up a ²_____ it will boil at a ³_____ temperature. The reason for this is ⁴_____ in air pressure. The lower the pressure, the lower the boiling point. Water ⁵_____ at 0°C, but if it is very ⁶_____ like sea water, it takes even lower temperatures of around -2°C to freeze. This is because the salt makes the water impure.

7   Find out more about boiling points of water and create a gap-fill activity for a partner to complete.

> **Extra challenge**
>
> Investigate the water cycle further using the internet or reference books. Sketch a copy of the diagram from page 277 and label the three processes that are part of the water cycle.

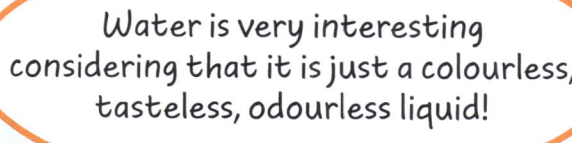

Water is very interesting considering that it is just a colourless, tasteless, odourless liquid!

Grammar builder

With your partner or in a small group, discuss the questions and tasks in each box together before writing down your answers. Look back through the unit if you need help.

Object pronouns
- What job do object pronouns do in sentences?
- List as many object pronouns as you know.

Extra challenge

Write a sentence that includes an object pronoun.

Parts of speech
- What exactly do we mean when we talk about "parts of speech"?

Extra challenge

What parts of speech are the words in bold in this sentence?
*The **boys** loved to **fish** in the river at weekends **but** they did not always catch anything.*

My grammar skills

Tenses
- What does the tense of a verb tell us?
- What are the three main tenses?

Extra challenge

What is the difference between present simple and present continuous? Give some examples.

Sentence types
- How do we know what type of sentence we are reading?

Extra challenge

Write a sentence that is an example of a **statement**.

Write a sentence that is an example of an **exclamation**.

Write a sentence that is an example of an **interrogative**.

Look at the questions and tasks for the four grammar skills again with your teacher. Be ready to share the responses and examples from your group.

Project 24 – The properties of water

ICT opportunity

Choose one of the four grammar skills from the chart. Use a computer to make a poster about it that can be printed out and used in a classroom display.

Self-check

1. How confident are you about using each of the grammar skills? List the skills and draw the emoji that matches how you feel about each skill.

2. If you are not completely confident about a skill, write what you can do to improve. If you are confident about a skill, say what you would like to learn next.

Grammar	☹	😐	🙂	What I can improve or learn next
Object pronouns				
Sentence types				
Tenses				
Parts of speech				

Let's write

Properties of water

Background

You have read that sea water has salt in it. Do you have any experience of this? How do you know sea water is salty? Read this text which explains how to get salt out of salty water.

> We can put some salty water into a shallow dish or saucer and leave it in a warm place. As the water dries up, we start to see the salt crystals forming at the edge of the salty water.
>
> Once all the water is gone, only the salt will be left. It will work faster if we use heat rather than just put the saucer in a warm place.

Task

Now use this information to make a science poster to show how to carry out this experiment.

Plan

- Write step-by-step instructions for the experiment:
    - Give the instructions a title.
    - List the materials you need.
    - Number the instructions.
    - Start each instruction with a verb that tells the reader what to do. For example: *Put…* or *Leave…*
    - Add some illustrations or diagrams.
- Think about the design for your poster.
- Research some additional facts about salt in water to add to your poster and to make it different from other posters. How can you personalise it in different ways?
- Share your poster with the class. Make a class collection of amazing posters about salt in water.

Project 24 – The properties of water

Extra challenge

Research online or in books other simple experiments to show the properties of water. Make posters for these, too.

Remember ☆☆☆

Writing instructions for a science experiment is non-fiction writing. You have to use specialist vocabulary and give clear instructions so the reader knows what to do and in what order.

Editor's checklist

Check your work carefully when you finish.

- Are all the instructions numbered?
- Did you personalise your poster and make it different?
- Did you plan the layout of your poster carefully?
- Have you used capital letters in your title?
- Have you used specialist vocabulary correctly?
- Look out for spelling, punctuation and grammar!

Reflect and review
Write a few bullet points for yourself about what did and did not go well. What do you want to improve?

Term 2 Unit 2 Review and assessment

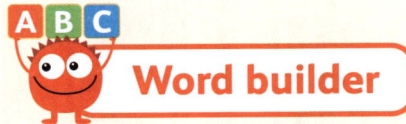

Word builder

1. The same suffix can be added to the word beginnings below to make verbs. What suffix is it?

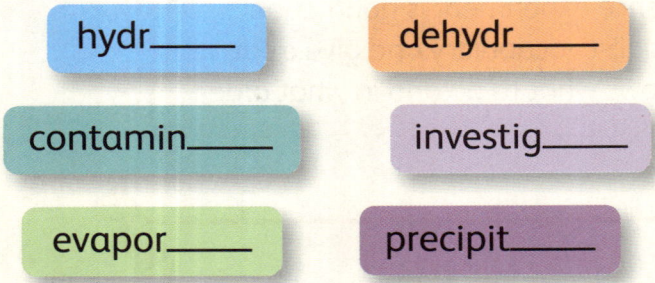

2. Choose three words from Activity 1. Write a short definition for each one.

3. Copy the table. Fill each column with at least three words related to water.

Sources of water	Uses of water	Processes involving water	Verbs to do with water

Let's read

The water cycle

1. Copy the diagram of the water cycle and label it with these words:

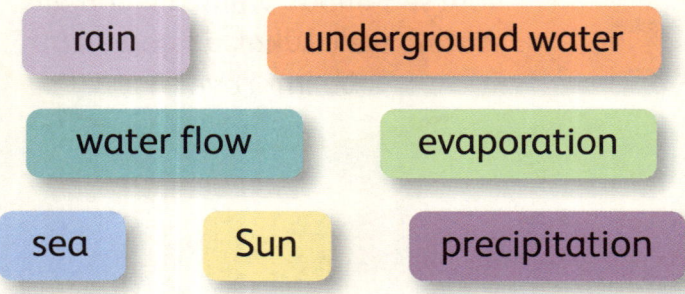

284

Review and assessment

2   What is the scientific name for rain, snow and other forms of water that fall from clouds?

G Grammar builder

1   Decide if each sentence is an interrogative, exclamation or statement and write the correct punctuation mark at the end.

   1   The water cycle is a natural process
   2   How much water do you use each day
   3   In a day we use enough water to fill 6000 kettles
   4   Will you pass that water bottle please

2   Write three sentences in the same way for a partner to complete.

3   Complete the text with the words below.

   For each word say what part of speech it is. For example: *blistering – adjective*.

It was another blistering hot day. As ¹_____ began his walk to

²_____, he could feel the ³_____ soil beneath his

feet starting to ⁴_____ between his ⁵_____.

285

4 Rewrite the paragraph in the past tense.

It is a strange day. The sky is colourless and the usual roar of the sea is softened. We walk side-by-side up to the top of the mountain and wait for the rain to begin. Pitter, patter at first and then heavier and stronger. Here it is at last. We begin to dance with relief. The drought is over.

_____

_____

_____

_____

_____

5 Look at these two sentences which are both in present tense.

- *I am washing the car.*
- *I wash the car at weekends.*

1 Write the sentences in the past tense.

_____

_____

2 Explain what is different about the verbs in the sentences and how the meaning changes.

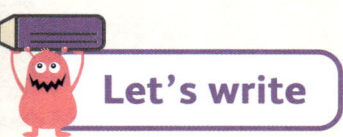

Let's write

Task

Write a short article or blog for a school magazine, or website about water. Choose one of the following topics:

1. Properties of water
2. The ways we use water
3. Drought and its effects

Plan

Copy and add to the table below to plan your writing.

Use noun substitutes	Water is essential. It…
Use different tenses • To state facts, use the present tense. • To give an example about an action that happened before, use the past.	Water **is** essential. Last year people **wasted** 10% of clean water according to National Water Commission (NWC).
Use different types of sentences • questions • statements • exclamations	Should we turn the tap off when brushing our teeth? We must all help to save water. A running tap uses six litres of water per minute!

Write

- Aim to write one or two paragraphs.
- Write your own "Editor's checklist" to show what you reviewed in your writing. Look at the "Editor's checklist" you have used before to get ideas.
- Why is an "Editor's checklist" important?

TERM 3

Unit 1

In this unit, you will learn how to talk about different aspects of the weather, using oral and written language.

Project 25

Speaking and listening

It does not matter where you live in the world, the weather is important to everybody. One of the first things most people do every day is look outside to see what is happening with the weather. The weather has a huge impact on daily life from what we choose to wear to what we eat.

1. Discuss how the weather affects the choices you make. For example, you may decide to skip football training because it is raining. Discuss with a partner and then share your ideas with the class.

> The weather can change suddenly. For many centuries, humans have tried to find ways of predicting the weather. Sailors and farmers, who relied greatly upon good weather, were amongst the first people who noticed signs in the natural world that could indicate the forthcoming weather. They began to make up sayings, many of which are still used today. These sayings are known as **weather lore**.

2. Read the rhyme that the boy is saying. It is an example of weather lore. Discuss it with a partner.

    1. What do you think it means?

    2. If you are not sure, how can you find out? Where will you search?

Red sky at night, shepherds delight. Red sky at morning, shepherds warning.

288

3 There are many examples of weather lore. Discuss with a partner.

   1   Which ones do you and your partner know?

   2   Share your weather lore and explain what it means to the class.

   3   Make a class book of weather lore. Can you make up any of your own?

Extra challenge

Why do you think it was sailors and farmers who first began to notice weather patterns? How was the weather important to them? Discuss your ideas with a partner and listen to what they think, too.

Word builder

This vocabulary is about the weather:

Vocabulary box

weather	instruments	thunder	chart
impact	patterns	observation	wind vane
ancient	temperature	predict	accurate
thermometer	rain gauge	civilisation	

1 Take turns to read the words with a partner. Discuss the word meanings and say a sentence for each. How do you pronounce the word *gauge*? Does it rhyme with *gorge*, *cage* or *barge*? Look up the pronunciation online.

Example:
People say the **weather** in Jamaica is predictable, but it sometimes rains when we don't expect it.

L👀k and learn

- **Stressed** syllables are pronounced slightly louder, more clearly and in a higher tone. For example: **'birth**day, has the first syllable stressed.

- In English, many **nouns** are stressed on the first syllable, but some are stressed on other syllables. The more you practise, the better you get at stressing words correctly.

- Look at the bold letters which show the stressed syllable. Which word is stressed differently from the others?

    '**wea**ther   '**im**pact   '**an**cient   ther'**mo**meter
    '**in**strument   '**pat**terns   '**tem**perature   '**gau**ge

- Often, if the stress is placed on the second syllable, it is a **verb**. For example: *predict*.

However, there are many rules so always check online for the pronunciation and stressed syllables if you are not sure. Then say the word out loud so you learn through practising.

2. Read the vocabulary words again and count the number of syllables by gently tapping your hand under your chin. Copy and complete the table so that every vocabulary word is placed in one of the columns.

One syllable	Two syllables	Three syllables	Four syllables	Five syllables

Extra challenge

Write the stress mark (') before the stressed syllable. For example: '*weather*. Check your work online or use a dictionary.

3. Rewrite each sentence and replace the word in bold with a vocabulary word that does not change the meaning.

   1. The weather can be recorded using scientific **equipment**.

   2. Maggie recorded the rainfall every day for a week and put her results in a **diagram**.

   3. We use instruments to give us **exact** measurements for weather conditions.

   4. Weather conditions have a big **influence** on choices we make every day.

Remember ☆☆☆

A **mnemonic** is a phrase or saying that spells out the letters of a word. For example: *I m*ostly *p*refer *a*pples, *c*arrots, *t*omatoes spells *impact*.

4. Choose two of the vocabulary words that you find difficult to spell and create your own mnemonic to help you to remember the spelling. Share your mnemonic with the class and listen to others. They may be helpful for you to remember the spelling.

Term 3 Unit 1

Let's read

Read this text.

1 What do you think? Discuss your answers to the questions on the next page with a partner and then write down your ideas in a paragraph.

Ancient weather myths and legends

Many ancient civilisations in different parts of the world had their own explanations for weather conditions. Some thought that their gods controlled the skies and sent the weather to them, so they would perform dances to please them in the hope the weather would be kind. Some believed that when the weather was bad, they were being punished by their gods.

The Mayan people believed in a rain god called Chac. They would give him gold, gems or even humans as offerings!

 The Hopi people (a native Indian tribe in the USA) performed a dance with snakes to encourage rain for their crops.

The Norse people believed that their god Thor created thunder with his hammer when he was angry.

 The Yoruba people of Nigeria sang songs to Shango, their god of thunder, because they believed this would keep storms at bay.

Look and learn

Myths are traditional stories that explain the early history of a people or some type of occurrence. They usually involve supernatural beings.

Legends are also traditional stories which explain historical events. These historical accounts usually remain unproven.

1. Why are the beliefs of these ancient people seen as myths and legends?

2. Do you think that the ancient people thought their beliefs were myths and legends?

3. Why do you think ancient civilisations had these beliefs?

4. What myths and legends do you enjoy reading?

2. Cover the pictures and text on the previous page. Rearrange and rewrite these words into the correct order to make sentences.

   1. Mayan people a rain god The believed in called Chac.

   2. Hopi people The performed a dance with snakes crops to encourage rain for their.

   3. with his hammer Norse people The believed that their god Thor created thunder when he angry was.

ICT opportunity

Use an internet search engine to find out more information about one of the ancient peoples and their beliefs. Write a short fact file with the information you discover.

Grammar builder

1 Work with a partner to test if you remember how contractions work. Take turns to say these words and test each other to say the contraction.

Vocabulary box

are not	he will	they have
we cannot	let us	it is

Remember ☆☆☆

A **contraction** is formed when two words are combined to form one shorter word.

You can recognise a contraction because it contains an apostrophe. For example: *can't, I'm, he's, let's*.

Look and learn

The words **will** and **shall** are special verbs known as **modal verbs**. They are often contracted, especially in speech. This is very useful when you are talking about things that you *will* or *won't* (and *shall* or *shan't*) do because of the weather. *Shall* is more formal than *will*.

Pronoun	Full form	Contraction	Verb
I, we, she, he, it, you, they	*will* or *shall*	'll	run
I, we, she, he, it, you, they	*will not* or *shall not*	*won't* or *shan't*	walk

2 Change the words in bold to the correct contraction.

1 It's raining today so **I will** wear my coat.

2 It's raining today so **I shall** go out.

3 It's raining today so **I will not** wear my coat.

4 It's raining today so **I shall not** go out.

3 Rewrite each sentence so that the words *will (not)* or *shall (not)* are replaced with a contraction.

1 It's sunny, so I will go to the beach.

2 I don't want to go, so I shall not go!

3 If it's too hot, I will not ride my bike.

4 We shall not go outside until the weather improves.

5 She will let us play outside if the rain stops.

6 Today he shall let us on the bus without a ticket.

7 He will not come out until it is cooler.

You can add 'll to any pronoun and it works the same way. For example: **he'll = he will, she'll = she will** and **we'll = we will**.

Extra challenge

Find out about other uses of *will* and *shall*. Create a tabletop fact file to help you remember when and how to use these verbs with or without their contractions.

Term 3 Unit 1

Let's write

Research and study skills

To better understand the weather, you should begin by recording weather conditions where you live. Some types of weather, like cloud cover and wind, can be recorded by observation and some weather can be recorded more scientifically using instruments.

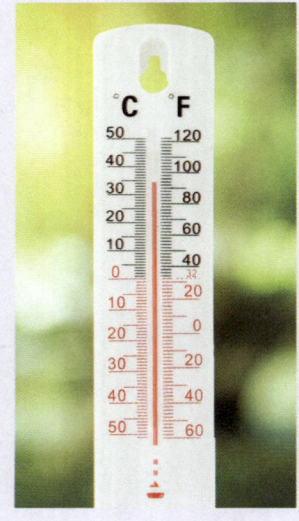

Thermometers measure temperature. Rain gauges measure the depth of rainfall. Windsocks and vanes show wind direction.

When you record weather conditions you need to be accurate. Keep your equipment in a safe place, so it does not get damaged. Carry out your recordings at the same time and in the same place each day.

1. Complete this weather chart and record the conditions for seven days in the place you live. In the last column, fill in your own piece of equipment and weather condition.

WEATHER CHART Date: ____ to ____ Location: ____				
Equipment used	Thermometer	Rain gauge	Observation	Wind sock
Condition	Temperature	Rainfall	Cloud cover	Wind direction
Day 1				
Day 2				
Day 3				
Day 4				
Day 5				
Day 6				
Day 7				

2. Choose two of the conditions that you have recorded and produce a graph to show your results. You could use a bar graph or a line graph. Look back at the "Research and study skills" section in Project 13 to revise graphs and charts.

> Remember to label the y and x axes.

Describe what the graph shows you about the conditions. What does the shape of the graph tell you?

....

Task

Use the information from the "Research and study skills" section to make a science poster that shows how you carried out this experiment. You may include pictures of the equipment used to illustrate your experiment and your graph from the "Research and study skills" section.

Plan and write

- Write your findings by writing a review of your weather-tracking experiment.
  - What went well and what went wrong?
  - What would you do differently next time?

> It was so windy that the old scarf we used as a windsock was blown away!

- Write a summary to describe the weather conditions your location experienced that week. Use adjectives to make comparisons, for example:

Temperature

Overall, it was a _____ week. Tuesday was warmer than Monday, but Friday was the warmest. The top temperature was _____ and the lowest temperature was _____.

Use similar structures for the other conditions: rainfall, cloud cover, wind and your own ideas.

- Mount your summaries on a separate piece of paper and attach it to your poster.

Editor's checklist

Check your work carefully when you finish.

- Did you use specialist vocabulary?
- Did you use adjectives to make comparisons?
- Is your report fact or fiction?
- Look out for spelling, punctuation and grammar!
- Have you used commas and apostrophes in the right places?
- Did you make good use of your weather chart to make statements?

Reflect and review
Write a few bullet points for yourself about what went well and what did not. What do you want to improve?

Project 26

Speaking and listening

1. Discuss weather forecasts. Are they important to you? Why or why not?
2. Read this weather forecast to yourself.

> Good morning, listeners, and welcome to the weather updates on Coast96. This morning, the south coast has clear skies and plenty of sunshine so get yourself down to the beach. Don't forget to cover up with sunblock as UV levels are high. Later today though, some clouds move in and rain is expected from about 3 p.m. Showers will persist until about 6 p.m. leaving us with a cooler night, temperatures down to 24°C overnight, before picking back up to 34°C by tomorrow morning.

3. Describe today's weather conditions in one sentence to your partner.
4. Write three questions about the text to ask your partner. Share and swap your questions.
5. With your partner, discuss whether this forecast is for a newspaper, television or radio. How do you know?

If you want to practise speaking and work on your own miscues, try recording yourself and then listen back to yourself. This can be very helpful!

6 Take turns to read the forecast out loud to each other. Read as if you are the character you imagine would be reading it. How would they talk?

1 As you listen to your partner, listen out for their miscues. Do they miss out any words, repeat any words or stumble on any words? Give your partner some useful feedback.

2 Compare your feedback and your partner's. Do you make similar mistakes? Have you both been able to help each other?

3 Read the forecast in different ways:

- as if you are really excited
- as if you are really bored
- with different speeds or pitches for good news and bad news sections.

How else can you vary your reading using your voice? What impact does it have?

ICT opportunity

Listen to and watch some weather forecasts online, on radio or on TV. Discuss how the presenters use their voices to deliver the messages.

Project 26 – Weather reports and forecasts

Word builder

This vocabulary is about reporting the weather:

Vocabulary box

sunblock	downpour	storm
lightning	forecast	technology
degrees	meteorology	prognostic
Celsius	ultraviolet (UV)	symbols
synoptic	meteorologist	drizzle

1 Take turns to read the words with a partner.

2 In groups of three, each student should look up the meaning of one column of words from the vocabulary box.

- Use a dictionary or online tool and make notes about the words you look up in order to explain the meaning to the other students in your group.

- If there are any words you cannot explain, write them in your notebook for the whole group to look up together.

- As a group, if you are still unsure of the meaning of any words, ask your teacher.

3 Which word is a proper noun? How did you recognise it?

4 Spot the suffix (word ending).

1 Copy and complete the table with words from the vocabulary box.

2 Then write another example of a word with that suffix.

Suffix	What is the word?	Another word with that suffix
-ing	lightning	thundering
-ology		
-gist		
-le		

Remember ☆☆☆

A **compound** word is a single word that is a combination of two other words, for example *wallpaper* is made from *wall* and *paper*. It is paper to go on the wall.

5 Read the vocabulary words again.

   1 Find three compound words. Write them down.

   2 Explain what the two words are within each compound word and say what the compound word means.

6 Challenge a partner to a *Spelling Bee*. Take turns to give each other a vocabulary word to spell out loud letter-by-letter. Who will spell the most words correctly?

ICT opportunity

On the internet, use a puzzle generator website to create your own word search, crossword or puzzle with words related to the weather. Give your puzzle to a partner to solve.

Project 26 – Weather reports and forecasts

Let's read

Weather forecasts

1 Read this text and look at the map.
  - What can you see?
  - What does it describe?

The scientific name for a weather map is a **synoptic chart**.

A weather forecast is usually a map that uses symbols to show the type of weather in different places. For example, a sun symbol means that the weather is sunny, or clouds with raindrops show it is raining. Some weather maps also show you the temperature by including numbers that represent degrees Celsius. Some weather forecasts tell you how the weather is and some predict it for the next days.

This weather map shows the weather in Jamaica on a day in September.

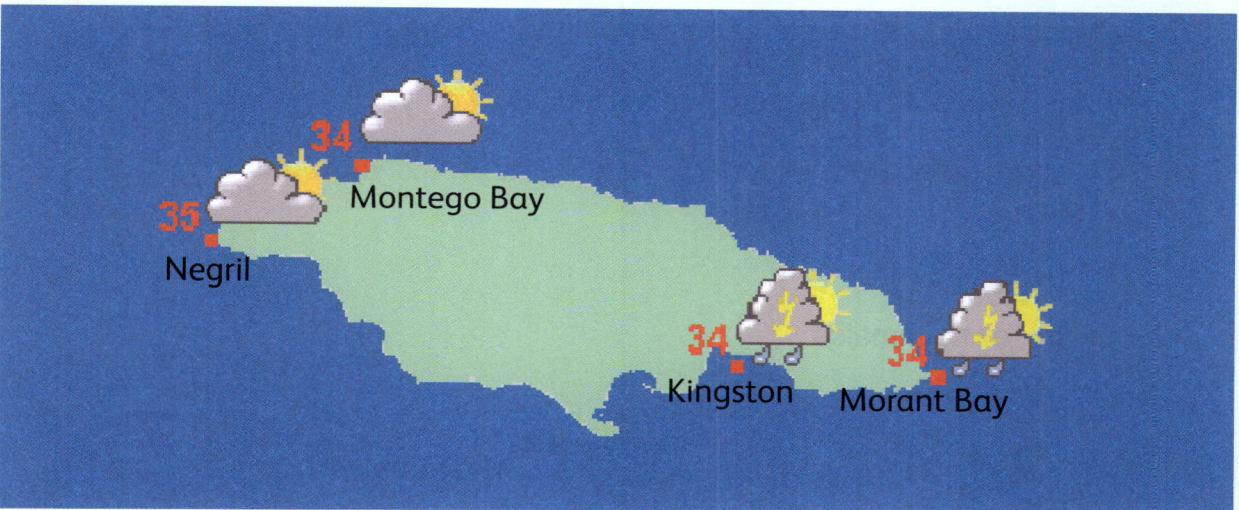

2 Look at the weather symbols.

  1 What do you think these symbols mean?
  2 What other symbols might you need?
  3 Design your own set of weather symbols.

3   Use the weather map and the symbols to help you answer these questions.

   1   Which place was warmer on this day: Kingston or Negril?

   2   Which place was drier on this day: Montego Bay or Morant Bay?

   3   What are the differences between the weather in Negril and Morant Bay? Are there any similarities?

4   Write a short summary of the weather conditions on this day that could be read out in a radio weather forecast. Remember to use the RAFT strategy if this helps you to focus on the important planning points.

5   Sometimes, weather forecasts don't have a map, they summarise the conditions in a chart, like the weekly forecast for Spanish Town below. Use the chart to help you answer these questions.

   1   Check the meanings of *precipitation* and *humidity*. How can you find out if you are unsure?

   2   What is the highest temperature expected? When is it expected?

   3   On which two days are storms expected? How do you know?

   4   If you are going for a walk on Sunday, what should you wear or carry with you?

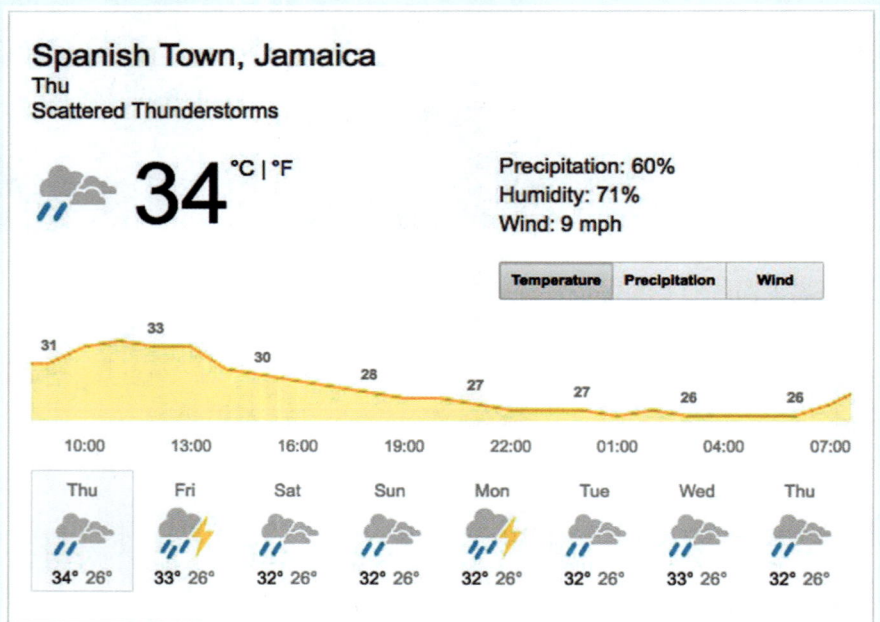

Grammar builder

Reflexive pronouns

Remember ☆☆☆

Pronouns are used as substitutes for nouns. You have already learned about **subject pronouns** and **object pronouns**:

Subject pronouns	Object pronouns
I	me
you	you
he, she, it	him, her, it
we	us
you	you
they	them

1 With your partner, say a sentence for each of the subject pronouns and its object pronoun in the table above. How well do you remember these?

> I asked Leo to give the map to **me**.

Look and learn

There is another group of pronouns called **reflexive pronouns**. Reflexive pronouns all end in either *-self* or *-selves*.

- Reflexives that end in *-self* refer to just one person.
- Reflexives that end in *-selves* refer to more than one person.

myself	ourselves
yourself	yourselves
himself / herself / itself	themselves

Here are some examples of reflexives in sentences:

*The south coast has clear skies and sunshine so get **yourself** down to the beach.*

*Zack forgot to go to the shop. I'll have to go **myself**.*

*The door shut by **itself**.*

*The children want to work it out for **themselves**.*

305

2 Choose the correct reflexive pronoun to fill the gaps in these sentences.

1. It's sunny, why have you dressed _____ in a coat?
2. The children were playing in the park by _____ .
3. It was such a lovely day so we decided to take _____ to the beach.
4. Jeffrey felt sad as he sat at the riverside by _____ .
5. I will never be able to do this by _____ .
6. Gemma absolutely refused to clean the kitchen _____ .
7. Boys, go and do it _____ .
8. Do you expect the kitchen to clean _____ ?

3 Write a story with all the reflexive pronouns jumbled up. Challenge a partner to fill the gaps.

4 Have some fun completing the silly rhyme. Use it to help you remember the pronouns.

Me, myself, I don't say goodbye.

You, yourself, you – never know what to do!

Him, himself, he – _____

Her, herself, she – _____

Its, itself, it – _____

Us, ourselves, we – _____

Them, themselves, they – _____

Project 26 – Weather reports and forecasts

Let's write

Background

Synoptic forecasts describe the weather when the forecast is given. They describe the weather conditions happening on that day. It is called *synoptic* because it gives a *synopsis* or summary of the current weather. **Prognostic forecasts** predict the weather. They tell you about the weather that is to come in a week or even further ahead. It is called *prognostic* because it gives a prognosis or prediction of the weather to come.

> A **synoptic forecast** uses the present tense because it is happening now, but a prognostic forecast uses the future tense because it is predicting the future.

Task

Write a script for a weather report for your local area. You can write about your parish or a larger area, like your region of the country. There are two parts to this weather report.

Part A: Synoptic forecast

Describe the weather that is happening today. What is happening in different places?

Part B: Prognostic forecast

Describe the weather that you expect to happen next week. Think about the following factors to help you to predict what the weather will be:

- What season is it?
- What has the weather been like in the last week?
- How often has it rained in the last week?

Plan

- Choose the area you will report on.
- Use RAFT if this helps you to focus.
- Think about the language you need to use for each part of your script.

Here are some phrases that you could use in your script:

Part A: Synoptic forecast
- Today we are experiencing…
- In the south there is…

Part B: Prognostic forecast
- And the forecast for the next few days is…
- Tomorrow, we will see…

Will you add any personal comments?

Hope you manage to dodge those downpours, folks!

- Draw a map of the area you are describing to go with your script. Use symbols to show the weather conditions that you are describing.
   - How does this help you to write your script?
   - How might this help you to remember your script if you are presenting?

Write and review

- Write your script.
- Use the "Editor's checklist" to review your weather report script.

Editor's checklist

Check your work carefully when you finish.

- Did you use specialist vocabulary and phrases?
- Did you use adjectives to make comparisons?
- Did you add some personal comments to the script to engage your audience?
- Look out for spelling, punctuation and grammar!
- Have you indicated on your script where you will pause to show any photographs, pictures, charts or maps?
- Did you use tenses correctly?

Project 26 – Weather reports and forecasts

Practise and present

Practise and present your forecast. Ask others for feedback.

Reflect and review
Write a few bullet points for yourself about what went well and what did not. What do you want to improve?

Extra challenge

Use technology to present your forecast as if you are on TV. Use cameras and video so you can play back your performance and review it.

Term 3 Unit 1

Project 27

Speaking and listening

Some people love the hot, humid, sunshine-filled days of summer. Other people love to be inside when it rains and listen to the raindrops bouncing off roofs and window panes. Some people get scared by the sounds of banging thunderclaps and lightning rods striking the sky.

1 In pairs, take turns to read the text to each other. Pause to think about the following questions. Discuss your responses with your partner.

   1 What stood out for you?

   2 Does the text connect with your memories and feelings?

2 There are three sentences in the text. Tell your partner what setting you think each sentence describes.

3 Discuss the weather with a partner and answer the following questions.

Example: Sentence one makes me think of birds singing, the green grass in the parks…

   1 What is your favourite type of weather?

   2 What type of weather do you like the least?

   3 How does different weather make you feel?

   4 Describe a time when the weather has made you or someone you know scared.

4 Compare the way you each feel about the weather. Do you have the same thoughts or feelings about weather?

310

5. Share your views with the class about how different weather conditions make you feel.

Remember

It is important to listen attentively and to respect other people's feelings. It is OK for someone to feel scared or frightened sometimes. Sit still and allow others to speak without interrupting them.

Extra challenge

Make a "sky of feelings". Cut out cloud shapes from white paper. Write a sentence on each cloud describing how you feel about different types of weather. Make as many clouds as you wish. What could you use as a background or border for this class display?

Word builder

This vocabulary is about describing weather:

Vocabulary box

wet	sweltering	soaking	strong
shining	freezing	blowing	blazing
warm	damp	pouring	humid
bright	blustery	torrential	

1. Take turns to read the words with a partner.
2. Discuss the word meanings and say a sentence for each.
3. With your partner, practise saying the words in the vocabulary box with the consonant clusters *br, sw, fr, bl, st* and stress the consonant clusters as loudly as you can.
4. Which vocabulary word ends with *-ial*? What other words end with *-ial*?
5. Copy and complete the table below by putting vocabulary words that could be used to describe the elements in the columns. You can put the same word in more than one column if you want to.

Sun	Wind	Rain	Air

Example:
According to the weather forecast, there's a **blustery** wind coming in over Montego Bay.

Remember

Consonant clusters **blend** letters **together** such as /br/, /sw/, /fr/, /bl/, /st/.

Look and learn

An **infinitive** is a verb that has not been changed to make any tense. It has the word **to** before it. For example: *to look, to listen, to play* and *to sing*.

312

6. Here are the words from the vocabulary box that end in *-ing*. Write down the infinitive of the verb that each word comes from.
   - shining
   - sweltering
   - freezing
   - soaking
   - blowing
   - pouring
   - blazing

7. Play a game of *Charades* with a partner. Write the words on small pieces of paper and turn them over or place in a box or bag. Take turns to pick a word and silently perform actions to help your partner to guess the word.

8. Write out the words in alphabetical order. Be careful with *bright*, *blowy*, *blazing* and *blustery*. Explain the strategy you used to decide the order of the words to a partner.

When you list words alphabetically, if more than one word starts with the same letter, then you have to look at the next letter along, or the next one. Keep going until you get letters that are different.

Let's read

1 Read the letter from Julie to her brother. Why is Julie writing to her brother?

Hey David,

We have just returned from our two-week Caribbean holiday. The weather was glorious! We stayed in Jamaica for a week and then went to Cuba. The sun shone brightly like a jewel in the sky almost every day. It was magical! The day we travelled from Jamaica to Cuba there was torrential rain. It was the heaviest rain in a thousand years! We were lucky because we were indoors at the airport and our flights were not delayed. The flight was bumpy like a fairground ride, but we arrived safe. When we got to Cuba we had flown out of the storm and into beautiful fine weather again. It was humid, though, after the rain which made us sticky, like we'd worked out in the gym really hard. Very different from the freezing winter weather we get in Chicago!

Julie

> **L👀k and learn**
>
> A **simile** is when one thing is compared to something else and the words *like* and *as* are used before the comparison. For example:
>
> *The girl sang **like** an angel.*
> *It exploded **like** a volcano.*
> *The rock was **as** big **as** a whale.*

2. Observe the similies Julie uses.

   1. What does she compare the Sun to?
   2. What does she compare the flight to?
   3. Find another simile and write down what is being compared.
   4. Why do you think Julie uses similes in her letter?

3. Fill the gaps to make your own similes.

   1. The sun shone brightly like a _____ almost every day.
   2. The flight was bumpy like a _____, but we arrived safely.

4. Write two more setences using your own similes.

5. Read the letter again and complete the following tasks.

   1. Find some examples from the text that are facts.
   2. Find some examples from the text that are Julie's opinion.
   3. What sort of language is Julie using? Why?

Grammar builder

Remember

Verbs tell us when an action happens; if it is happening now, in the **present**, if it happened in the **past**, or if it will happen in the **future**.

1 With your partner, say this sentence using different tenses.

  1 Say it in the present simple.

  2 Say it in the present continuous (add *-ing*).

  3 Say it in the past simple.

  4 Say it in the future simple.

The weather is annoying!

How well do you remember what you learned about tenses?

2 Make up your own sentence and say it in the present simple, the present continuous, the past simple and the future simple.

Look and learn

Look at this table describing the perfect form of the present, past and future tenses:

Subject or Pronoun	Present perfect	Past perfect	Future perfect	Main verb
I	have	had	will have	seen
you	have	had	will have	eaten
he/she/it	has	had	will have	finished
we	have	had	will have	stopped
you (plural)	have	had	will have	sheltered
they	have	had	will have	swum

Use the perfect tenses to show that something has finished or had finished:

- **Present perfect:** *I **have walked** the dog.* (It is done.)
- **Past perfect:** *I **had walked** the dog.* (It was done in the past.)
- **Future perfect:** *I **will have walked** the dog.* (It will have been done in the future.)

3   Rewrite the sentences. Use the table on the previous page to fill the gaps.

   1 To form the present perfect, use the words _____ or _____ + the main verb.

   2 To form the past perfect, use the word _____ + the main verb.

   3 To form the future perfect, use the two words _____ _____ + the main verb.

4   Write three sentences of your own for each of the three perfect tenses.

5   Are the following sentences in present, past or future perfect?

   1 Andrew has put on his coat.

   2 It had started when I got there.

   3 She will have heard it before.

   4 It had rained every day for a fortnight.

   5 They will have arrived by noon.

   6 I have just cleaned that!

6   Change the perfect tenses from Activity 5 to a different tense and write the sentences.

7   Write a reply to each question using a perfect tense.
   - What have you done now?
   - What had you eaten to make you so ill?

8   Here is a reply to a question:

   Yes, I will have arrived by ten o'clock.

   What could the question have been?

Extra challenge

Write two more questions of your own. Ask a partner to answer, using the perfect tenses.

Write two more answers of your own. Ask a partner to say what the question was. Then swap.

Let's write

Background

Think back to when you shared your thoughts and feelings about the weather at the start of this project.

Task

Write a personal account expressing what you like and dislike about the Caribbean weather.

- You can add thoughts about your "dream" and/or "nightmare" weather, especially if you have visited another Caribbean country and have experienced something quite different.
- You will share this with your class so include some humour as well as some serious experiences.

Make it entertaining!

Plan

- Firstly, make a list of your likes and dislikes about Caribbean weather.
- Draw a line down the middle of a piece of paper.
- Label one column *Like* and the other column *Dislike*.
- Add a section at the end of your columns for thoughts about weather experiences that are neither good nor bad. Consider these questions:
  - Which weather conditions do you like/dislike? Why?
  - What words describe those conditions?
  - How do those conditions make you feel?
  - Do you remember a particular experience that happened to you because of the conditions?
  - What is your "dream" weather and why?
  - What is your "nightmare" weather and why?

Think of one simile (comparison) to describe the conditions that you like and dislike. This will make your writing more exciting and vivid!

Here is an example of how one student started their planning lists:

Like	Dislike
sunshine – glorious, shining	hurricanes – wild
relaxing	terrifying
fun times – cricket	lost our roof

Other weather

Write

- Use your ideas in your planning lists to write a first draft.
    - How will you organise your ideas?
    - How will you make your writing funny?
    - How will you explain the serious bits?
- Write complete sentences. Use paragraphs.
- When you finish your first draft, swap with a partner. Proofread each other's work. Check for spellings, punctuation and verbs.
- Write your final draft neatly in your best joined handwriting. Alternatively, use a word processor on the computer to type it up.

Review

Review your personal account of the weather using the "Editor's checklist".

Editor's checklist

Check your work carefully when you finish.
- Did you recall some personal experiences?
- Did you use adjectives to make comparisons and add detail?
- Did you add funny bits as well as serious ideas to engage your audience?
- Look out for spelling, punctuation and grammar!
- Have you used tenses correctly?
- Have you used similes?

Reflect and review
Write a few bullet points for yourself about what went well and what did not. What do you want to improve?

Project 28

Speaking and listening

Singing about weather

The weather has inspired artists throughout history from painters and writers to poets and song writers. Many songs mention weather. Sometimes the weather is used to mirror people's feelings or emotions. For example, when it's raining, people might feel sad or when the sun is shining, people might feel happy.

1. Discuss how different types of weather make you feel.

> When it rains, I feel…

> When there's thunder, I feel…

> When it's very hot, I feel…

2. Here are some famous songs that mention weather:
   - *I Can See Clearly Now*
   - *Raindrops Keep Falling on My Head*
   - *Walking on Sunshine*
   - *Singin' in the Rain*

   1. Have you heard them before? Can you sing some lyrics?
   2. What other songs do you know about the weather?

ICT opportunity

Use an online music streaming service to search for and listen to songs about the weather.

The words of a song are called the **lyrics**.

3 Here are some lyrics. Which song do you think they belong to? Why?

A
Let the stormy clouds chase
Everyone from the place,
Come on with the rain,
I've a smile on my face.

B
Gone are the dark clouds that had me blind.
It's gonna be a bright (bright),
bright (bright) sunshiny day.

C
I feel alive, I feel the love, I feel the love that's really real.

D
Crying's not for me
'Cause, I'm never gonna stop the rain by complaining.

1 Find a YouTube video of the song and lyrics for *I Can See Clearly Now* by Johnny Nash. Discuss with a partner what you think the lyrics mean.

Example:

"Look all around, there's nothin' but blue skies"

I think this line is saying that even if you have problems, if you look around there are a lot of good things in your life.

2 After your discussion, share your ideas with the class. Sing or read out some of the lyrics.

Project 28 – Artists inspired by weather

Word builder

This is descriptive vocabulary about the weather:

Vocabulary box

rumble	puddles	rainbow	blinding
roar	chase	trickle	burst
shake	crying	break	shining
stumble	wonder	humble	

1. Take turns to read the words with a partner. Circle the words you are unsure about and look them up in a dictionary or online.

2. In pairs, each student creates a table with three columns in their notebook, as in the example below.

1 Copy	2 Practise	3 Write
rumble roar	rumble roar	

   1. Copy the words from the vocabulary box into column 1.

   2. Practise writing each word in column 2.

   3. Then cover the first two columns and listen as your partner reads the words aloud while you write the words in column 3. Then swap.

3. Which vocabulary words end with -le? Add more words that end with -le.

4. Copy and complete the table.

   1. Read the vocabulary box words. Find pairs of words that rhyme. Write them in the table.

   2. Write a sentence that includes both rhyming words.

Words that rhyme	Sentence with rhyming words
shake/break	The wind might shake the tree and make it break.

Term 3 Unit 1

> **Extra challenge**
>
> Choose three vocabulary words that don't rhyme with any others. Think of other words that will rhyme with them. Write them down.

> **Remember** ☆☆☆
>
> All letters are either **consonants** or **vowels**. The **vowels** are **a**, **e**, **i**, **o** and **u**. All of the other letters are **consonants**. Consonant clusters can be:
>
> - a combination of **two letters** representing **one sound**, as in /th/ or /wh/
> - **two or three consonants** which are blended together as in /br/. They sound like one sound, but the sounds are separate.

5 A blend sound is often found at the beginning of a word. Copy and complete the table by filling in the vocabulary words for each blend sound.

/bl/	/tr/	/sh/	/ch/	/br/	/st/	/cr/

There are two types of blends in the table. One type makes one sound; the other type makes two sounds. Put the blends in the correct column. The first one is done for you.

One sound	Two sounds
/sh/	/bl/

Project 28 – Artists inspired by weather

6 Choose a vocabulary word to match each definition.

1 to trip or fall　　　　　　　　　　　　_____

2 pools of water on the ground　　　　_____

3 high-speed race　　　　　　　　　　_____

4 small flow of water or other liquid　　_____

5 band of colours in the sky after rain　_____

7 Play *Shannon's Game* with a partner.

1 Choose a vocabulary word.

2 Write the first letter of the word followed by a dash for each of the other letters. For example: h _ _ _ _ _ .

3 Your partner then predicts the next letters one by one until they can guess or read the word.

4 Try to guess the word ten times. If you are unsuccessful, the game is over. Then swap partners.

Let's read

1 Read these weather poems to yourself. Pause to think about their meaning.

I like to see a thunder storm

I like to see a thunder storm,
A dunder storm,
A blunder storm,
I like to see it, black and slow,
Come stumbling down the hills.

I like to hear a thunder storm,
A plunder storm,
A wonder storm,
Roar loudly at our little house
And shake the window sills!

by Elizabeth Coatsworth

Rain Rain

Rain rain
falls on the street,
mud in puddles
cleaning my feet.

Thunder thunder
rumble and roar,
close the windows
and lock the door.

Clouds clouds
black and gray,
heavy with water
to drop all day.

Sun sun
is breaking through,
clouds are moving,
the rain stops too.

Rainbow rainbow
across the sky,
see-through colours
to tickle my eyes.

by James Hörner

The weather is an incredible inspiration for poetry!

2 Read the poems aloud and complete the following tasks.

1. In a small group, read the poems out loud. Take turns to read lines or a stanza each. Think about the rhythm of the poem and how you can change your voice for different effects.

2. Say the stanza below in these different ways:
   - using volume, for example, speaking loudly and then whispering
   - with rising intonation as if it is a question
   - with stress on the first word of each line
   - with stress on the last word of each line
   - adding rhythm and stressing rhyme.

   Rain rain

   falls on the street,

   mud in puddles

   cleaning my feet.

3. Can you think of any other ways to say this stanza differently?

3 Answer the questions and complete the tasks about the poems.

1. List all the adjectives and adverbs that are used in the poems to describe weather conditions.

2. Look at *Rain Rain* again. Find the rhyming words in each stanza. What do you notice about their spellings?

3. Which verb is used in both poems to refer to thunder?

4. Which poem do you prefer? Why?

Extra challenge

What do you notice about the punctuation in the poems? Why do you think the poets have done that? Choose one of the poems. Draw a picture of what you can see in your mind as you read the poem.

Grammar builder

Look and learn

You already know a lot about verbs and how to use them. Now you are going to look at some verbs that are used with another verb to express a mood or tense. These words are known as **modal auxiliary verbs**.
Here are the most common ones.

Vocabulary box

must	may	shall	can	will
ought to	might	should	could	would

Look at these examples:
It **will** rain tomorrow.   **Could** I ask a question?
You **must** tidy your bedroom.   You **should** know better.

1 Underline the modal auxiliary in each sentence.
   1 Mark can fix it.
   2 You really ought to go and see a doctor.
   3 We will be late.
   4 Could you speak up, please?
   5 I would walk, but it is raining.
   6 You must be careful and follow instructions.
   7 Adam said he might go to the pool.
   8 I shall not let it bother me.
   9 Please may I go to the toilet?
   10 They should arrive by train around 8 o'clock.

> I often use these words. I never knew I was using a fancy part of grammar when I did!

Project 28 – Artists inspired by weather

2 Copy and complete the table.

1. Choose one sentence from Activity 1 and write it using each of the modal auxiliaries. Use the table below as an example and template for the sentence you choose.

2. How does the meaning change? Add an ending to the sentence to make the change in meaning clearer.

3. Compare your table with a partner who chose a different sentence to you.

Modal auxiliary	Sentence	Sentence ending to make meaning clearer
can	Mark can fix it	as he's an expert.
could		
may		
must		
might	Mark might fix it,	but don't rely on it.
ought to		
shall		
should		
will	Mark will fix it,	but in his own time.
would		

3 1. Rewrite the poem *I like to see a thunder storm* using modal auxiliaries.

2. Write your own short rhyming poem involving modal auxiliaries. For example:

You should sing, but you shouldn't cry,

You mustn't worry, but you must try.

Extra challenge

Complete the table with another sentence from Activity 1. The more you practise creating sentences with modal auxiliary verbs, the more fluent your writing will become.

Let's write

Background

Poems don't have to rhyme, but it is fun to write poems that do rhyme. You have read many poems about weather. Now it is your turn to write your own rhyming poem.

Task

You are going to write a poem of your own that is inspired by the weather of Jamaica.

- You may choose any weather condition that you wish or you can include several different types of weather in your poem.
- Your poem should rhyme and it should be written in stanzas.
- Use adjectives and similes to make your poem more vivid and descriptive.

Plan

- Jot down some ideas in a mind map or thought bubbles to help you to get started.
- Make pairs of rhyming words as you go. This will help when you come to write your poem.

> **Remember**
>
> A **simile** is when something is compared to something else using the words *like* or *as*.

Sea is **blue**
And the sky is, **too**.

The sun is fading **fast**…
Why, oh why can it not **last**?

Sharks need to stay **away**,
so fish can enjoy their **day**.

Look and learn

- Question marks are needed for **direct** questions.
- When writing what you're wondering about, then it is an **indirect** question and it should not have a question mark.
- When reading poetry or other texts, you need to decide whether the writer is asking a question or simply wondering about an outcome.

Project 28 – Artists inspired by weather

- You may use an existing poem like the one below to help you to structure your own. Or you can change it completely!

I wonder

I wonder why the grass is green
And why the wind is never seen?

Who taught the birds to build a nest,
And told the trees to take a rest?

O, when the moon is not quite round,
Where can the missing bit be found?

Who lights the stars, when they blow out,
And makes the lightning flash about?

Who paints the rainbow in the sky,
And hangs the fluffy clouds so high?

Why is it now, do you suppose,
That Dad won't tell me, if he knows?

by Jeannie Kirby

I wonder

I wonder why _____
And why the _____?

Who taught _____,
And told _____?

O, when the _____
Where can _____?

Who lights _____
And makes _____?

Who paints _____
And hangs _____?

Why is it now, _____,
That _____?

Write

- Use your ideas from your mind map or thought bubbles and rhyming pairs to write your first draft. Read it out loud to hear the rhythm and rhyme. Then make some adjustments.
- Ask a friend for feedback.
- Make your final copy.
- Add your name as the poet.

ICT opportunity

Type up your poem on the computer and print it out. Add some drawings of your own around your poem. Put it on the wall with others to make a weather poetry display.

Review

Review your rhyming poem inspired by the weather using the "Editor's checklist".

Editor's checklist

Check your work carefully when you finish.
- Does your poem include any similes?
- Does your poem rhyme well?
- Does your poem use rhythm or repeated lines?
- Is all the end of sentence punctuation correct?
- Is there a capital letter for each new line of the poem?
- Does your poem use lots of descriptive language?

Reflect and review
Write a few bullet points for yourself about what went well and what did not. What do you think of your poem? Mark yourself out of 10. What could you improve?

Project 29

Speaking and listening

1 Discuss your experiences of hurricanes or the experiences of people you know. Be sensitive to those friends who may have suffered family loss or damage and still feel upset. Be kind whilst you talk and listen.

2 Hurricane Gilbert was a hurricane that hit Jamaica in 1988 and caused catastrophic devastation. As a class, research if there are any songs about this hurricane.

3 After researching, listening and talking about Hurricane Gilbert, discuss these questions.

   1 Did you find a poem or song about the event? Discuss your findings and how this poem or song helps you understand the event.
   2 What kind of damage did Hurricane Gilbert do?
   3 What effects did Hurricane Gilbert have on everyday life?
   4 What did you think people had to do when the hurricane hit?
   5 How do you think people felt at that time?

4 Ask your parents and grandparents what they remember about Hurricane Gilbert. Ask them for permission to share those stories with your classmates. If they give you permission, report back to the class and listen to other students' stories of Hurricane Gilbert.

Project 29 – Hurricanes

Word builder

This vocabulary is about wild weather:

Vocabulary box

hurricane	spinning	protection	frightening
preparedness	evacuation	swirl	category
recovery	forceful	catastrophe	rebuild
cyclone	hazard	devastation	

1
  1. Take turns to read the words with a partner. Circle the words you are unsure about and look them up in a dictionary or online.
  2. Discuss the word meanings. What is your favourite strategy for working out a word meaning when you need to check it?
  3. Which words end with *-tion*? Add more words that end with *-tion*.

2 Read the words again and count the number of syllables by gently tapping your hand under your chin. Copy and complete the table so that every vocabulary word is placed in one of the columns.

One syllable	Two syllables	Three syllables	Four syllables	Five syllables

3 Use a thesaurus. Find three synonyms for each of these vocabulary words. Record them in word wheels like this:

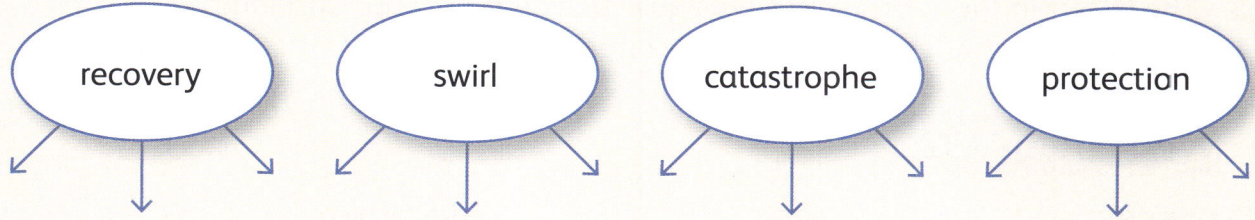

Look and learn

A **thesaurus** is a book that is similar to a dictionary, but instead of giving the definition of a word, it lists other words that have the same or similar meanings. In other words, it gives you synonyms.

ICT opportunity

If you don't have a thesaurus, you can look words up online. Just as there are dictionary websites online, there are many thesaurus websites, too. In fact, most websites that offer a dictionary also offer a thesaurus. Check them out.

4 Read this text about disaster management in Jamaica. Find and write the vocabulary words that are used in the text.

In Jamaica, a government organisation called the Office of Disaster Preparedness and Emergency Management (ODPEM) is responsible for advising, preparing, planning, managing and helping in the recovery of the country when natural hazards such as hurricanes strike.

Extra challenge

Add another sentence to this description using the same style of language and vocabulary.

5 The letters in the vocabulary words have been jumbled up! Unscramble the letters so that each word is spelt correctly.

Vocabulary box

ngeigrnhft	loecnyc	aprechsoatt
ouefcflr	yteoragc	drpepesensra
ehrcunari	nrocttpeio	atncoeviua
uibredl	ginnipns	eocvrrey
ndatavetsoi	swilr	rahadz

Project 29 – Hurricanes

Let's read

1   Read this extract from *A High Wind in Jamaica* by Richard Hughes and answer the following questions.

> That Sunday evening they ran out as soon as they saw him coming, in spite of the thunderstorm that by now was clattering over their very heads – and not only over their heads either, for in the Tropics a thunderstorm is not a remote affair up in the sky, as it is in England, but is all round you: lightning plays ducks and drakes across the water, bounds from tree to tree, bounces about the ground, while the thunder seems to proceed from violent explosions in your own very core.
>
> "Go back! Go back, you little fools!" he yelled furiously: "Get into the house!"
>
> They stopped, aghast: and began to realise that after all it was a storm of more than ordinary violence. They discovered that they were drenched to the skin – must have been the moment they left the house. The lightning kept up a continuous blaze: it was playing about their father's very stirrup-irons; and all of a sudden they realised that he was afraid. They fled to the house, shocked to the heart: and he was in the house almost as soon as they were. Mrs Thornton rushed out:
>
> "My dear, I'm so glad…"
>
> "I've never seen such a storm! Why on Earth did you let the children come out?"
>
> "I never dreamt they would be so silly!"

1   Are the family Jamaican? How do you know?

2   What words tell you how the children's father feels when he sees them outside?

3   Why were the children *aghast*? What does that mean?

4   Why did the children rush out into the storm?

5   How many exclamation marks can you see in this extract?
    Why does the author use so many?

6   What do you think happens next in this story?
    Try to think of two different outcomes.

Extra challenge

Go to the library or online to find this book.
Find out what really happened next.

337

Term 3 Unit 1

Grammar builder

1. What are the ten common auxiliaries? List them with a partner.
2. Look at how modal auxiliaries change the mood of a sentence:

    1. *They **will** go back to the house now.* What does *will* tell us in this sentence?

    2. *They **ought to** go back to the house now.* What does *ought to* tell us in this sentence?

Remember ☆☆☆

Modal auxiliaries appear before the main verb in sentences and tell us more about the tense or mood of the sentences:

| must | may | shall | can | will |
| ought to | might | should | could | would |

These words are very helpful. I can express myself more clearly by using them.

L👀k and learn

- **Modal auxiliaries** can tell us if something is allowed.

    You may not enter.

- They can tell us if something is likely or unlikely.

    I might join you later.

- They can be used to give advice.

    You must stay here.

338

3 It is important to listen to advice about staying safe when there is a hurricane. You should know what to do if a disaster happens.

  1 Write your own sentences based on the examples in the "Look and learn" box. Make them fit with the theme of hurricanes.

  2 Use different modal auxiliary verbs if you can.

4 Read the advice. Underline the modal auxiliary in each case:

  1 You ought to know and understand the hurricane warning system.

  2 You should stay in close contact with your neighbours and local community.

  3 You may lose power so have flashlights and lamps ready.

  4 You must stay calm and listen to instructions.

  5 You can prepare a box of food supplies in advance and store it away.

5 What other advice would you give? Add to the list.

6 Design a poster that gives tips and advice for people to follow when they are expecting a hurricane or during a hurricane. Give the advice as a series of bullet points. Each bullet should contain a modal auxiliary.

Make a class display. Explain why you chose your bullet points and what you hope people may learn from them. Listen to others' ideas, too.

Let's write

Background

At the beginning of this unit you shared experiences of hurricanes. It is likely that you will have experienced stormy weather. Look back at those ideas you shared.

- How can you use those experiences to write a short story?
- How can you use storm experiences you may have read about to write your own story?
- How can you use what you and your family know about storms?

Task

Use your experiences and knowledge to write a short story in which the characters are greatly affected by a hurricane or storm.

- It is likely that you will have experienced stormy weather; you may even have experienced a hurricane before. What can you remember about your experiences?
- Using your own experiences for inspiration, write a short story in which the characters are greatly affected by a hurricane or storm.
- Your story should contain three main elements. Write a first draft by splitting a piece of paper into thirds and making notes about these three aspects of the story:
  - A little background about the lead up to the event happening.
  - Details about what happened during the event.
  - Some indication of what happened or will happen next.

Plan

Your story should contain three main elements.

- A little background about the lead up to the event including characters and setting. Think about how many characters there are. Are they all human? Are they on land, at sea or in the air?
- Details about what problem occurred and what happened during the event. Was it a normal scare or did something special or extraordinary happen?

- Some indication of what happened or will happen next. What sort of ending will you choose? Will it be happy, sad or mixed? Or will you end with a mystery, such as an unanswered question? Divide a piece of paper into thirds and make notes about these three aspects of the story. Here is an example:

Background	Details of problem and events	Outcome (What happened next?)
Characters – me, Mom, Josie Setting – my town	Hurricane watch turned to hurricane warning. Scared / frightening	Evacuate house Stay safe Town floods

Write

- Use your planning chart to write your first draft.
- Try to use adjectives, adverbs and similes in your writing to help to bring it to life.
- Read your first draft to yourself and think about the flow of the story. Read it aloud. Does it make any difference?
- Ask a friend for feedback.
- Make your changes.
- Add a title.

Remember ☆☆☆

A **simile** is when a writer makes a comparison using the words *like* or *as*. For example: *We were **as** scared **as** rabbits, caught in the lights of a juggernaut.*

> The title for your story needs to relate to what happens and should make the reader want to pick it up and read it. However, it should not give too much away!

Review

Review your story about people greatly affected by a hurricane using the "Editor's checklist".

> **Editor's checklist**
>
> Check your work carefully when you finish. Do not give too much away!
> - Did you use adjective, adverbs and similes in your story?
> - Did you make sentences longer by using linking words?
> - Does the story have a strong beginning, middle and end?
> - Did you give your story a suitable and effective title?
> - Look out for sentence punctuation.
> - Did you use capital letters for your characters' names?
> - Did you check your handwriting to make sure it is easy to read and neat?

> **Reflect and review**
> Write a few bullet points for yourself about what went well and what did not. What do you think of your story? Mark yourself out of 10. What could you improve?

Project 30

Speaking and listening

1. Think and discuss any experiences you may have of floods. What do you already know?

2. Read this article from the *Jamaica Observer*. In a small group, take turns to read the paragraphs. Listen carefully and follow with your finger on the text as other students are reading.

Remember ☆☆☆

Be sensitive to those friends who may have suffered family loss or damage in a flood and still feel upset. Be kind whilst you talk and listen.

KINGSTON, Jamaica – A Flash Flood Watch is now in effect for low-lying and flood-prone areas of St Mary, Portland, St Thomas, Kingston and St Andrew, until 5:00 a.m. tomorrow, the Meteorological (Met) Service is reporting.

According to the Met Service, a tropical wave is currently affecting weather conditions across the island and it has forecast periods of light to moderate and, at times, heavy showers and thunderstorms to continue affecting the island this evening into tomorrow morning.

The Met Service added that a trough induced by Hurricane Jose is expected to contribute to shower activity through Monday.

A Flash Flood Watch means that flash flooding is possible and residents are advised to take precautionary measures, keep informed by paying attention to further releases from the Met Service and be ready for quick action if flooding is observed or if a Warning is issued.

3 Discuss these questions in your group. Look for answers in the text on the previous page.

  1. What is the weather going to be like?
  2. What is causing this weather?
  3. What effects might this weather have?
  4. What should residents in the area be doing?
  5. What is a flash flood watch? Who decides?
  6. What are "precautionary measures"?
  7. How is a warning issued? What is a warning like?
  8. Why are some areas more likely to flood than others?

My mom made me put my favourite toys in plastic bags to protect them last time we had a flood warning.

4 Share your answers with the class. Listen to the ideas from other groups as well.

ICT opportunity

Research more about flooding and its effects either online or in books.

Project 30 – Flooding in the news

Word builder

This vocabulary is about flooding:

Vocabulary box

intense	coastal	channel	gushing
flood-prone	storm surge	fronts	shelter
burst	banks	drainage	bridge
low-lying	saturate	severe	

1 Take turns to read the words with a partner. Discuss the word meanings and say a sentence for each.

> **Example:**
> We live in a **low-lying** area. Whenever there is a **storm surge**, our drains are **gushing** with water.

Look and learn

Sometimes, two words are joined together with a little line called a *hyphen*. This creates a new word. These are called **hyphenated** words. For example: *check-in* and *far-off*.

2 1 There are two hyphenated words in the vocabulary box. What are they?

  2 Match a word in the first column with a word in the second column to make a hyphenated word. Write a sentence for each hyphenated word you have made.

no	handed
hand	made
time	saving
left	new
brand	one

345

3 Look up the word *channel* in a dictionary. It has several meanings (homographs). They are not all related to water or flooding.

  1 How many meanings can you find?

  2 Write two sentences. Each sentence must use the word *channel* in a different way.

4 Play a game of *Charades* with a partner. Write the vocabulary box words on small pieces of paper and turn them over or put them in a box or bag. In turn, pick one of the pieces of paper and try to describe it to your partner without actually saying the word itself or any words derived from it. For example, if you are describing the word *coastal*, you can't say the word *coast* in your description. However, you could say "the first syllable rhymes with toast".

A good way to help people to guess the word you are thinking of is to tell them an antonym for it. Antonyms are opposites. For example, you could say, "This is a structure that is the opposite of **underwater tunnel**."

Let's read

1 Read this news report and answer the following questions.

> # Massive flooding in Clarendon as heavy rains continue to lash Jamaica
>
> JAMAICA – Heavy rain has wreaked more havoc in Clarendon. Roads in Ballards River, Pennants, Green River, Ettrick Hall, Commissary and 19 Miles are flooded.
>
> The police are advising motorists to avoid the locations. Member of Parliament for Clarendon Northern, Horace Dalley, late last night said persons were preparing to evacuate.
>
> Two bridges in Frankfield have been washed away. The police are also reporting that Bombay in Manchester is also flooded and there are landslides.
>
> The repair bill following the heavy rain which has affected Clarendon since last weekend has so far exceeded $100 million. Several communities in the parish were flooded. Others are grappling with land slippages.
>
> Local Government Minister Desmond McKenzie told RJR News that based on reports from technical teams and the Municipal Corporation, Clarendon has been hard hit.
>
> Meanwhile, approval has been granted for the release of $175 million in emergency funds to carry out repairs to critical infrastructure in six parishes following the heavy rain. The Local Government Minister says priority will be given to restoring access to communities in Clarendon, St. Elizabeth, Manchester, St Thomas, Portland and Westmoreland.

1 What advice have the police given to people?

2 Who is Horace Dalley? What information did he provide for this article?

3 How much is it likely to cost to repair the damage and what will the money be used for?

2 Some words have double consonants.

1 Find the words *grappling* and *slippages* in the report. Check their meanings.

What is the double letter in each word?

2 Write some other words that feature double letters and, if possible, are linked to the topic.

3 Make a summary of the facts of this report in notes.

Begin like this: *Six roads in Clarendon flooded badly. Avoid...*

4 Look at the article again. Do you think that you could have read this text in Grade 3? Discuss some ways you think you have improved your reading in Grade 4.

Grammar builder

1. With your partner, or in a small group, discuss the questions and tasks in each box before writing down your answers.

2. Look at the questions and tasks for the four grammar skills again with your teacher. Be ready to share the responses and examples from your group.

My writing is so much better now because I can confidently use grammar in my work!

Reflexive pronouns
- What job do reflexive pronouns do in sentences?
- List as many reflexive pronouns as you know.

Extra challenge

Write a sentence that includes a reflexive pronoun.

Modal auxiliaries
- List as many words that are modal auxiliaries as you can remember.

Extra challenge

Write two sentences giving advice about flood prevention that contain a modal auxiliary.

My grammar skills

Contractions

What contraction could you make in each of these sentences?
- "It's windy today so I will stay at home."
- "I shall not tell you again!"

Extra challenge

Write a sentence of your own that contains a contraction made from *will*.

Write a sentence of your own that contains a contraction made from *shall*.

Perfect tenses
- What words do you need to use with verbs to form the perfect tenses?

Extra challenge

Write a question that requires an answer using a perfect tense.

Challenge a partner to answer the question. See if you can write an answer for your partner's question.

ICT opportunity

Choose one of the four grammar skills from the chart. Use a computer to make a poster about it that can be printed out and used in a classroom display.

Self-check

1. How confident are you about using each of the grammar skills? List the skills and draw the emoji that matches how you feel about each skill.

2. If you are not completely confident with a skill, write what you can do to improve. If you are confident about a skill, say what you would like to learn next.

Grammar	☹	😐	☺	What I can improve or learn next
Reflexive pronouns				
Contractions				
Perfect tenses				
Modal auxiliaries				

Let's write

Background

Floods are a common problem for many people in Jamaica. Flooding is often caused because of weather conditions happening in the Caribbean. Hurricanes can bring rain and storm surges and cause wind damage. Hurricanes are named after Hurican, the Carib God of Evil. There are usually about 40 to 50 hurricanes per year worldwide.

ICT opportunity

Look online for live cameras on beaches or film footage that shows examples of hurricanes, flooding and tropical waves.

Task

Imagine that you are a news reporter for a local newspaper or website. Your task is to do some research about a flood that has happened in Jamaica and write an article about it.

- You should write at least two paragraphs about how a flood has affected the landscape you have chosen.
- Use adjectives and adverbs to make your work vivid and realistic.

Extra challenge

Include quotes from an interview with a local person whose life has been affected by the flood.

Plan

- Use a writing strategy such as RAFT to help you to plan your first draft.

R	**R**ole	News reporter, paper or online
A	**A**udience	Viewers, local people
F	**F**ormat	Report, include photographs or pictures
T	**T**opic	Effects of flooding

- You can use the internet, books or newspapers to do research for your article.
- A news report is a factual piece of writing so you need to include the following information:

Function	Example
Headline	Horrifying Hurricane Hits Homemakers
Introducing the topic	The names of specific places that were flooded. The cause of the flooding.
Fact 1	A description of the weather conditions. (It may include a quote from an interview.)
Fact 2	A description of some of the damage that was done. (It may include a quote from an interview.)
Fact 3	Information about how the local people managed during the flood. (It may include a quote from an interview.)
Some reassurance and hope	Details about what happened or will happen after the flood, including costs for recovery.
Exit message	Promise to continue to report on the situation as people recover.

Write

- Use your planning sheets to write a first draft.
- Write your article neatly, separated into paragraphs and columns. Alternatively, type it out and format it using a computer.

ICT opportunity

Only use the websites of trusted sources of information for research. Visit the *Jamaica Gleaner* or *Jamaica Observer* websites to read articles about floods. Visit official government websites like *www.odpem.org.jm* for information about how to manage in a flood.

Editor's checklist

Check your work carefully when you finish.

- Did you keep focused on the topic?
- Did you use rich adjectives to make it interesting to read?
- Does it have both facts and personal opinion?
- Look out for spelling, punctuation and grammar!
- Have you used commas and apostrophes in the right places?
- Did you use formal language?

Reflect and review
Write a few bullet points for yourself as a journal entry to say what went well and what did not. What do you want to improve?

Term 3 Unit 1 Review and assessment

Word builder

1. Create a mind map of different nouns for weather conditions.
2. Choose two of the weather conditions on your mind map and add adjectives for them on the same mind map.
3. Hurricanes and floods are types of natural disaster. Copy and complete the table by filling in at least six words that you could use when you are writing about each disaster.

Hurricane	Flood

4. Say what a meteorologist is and write a definition in your own words. Name as many things as possible that meteorologists might use to do their work. You cannot repeat words from any previous activities.

   _____
   _____

5. Use each word ending (suffix) to write a word that is weather related.
   - -ble   _____
   - -ation   _____
   - -ology   _____
   - -ture   _____
   - -tion   _____

Let's read

1 Read the news report and fill the gaps with a word from below.

> temperature   clear   high   rain   sunshine   clouds   cooler

Good morning, listeners, and welcome to the updates on Coast96. This morning, the south coast has ¹_____ skies and plenty of ²_____, so get yourself down to the beach. Don't forget to cover up with sunblock as UV levels are ³_____. Later today though, some ⁴_____ move in and ⁵_____ is expected from about 3 p.m. Showers will persist until about 6 p.m. leaving us with a cooler night; the ⁶_____ will drop to 24°C overnight before picking back up to 34°C by tomorrow morning.

2 Decide whether the following statements are true (T) or false (F).

1 The weather in the morning is ideal for swimming. _____

2 You will need an umbrella after 6 p.m. _____

3 It might be a good idea to wear something warm in the night. _____

4 The temperature will stay the same overnight and the next morning. _____

Review and assessment

Grammar builder

1 Rewrite these sentences. Insert a reflexive pronoun.

  1 I think I can do it by _____.

  2 Why can't you do it _____?

  3 Why can't they work by _____?

2 Rewrite these sentences and insert a contraction.

  1 It's a lovely day so we will go to the beach.

  _____

  2 It's cloudy so we shall not go to the beach.

  _____

3 Write a reply to each question using a perfect tense.

  1 What have you read so far this year?

  _____

  2 Where had you hoped to go on holiday?

  _____

4 Circle the modal auxiliary verb in each sentence.

  1 You should wait until it is safe to go outside.

  2 Ruby said she might be late.

  3 You may need to evacuate.

  4 If you want to learn, then you must listen.

5 Give someone some advice about what to do in a hurricane. Use a modal auxiliary verb.

  _____

Let's write

Choose either hurricanes or floods to complete this task. You can write about a real or a fictional event.

Task

Choose a writing activity:

- Search and select three weather-related pictures to help you to plan a short story about a wild weather adventure.
- Write a poem about the power of the weather. It does not have to rhyme. Use adjectives, similes and rich, exciting vocabulary.
- Write a diary entry reflecting on a weather event in your area. Write using "I" and include a range of tenses.

Plan

In your writing, demonstrate that you can:

- use planning strategies (mind maps, RAFT, thought bubbles or any charts you have used and found helpful)
- include your own creative ideas
- use some of the grammar from this unit, such as reflexive pronouns, contractions, perfect tenses and modal auxiliaries.

Remember to keep your writing natural.

Write

- Use any planning tools to write a first draft.
- Share with a friend and ask for their feedback.

Review

- Proofread your writing when you finish in order to spot any errors before submitting your assessment work. What will you check for?
- Write your own "Editor's checklist" to show what you reviewed in your own writing. Look at the "Editor's checklists" you have used before to get ideas.
- Why is an "Editor's checklist" important for proofreading?